DISCARD

Violence at Work

Dedicated to the memory of all those who lost their lives at work on September 11 2001.

Violence at Work
Causes, patterns and prevention

Edited by

**Martin Gill, Bonnie Fisher
and Vaughan Bowie**

WILLAN
PUBLISHING

BAS PS

Published by

Willan Publishing
Culmcott House
Mill Street, Uffculme
Cullompton, Devon
EX15 3AT, UK
Tel: +44(0)1884 840337
Fax: +44(0)1884 840251
e-mail: info@willanpublishing.co.uk
website: www.willanpublishing.co.uk

Published simultaneously in the USA and Canada by

Willan Publishing
c/o ISBS, 5824 N.E. Hassalo St,
Portland, Oregon 97213-3644, USA
Tel: +001(0)503 287 3093
Fax: +001(0)503 280 8832
e-mail: info@isbs.com
website: www.isbs.com

First published 2002
Reprinted 2003

ISBN 1 903240 62 X Hardback

British Library Cataloguing-in-Publication Data
A catalogue record for this book is available from the British Library.

Printed and bound by T. J. International, Padstow, Cornwall
Typeset by PDQ Typesetting, Newcastle-under-Lyme, Staffordshire

49.50   1/4/07

Contents

List of tables and figures

Acknowledgements

This book came out of discussions held while we were all at the Scarman Centre, although never at the same time! Bonnie visited for a six-month sabbatical in the first half of 2000, and Vaughan made a shorter visit in 1999, but the seeds were sown. Initially we co-operated on a special issue of the *Security Journal* and, such was the success of this volume we were encouraged to consider a book tackling a range of issues at the forefront of concern for those involved in different ways in tackling violence at work. We are grateful to Karen Gill of Perpetuity Press for encouraging us to develop our ideas.

We would especially like to thank all the contributors for answering our questions and responding speedily to our requests. As editors we have been encouraged by the wonders of technology, which have certainly facilitated easier communications. However, given our location (the UK, the USA and Australia), we were constantly being reminded that things would have been a great deal easier if someone had invented a way of circumventing time zones!

Martin Gill would like to thank the University of Leicester for granting him a sabbatical to complete his work on this book.

Martin Gill
Bonnie Fisher
Vaughan Bowie
September 2001

Notes on editors and contributors

A. Giles Arway is the president and owner of Executive Training and Consultation (ETC), a US-based firm which focuses on a broad range of human resources issues including EEO investigations, workplace violence, and management style and interaction training. Giles has a BS in Behavioral Science, Masters in Human Services and a Doctorate in Business Administration. He has extensive experience working on personnel and staffing issues in both governmental/municipal and private industry. In addition, Giles has experience in law enforcement and security operations.

Oonagh Barron has been researching and working as a practitioner in the area of workplace bullying and violence since 1997. She has presented papers on her research at a number of conferences and seminars. Her work has been published in the *Journal of Occupational Health and Safety Australia and New Zealand* and the *Security Journal*. Oonagh has a Postgraduate Diploma in Industrial Relations, and is currently contracted by the Victorian WorkCover Authority to assist in the development of a code of practice on the prevention of workplace bullying.

Vaughan Bowie is a lecturer at the University of Western Sydney Australia. He has researched and written on the topic of workplace violence over the last fifteen years and achieved a wide sale internationally for his book *Coping with Violence: a guide for human services*. Vaughan has trained thousands of workers around the world in violence management including health and welfare staff, police and correctional workers, youth workers and a variety of other front-line workers and management personnel. He has consulted with organizations in violence and aggression management in places as diverse as London, Amsterdam, the Bronx NY, Belfast, and Soweto in South Africa. Vaughan has appeared regularly as an expert witness in court cases where workplace violence has occurred. He is currently co-authoring a book on workplace violence from a management perspective.

Mark Braverman received his Ph.D. in Psychology from Boston University. He is a founder and Principal of *CMG Associates, Inc.*, in Newton, Massachusetts. Dr. Braverman is a pioneer in the field of traumatic stress in the workplace, was a founding member of the Harvard University Psychological Trauma Center and served as Instructor in Psychology at Harvard University Medical School from 1987 to 1990. He established the Taskforce on Workplace Trauma for the International Society for Traumatic Stress Studies. He is a member of the Taskforce on Workplace Violence of the American Psychological Association. Dr. Braverman has lectured, trained and consulted to businesses, governmental agencies, and academic and professional groups in both the USA and internationally. He has written widely on the subjects of workplace trauma intervention, the management of organizational change, the causes and prevention of workplace violence, and occupational mental health. He is the author of *Preventing Workplace Violence, a Guide for Employers and Practitioners*, published by Sage Publications in 1999, and co-author of *The Violence-Prone Workplace*, published by Cornell University Press in the same year.

Bonnie S. Fisher is an Associate Professor in the Division of Criminal Justice at the University of Cincinnati and a senior research fellow at the Criminal Justice Research Center. Her most recent work examines the gender issues and workplace violence, women's security and cyberagression, and evolution, controversies, and future research efforts of the measurement of the sexual victimization of women. She recently completed two national-level studies funded by the National Institute of Justice and the Bureau of Justice Statistics that examine the extent and nature of sexual victimization and violence against college women, respectively. She is co-editor, with Professor Martin Gill, of the *Security Journal*. She has published over 70 articles and chapters that address issues concerning victimization.

Raymond B. Flannery, Jr., Ph.D., a licensed clinical psychologist, is Associate Clinical Professor of Psychology, Department of Psychiatry, Harvard Medical School; Adjunct Assistant Professor of Psychiatry, The University of Massachusetts Medical School; and Director of Training, The Massachusetts Department of Mental Health, Boston, MA. He has lectured extensively in Canada, Europe, and the United States and is the author of over one hundred peer-reviewed articles on stress, violence, and victimization in the medical and science journals. His work has been translated into four foreign languages. Dr. Flannery designed and fielded the Assaulted Staff Action Program (ASAP) and has overseen its development during the past twelve years.

Martin Gill is Professor of Criminology and Director and Head of Department of the Scarman Centre at Leicester University. He has published extensively in the field of criminology and security management, his most recent books being the *Crime at Work* Series (Perpetuity Press) and *Commercial Robbery* (Blackstone Press). He is co-editor of the *Security Journal* and co-editor of *Risk Management: an International Journal*, and is presently involved in several studies related to different aspects of crimes against organizations. This includes a study of the impact of money laundering regulations, the effectiveness of different types of security measures and especially closed-circuit television in a range of environments, shop theft and in particular the perspectives of shop thieves, and burglary reduction initiatives. Much of his present work involves evaluating 'what works'.

Matt Hopkins is a research consultant for Morgan Harris Burrows. Formerly a lecturer in criminology at Nottingham Trent University he completed his Ph.D thesis on Abuse and Violence against Small Businesses in 2000. He has published in *The International Review of Victimology*, the *Security Journal*, *The International Journal of Risk, Security and Crime Prevention*, and also completed a chapter on business crime for the *Crime at Work* series (volume 2) in 1998 published by Perpetuity Press.

James F. Kenny received his Ph.D. in Criminal Justice from Rutgers University. Before being selected as an Assistant Professor at the School of Criminal Justice at Fairleigh Dickinson University, he served the US Treasury Department as Chief of Advisory, Chief of Review, District Quality Officer, Group Manager of Field Investigations and Treasury Officer. He has facilitated professional seminars, coordinated professional conferences, appeared on TV and radio shows, been interviewed for magazine articles involving violence prevention and security. He served on the US Justice Department/National Victim Center Work Group on Workplace Violence and the Middlesex County Superior Court Juvenile Conference Committee. His research interest include gender violence in the workplace, violence and the process approach, domestic violence and helpseeking, gender discrimination in law enforcement, stalking and domestic violence in the workplace and corporate security.

David Leadbetter is a recognized authority on work-related aggression, with over 25 years' experience of training in this area – experience that combines an early recreational involvement in the martial arts with an academic and professional background in social work, first as a field social worker and later in a variety of training roles. He retains a continuing involvement in UK national policy and training development initiatives and acts in an advisory capacity to various national bodies. He has studied the topic of occupational violence at an advanced academic level, undertaken and published research and continues to write extensively on the issue of occupational violence, challenging behaviour and related issues. He developed the now widely used CALM system of aggression management training in response to concerns about the ethics and effectiveness of available approaches. He is currently the Director and Programme Coordinator of the CALM programme.

Claire Mayhew is Senior Research Scientist at the National Occupational Health and Safety Commission of Australia, an Associate of the Industrial Relations Research Centre at the University of New South Wales, and has recently been seconded to the Australian Institute of Criminology to work on a range of occupational violence prevention strategies. Claire has conducted ten large-scale studies of occupational health and safety over the past decade, all of which to some extent included assessment of occupational violence. She has published widely in Australian and international journals, written a number of books and monographs, and is currently evaluating mechanisms that may help prevent violence associated with hold-ups in small businesses. She will shortly be embarking upon a major empirical study of the incidence and severity of different types of occupational violence experienced by health workers, being seconded to the Task Force on Prevention and Management of Violence in the Health workplace, based at the New South Wales Department of Health.

Brodie Paterson is a Lecturer with the Department of Nursing and Midwifery of the University of Stirling in Scotland. He has degrees in psychology and education and qualified as a mental health nurse. He developed the world's first degree programme in Forensic Psychiatric Nursing and has a longstanding interest in the management of aggression and violence in the workplace, with a particular interest in evaluating the effects of training and in reducing the risks associated with physical interventions in health and social care settings. He has published extensively on the issue of aggression and violence in the UK, US and Germany and has been actively involved in a number of national and international initiatives including the European Violence in Psychiatry Research Interest Group (EViPRG).

Anthony Pizzino is the National Health and Safety Director for Canada's largest union, the Canadian Union of Public Employees (CUPE). He is responsible for overseeing CUPE's national health and safety and environment programs. For the past ten years, he has researched, written and conducted numerous workshops and seminars on a wide range of occupational health and safety issues, including workplace violence. He was the labour spokesperson on a government committee that drafted Nova Scotia's Violence in the Workplace Regulations. He currently represents Canada's central trade union body, the Canadian Labour Congress (CLC), on a tripartite federal working group developing a violence regulation under the federal Canada Labour Code. Mr. Pizzino is a Governor in Council of the Canadian Centre for Occupational Health and Safety (CCOHS) and also represents labour on a wide variety of regulatory and standard setting organizations.

Shannon A. Santana, is an advanced doctoral student at the University of Cincinnati. Her most recent publications have appeared in the *Security Journal* and the *Justice System Journal*. Her research interests include gender and workplace violence, rehabilitation, and violence against women. She is the co-project director for the National Crime Policy Survey which is being administered through the Criminal Justice Research Center at the University of Cincinnati.

Noreen Tehrani is a chartered occupational, counselling and health psychologist. She formed her own organization in 1997 to assist organizations and employees to maximize their effectiveness and efficiency through the identification of the blocks to achievement and the development of support which is tailored to the needs of the organization and the individual. Noreen was the Head of the UK Post Office's Employee Support service and has had a varied career working as a medical researcher in the NHS, in industry as an operations manager, as a marital counsellor with Relate and as the director of an Employee Assistance Programme. She has combined her commercial, psychological and counselling knowledge and experience to develop an approach to supporting employees, which meets the needs of both the organisation and the employees. Noreen's special interests include trauma care, burnout, bullying and harassment and stress auditing. Noreen has been internationally recognized for her work presenting papers at conferences in the UK, Europe and Australia.

Dedications

Martin's father: Reginald Frederick Gill

Bonnie's children: Olivia Fisher Williams and Camille Fisher Williams

Vaughan's parents: Victor Bowie and Ruth Bowie

Introduction

Martin Gill, Bonnie Fisher, Vaughan Bowie

The emergence of workplace violence as a growing concern in our interdependent global economy has provided us with a new opportunity to rethink and address a variety of issues concerning violence at work. As the editors of this volume, we have brought together a mixture of academics and practitioners to share their innovative knowledge of workplace violence issues. Capitalizing on the distance between us (the UK, the USA and Australia), we have included contributors from our respective countries and beyond. In doing so, we have sought to provide the reader with perspectives and experiences of workplace violence experts located around the world that, we hope, will be of use to both researchers and practitioners.

One of the drawbacks to examining workplace violence from a global perspective is that it is so broad that any single edited volume would be too small to cover all relevant topics in sufficient detail. Indeed, in our view it would be a mistake to try to do so. Therefore, our challenging task was to decide which topics to include and which ones to leave out. We agreed on three key principles to guide our efforts.

First, our title – *Violence at Work* – reveals a broad interest in issues surrounding violence at work and, specifically, we are keen to encourage innovative thinking about the causes of, and approaches to, reducing and preventing different types of violence at work. All the chapters contribute to these aims, albeit from very different perspectives. Indeed, we believe that among the strengths of this volume is that the respective contributors' perspectives and approaches are different from one another and, thus, encourage new and revised thinking.

We have included a range of issues that are at the forefront of present concerns about violence at work. Collectively, the contributors address a variety of topics and, in that process, review and critique previous workplace violence studies, identify and assess trends and patterns of violence at work, and reapply traditional theories of victimization and approaches to prevention, security and safety. It will become clear they have different perspectives and different priorities for change.

Secondly, preventing violence, in all its forms, ultimately has to be informed by theory and tested by research and practice if it is going to be more than a hit or miss affair. If this volume encourages rethinking the theories of violence at work, and influences innovative practice that is guided by informed frameworks, then we will have met a major aim. We are optimistic that the contributors' ideas will provide a foundation on which others can develop new theories and improve current theories better to explain, predict and understand workplace violence and to develop more effective prevention strategies.

The third and final principle is that we want to encourage a comparative element and provide a basis for learning across borders and seas. We are aware that a truly international text would draw together studies from more countries (not least third-world and developing economies). We do believe, however, that by bringing together the contributors included in this volume we have set in motion the first step for those interested in workplace violence issues to rethink research and practice concerning workplace violence within a global perspective. Hopefully, more communication of new and revised knowledge and collaboration on effective strategies and approaches from researchers and practitioners around the world will be encouraged.

Structure of the volume

Vaughan Bowie (Chapter 1) begins the book with a discussion about definitions and typologies of violence. He traces the history of workplace violence to assess what it is, how it is defined and the links that exist between workplaces and violent incidents. From this analysis and other work he proposes a fourfold classification of violence that builds upon and extends the Californian Division of Occupational Health and Safety definition. Bowie suggests it is helpful to think of a four-way classification or, more specifically, of four types of workplace violence: 1) intrusive violence; 2) consumer-related violence; 3) relationship violence; and 4) organizational violence. For Bowie, the lack of a clear definition has generated a number of problems. These include the undermining of research that has complicated comparison of findings, a fragmented pathway to strategy that often includes totally inappropriate policies, as well as the uncritical acceptance of untested approaches.

Claire Mayhew (Chapter 2) continues this theme and argues there is an epidemic of occupational violence in certain jobs across countries. Via a review of the research evidence, Mayhew is able to identify a range of risk factors – that is, features or characteristics of employment that are likely to render an employee more susceptible to violence. These include handling cash, more face-to-face customer contact and reduced job security. She also reveals there are gender differences too: women appear to suffer more verbal abuse than men, whereas men experience more threats and assaults than women. As Mayhew notes, as more jobs become less secure so the dangers of violence become greater, and these types of violence may not always appear in 'official' workplace violence statistics.

Giles Arway (Chapter 3) looks at violence from the viewpoint of human resource managers. A part of his chapter reports on a study eliciting their views on violence at work, recognizing that this group is responsible for recruiting some of the aggressors. Arway considers the causes of violence at work and notes that aggressive tendencies in individuals are usually developed in society; he reviews a range of theories to illustrate this point. Clearly there are limits as to how much employers can control the factors that breed aggressiveness but, within work, there are a range of viable strategies that provide a clear understanding of causes and triggers. If human resource managers are to be believed, then interpersonal relationships, the culture of the organization and the way it operates and the baggage employees bring to the workplace all contribute. Herein, he argues, lies the challenge for policy and practice.

Matt Hopkins (Chapter 4) also theorizes about the causes, adapting the principles of lifestyle theory and routine activities theory to develop a theoretical framework for understanding patterns of abuse and violence in business. For Hopkins, lifestyles create contexts that are conducive to violence and abuse, and he offers a model of context, triggers, process of events and result to explain how violence occurs and the various triggers that either escalate incidents into violent ones or de-escalate them. He includes a review of his findings from interviews with 894 businesses, showing why some are disproportionately victimized. His findings show that the higher victimization of Asians can only partly be explained by racial motives.

For James F. Kenny (Chapter 5), violence at work is not an irrational act, which is how it often appears, but the logical outcome of a sequence of events or behaviours. The identification of rational actors lends support to the need for situational prevention measures. This chapter is important in that it seeks to look at violence at work from the viewpoint of the perpetrator, and Kenny traces the stages that can lead to the 'workplace time bomb' exploding. Essentially one needs to look at the situational risk factors that combine with people's behaviours and traits as opportunities to tackle violence – that is, to defuse the time bomb.

Shannon A. Santana and Bonnie S. Fisher (Chapter 6) explore gender differences in the victimization patterns of violence. They review a range of research evidence in the USA including woman's comparative exposure to homicide, rape, sexual assault, robbery, stalking, cyber aggression and assaults, and they report major differences in victimization patterns. For example, they show that homicide is the leading cause of death for women at work and that they are more likely to be victims of sexual assault, rape and stalking by co-workers and of violent cyber crimes. They call for more research but, in the meantime, draw attention to the fact that different victimization patterns highlight the needs for different and focused prevention strategies.

Marc Braverman's chapter (Chapter 7) looks at the management of violence from a systems perspective or, more specifically, at an organization's ability to respond to different types of crises. Braverman's starting point is that events within organizations are connected. Thus, what happens in one part of the organization will affect what is happening in another; the warning signs for violence can be found in the level of grievances, the requests for increased security or just one employee complaining about harassment. An alert organization (crisis prone) will respond to these signs early and prevent the development of a crisis. Thus a broad range of organizational strategies is needed both to identify problems and then to tackle them before they develop. The problem for Braverman is that many systems are flawed and so he outlines a new approach.

Brodie Paterson and David Leadbetter (Chapter 8) critique the unregulated world of management training, which, they argue, has a negative impact on quality, and this is certainly the case with regards to managing violence. In their chapter they outline the key components of a properly organized programme. This includes the need to identify and include relevant research findings but, more importantly, to identify the objectives. Here they pick up on a theme that runs through a number of chapters: that patterns vary for different groups in different locations and that no one solution solves all problems. They identify a number of key issues that need to be addressed in assessing the suitability of training: ensuring the techniques advocated for controlling violence are relevant to the situation and that relevant risks have been adequately assessed are but two.

Oonagh Barron (Chapter 9) also approaches the topic from the practitioner's viewpoint. Barron's point is that different types of violence require different responses, and she illustrates this by comparing assaults with bullying: not only do they have different behavioural characteristics but the legal implication of each type of behaviour are different. In looking at solutions, Barron advocates an occupational health and safety paradigm as a framework for developing solutions.

Anthony Pizzino's chapter (Chapter 10) addresses the responses of trade unions to tackling workplace violence. Pizzino believes that newspaper headlines have focused on the atypical, thereby distorting impressions about the real problems, while some government strategies have aggravated the problem and some employer policies designed to tackle violence have violated employee's rights or left them feeling they were blameworthy for their own victimization. While there can be no quick fix there are logical steps that can be taken to reduce risks, and Pizzino outlines the role unions have played in raising awareness and developing responses. In so doing he highlights the advantages of collective bargaining, legislation, employee involvement and employer commitment.

Raymond B. Flannery's chapter (Chapter 11) is about assaults in healthcare locations and specifically about the Assaulted Staff Action Program (ASAP), a volunteer initiative. His chapter reviews the work of the 16 ASAP teams operating in three US states which have so far dealt with over 900 cases. These have generated some interesting data from a range of studies that have been undertaken to test the effectiveness of the programme. Flannery reviews the preliminary findings, showing that the programme has the potential to be effective and cost-effective while advocating the need for more and better research.

Noreen Tehrani's chapter (Chapter 12) is focused on a different aspect of supporting victims – that is, safeguarding the (psychological) well-being of those who have been victimized by traumatic incidents at work. Tehrani begins by defining four types of traumatic events, not all of which would be typically considered violent, and then outlines the essential elements of a trauma care programme based upon a system of crisis management. A scheme operated by the UK Post Office is discussed and evaluated. A key finding that mirrors findings from research on other initiatives is the need to integrate the programme into the core of the business. Tehrani highlights the need for all organizations to have in place a strategy for tackling all forms of violence, and for these to be evaluated.

In summary, we have concentrated on cutting-edge violence at work issues. These contributors are at the forefront of thinking, research and practice in the workplace violence field. We hope you will enjoy the collection of chapters and that you will benefit from the many theoretical and practical ideas presented in this volume.

Chapter 1

Defining violence at work: a new typology

Vaughan Bowie

Introduction

Workplace violence has always been present in one form or another wherever people have worked together. Despite this long history the western world first began to give attention to this issue in the 1960s and 1970s when it became an area of interest and concern to workers and unions.[1] This concern was later taken up by academics, researchers, governments and employers.

Over this thirty-year timespan, a number of key issues and trends have emerged which are still under debate.[2] Some of this ongoing uncertainty and confusion in understanding and approaches have arisen because of lack of clarity around such fundamental issues as:

- What is workplace violence?
- How do we define the workplace?
- What is the link between the workplace and violence?

In this opening chapter an attempt is made to identify and clarify some of these issues through a more comprehensive definition and typology of workplace violence in order to lay the foundation for a more informed analysis and response to this critical issue throughout the book.

What is workplace violence?

There still are in many instances no definitive answers to this question, which is still being hotly debated. Diamond (p. 232)[3] summarizes some of the varied individual, contextual, organizzational and historical variables that need to be faced in defining workplace aggression and violence: 'Workplace aggression is a dialectical and intersubjective phenomenon in which external realities such as social class, unemployment, organizational downsizing, organizational structure, work processes, roles and culture, and internal worlds of emotions, fantasies, motives, wishes, perceptions, anxieties, and the like collide. Economy meets psychology.'

In the light of such complexities researchers and others have struggled with the issue of defining workplace violence and the broader issue of violence generally. There is much ongoing debate about the nature and definition of workplace violence. Bulatao and VandenBos[4] identify the three key issues as follows: '...it is important to understand what workplace violence actually covers. Researchers and government officials are still struggling towards a consensual definition. Essentially they face three issues: (a) how broadly to define violence, (b) how to define the workplace, and (c) whether to focus on the link between violence and work.'

Budd[5] makes some similar observations within the British context: '... there remains no consensus about how violence at work should be defined. There are two hurdles to defining violence at work. The first is defining "violence" itself and the second is defining "at work".' He goes on to comment:

> The definition of violence itself is contentious. Definitions of violence form a continuum ranging from those which only include physical assaults to broader definitions which also include threats, intimidation, verbal abuse, and emotional or psychological abuse. Those who favour the inclusion of non-physical acts argue that the consequences of non-physical violence may well be as serious for the victim as physical assault. However methodologically it is more difficult to measure non-physical violence.[6]

The experience of aggression and violence is subjective in that each individual perceives such acts uniquely in the light of his or her own experiences, skills and personality. Thus the same violent incident may have a quite different impact upon the different people involved. In some instances, for example, someone witnessing an attack on one of his or her colleagues may be more distressed than the actual target of the aggressive incident.

Littlechild (p. 222)[7] comments:

every individual experiences certain types of behaviour differently. One person may view a situation as violent and threatening, whereas a colleague may not. It is important that we allow the threatened person, or the person who has been victimised, the reality of their perceptions. This means we cannot define violence just in terms of physical contact...

Budd[8] notes this subjective experience in a survey of crime at work: '...Victims of threats were if anything slightly more effected than victims of assault. Those who had been threatened were particularly likely to say they felt frightened.'

Therefore in defining and responding to workplace violence the threat must be taken equally seriously as actual physical violence by managers and others. The level of physical 'damage' is not necessarily a good indication of the level of psychological trauma experienced by targets of violence at work. Some early response strategies based the intensity and type of the response on the level of physical trauma suffered by the individual and ignored or downplayed the equally important psychological impact of workplace violence.

Perone[9] comments on this twin problem of being too narrow or over-inclusive in such definitions:

> ...if the definitional parameters of violence are drawn too narrowly, there is a risk of over-concentrating on what are essentially sensational, though rarely enacted forms of occupational violence while overlooking the more prevalent, though insidious manifestations, which may have longer lasting effects, and which represent more of a financial drain on our health system and our economy generally.
>
> On the contrary, if the term violence is defined too broadly, then it is important to question the value of treating violence in the workplace as a phenomenon separate from the larger universe of violence.

Interestingly Perone[10] notes that the US Department of Labor includes work-related suicides in its definition of workplace violence, a definition that some might argue as being far too broad.

Reflecting this dilemma, some definitions of workplace violence focus only on those events of physical assault in the workplace; other expanded definitions also include the threat of assault. Early definitions of workplace violence focused on the physical impact of violence and ignored or minimized the potential emotional trauma of threats of violence.

Another commonly used definition of violence is that recently agreed to by the European Commission: 'Incidents where persons are abused, threatened or assaulted in circumstances related to their work, involving an explicit or implicit challenge to their safety, well-being or health.'[11] An even broader, somewhat circular definition of workplace violence has been suggested by WorkCover NSW Australia[12] in which workplace violence is whatever the 'victim' of such aggression perceives and describes as violence towards him or her. Folger and Baron's[13] expansive definition includes 'any form of behaviour by individuals that intend to harm current or previous co-workers or their organisation'.

It would seem from the above attempts at defining what is violence as well as from data from current research that a comprehensive definition of workplace violence would need to include at least the following characteristics:

- *Target*: whom is the violence aimed at?
- *Source:* where is the violence coming from?
- *Perception of the act*: the target(s) perceive it as a violent act.
- *Impact*: the act has some physical and/or emotional impact on the target(s).
- *Work related*: the violence occurs while undertaking work related duties.

Standing and Nicolini[14] further remind us on this issue of defining workplace violence that:

- *Any working definition should be produced locally...* A working definition should hence take into account the context and culture of the organisation, and should be developed as a flexible tool for understanding, building commitment, and developing policies, procedures and working practices.

- *Any working definition should be broad enough* so that it encompasses different types of violent occurrences, not only that coming from the 'public'.

- *Any definition should refer to a range of phenomena embodying the idea that aggressive behaviour and violent assaults belong to a continuum* that can only be artificially divided into working categories. Accordingly, any definition of violence is bound to refer to the partially overlapping phenomena of sexual and racial harassment or bullying.

In order to address many of the issues raised in trying to define workplace violence, Bowie has elsewhere defined it as 'a perceived or actual verbal, emotional threat or physical attack on an individual's person or property by another individual, group or organisation' (p. 5)[15] while undertaking work-related duties. This definition incorporates a number of the aspects mentioned previously. These include both perceived and real violence of both a verbal and physical nature as well as encompassing 'damage' to individuals as well as their property. A final aspect of this definition is the recognition that violence may also come from a group or an organization. As Standing and Nicolini suggest, there is no perfect definition and the one offered above by this author would need to be contextualized and adapted to each workplace.

The struggle outlined so far to define workplace violence may seem a somewhat academic, unachievable task. However it is important to continue to wrestle with this issue for a variety of reasons, both practical and theoretical. Without a common definition of workplace, or at least clarity as to how violent incidents are defined and recorded in individual research projects, research on the topic and the collection of meaningful and comparable statistics are extremely difficult. Also any definition must, as Standing and Nicolini infer, take into account the other two key aspects of what types of occupational violence there are and what the relationship is between the violence and the workplace.

What types of workplace violence are there?

Equally important as defining workplace violence is the source or type of this violence. Without a comprehensive typology of workplace violence the research focus may be too narrow and attempts to identify and manage such violence too limited. Therefore, as Standing and Nicolini commented above any classifications of workplace violence need to be broad enough to encompass a continuum of types that may to some extent overlap.

A widely used classification mentioned throughout this book and other research is the typology developed by the Californian Division of Occupational Safety and Health (OHSA).[16] This model is probably the most generally accepted one in current legal, occupational health and safety, criminology and security circles. This original schema identifies three types of workplace violence this author has titled 'intrusive', 'consumer-related' and 'relationship' violence. This author feels strongly that, to these already-identified subcategories, should be added a number of types that so far have been omitted from existing typologies. Thus the author suggests that a new expanded typology based on the existing OSHA classifications should be developed (see Table 1.1) including the following categories.

Table 1.1 Expanded workplace violence typology

Type 1: intrusive violence
- Criminal intent by strangers
- Terrorist acts
- Mental illness or drug-related aggression
- Protest violence

Type 2: consumer-related violence
- Consumer/clients/patients (and family) violence against staff
- Vicarious trauma to staff
- Staff violence to clients/consumers

Type 3: relationship violence
- Staff-on-staff violence and bullying
- Domestic violence at work

Type 4: organizational violence
- Organizational violence against staff
- Organizational violence against consumers/clients/patients

Type I: intrusive violence

Originally type 1 was largely considered to be violence used in the committing of a crime such as robbery or sexual assault. These involve external perpetrators who have no legitimate relationship to the workplace. The early stages of awareness of this type came from staff working in a variety of settings subject to external violence from assaults and robberies especially in banks and other cash-handling business.

Thus the initial common perception of workplace violence was mainly around high-profile incidents of staff traumatized by external robberies and assaults by strangers. However, there are other less frequent but equally important types of this violence that also need to be part of a comprehensive awareness of intrusive violence. These include the following:

- Those pursuing acts of sabotage, kidnapping or terrorism using violence. This may occur in incidents of plane hijackings or bombing of embassies. We have seen such tragic events occur recently in America and Africa.

- Mentally ill, homeless or drug-affected people who find shelter within an organization such as a public library and who may strongly resist being moved on.

- Those protesting in a violent way against an organization's policies or practices, such as multinationals that pollute the environment or exploit third-world countries.

Thus the existing OSHA typology needs to incorporate these additional aspects of workplace violence.

Type 2: consumer-related violence

The most widely recognized aspect of type 2 violence involves aggressive acts by customers/clients/patients (or their relatives and friends) against staff of a service or a business. However, type 2 violence should also be expanded to include at least two other types of violence. These are vicarious trauma and staff violence against others they are 'serving'.

Vicarious trauma

During the 1980s and 1990s researchers became aware of a number of front-line workers suffering from 'burnout' who were displaying signs of traumatization as a result of dealing with violent clients. These symptoms came from not only having to deal with physically threatening patients and clients but also by being exposed to the emotional trauma of these aggressive clients' previous horrendous histories of abuse against them.

This is another type of client/consumer-related violence that can occur to those in the 'care and control' professions, such as police officers, lawyers, judges, social workers, rape counsellors and child protection specialists. Journalists and international peace keepers may also be exposed to such trauma.[17] These staff may have to deal with a 'double dose' of both direct violence from their clients as well as the 'horror' of helping their clients face what they have done to others or have experienced themselves. Such experiences by staff are now referred to by various terms, such as secondary trauma or vicarious traumatization. Kyle and Hampshire[18] comment:

↓ Vicarious trauma is best described as a series of layers which result from working with survivors of violence and abuse and can involve changes to feelings, perceptions and behaviours. Each of the layers can be very painful and difficult for workers. Together they can be overwhelming.

We see the different layers which make up the trauma experienced by those who work with the survivors of violence and abuse as:

- The nature of clients' experiences and stories
- Workers' exposure to threat from others
- Alienation and isolation from others.

Kyle and Hampshire also note that some of these survivors are also perpetrators.

This indirect violence can also be experienced by those teaching or training workers[19] or undertaking research in prisons or amongst certain types of offenders, such as paedophiles or rapists. The effects of this trauma can sometimes be quite subtle and denied by staff, and largely unnoticed by managers and supervisors. Thus any risk assessment needs to factor in the possibility of such trauma occurring and to take steps to manage or prevent it.

Violence by staff against clients/patients
There is another kind of type 2 violence – that of violence by staff against consumers/clients/patients that is largely denied or overlooked. This can range from neglect and withholding of services to verbal abuse by staff through to sexual assault and even homicide. Some specific subgroups of clients may be especially vulnerable to violence, including state wards (such as children and the mentally ill) and those with physical and intellectual impairments, prisoners, refugees and the aged.

The possibility of such incidents occurring has been validated through a number of recent high-profile cases of health workers committing serial homicide against their patients, and child abuse by staff in residential child-care facilities especially within the UK. The recent charges brought against Dr Shipman in England are a case in point. Kinnell[20] as regards the Shipman case and others throughout several centuries, comments: 'medicine has arguably thrown up more serial killers than all the other professions put together, with nursing a close second.' In the same light, Kohnke (p. 257)[21] comments about abusive nurses:

> The nature of the abuse delivered by nurses to patients is often subtle: rarely...do we see actual physical abuse. The more primitive, isolated and poor the institutions, the more likely they harbor the actual physical abusers. The better financed, more modern institutions where patients are more in control of the environment, see the more subtle forms of abuse.

Similar observations are made by Rylance (p. 31)[22] based on a survey of 454 mainly social workers, counsellors and psychologists; she comments: 'in addition to clients being abusive to workers, service users can experience similar behaviours by workers.'

The existing typologies have not generally as yet identified such a staff-based source of workplace violence. The lack of recognition of such an issue has partially occurred because of denial or disbelief that staff-based violence is potential reality. Also the union mandate to defend the rights of aggressive staff sometimes puts them in the difficult position of having to support such workers to remain at work even though these labour representatives recognize that these aggressive employees presented in some instances a real threat to their own members or the clients or patients who were in their care. At the same time this support function sometimes put the unions in direct opposition to the employer's approach to aggressive workers.

In some instances even well intentioned co-operative approaches may prove ineffective or even counterproductive for the welfare of the employee.[23] This also demonstrates a lack of clarity as to what co-operative approaches should be used in dealing with staff that do not 'tear' staff apart yet provide appropriate responses to staff who are both 'troubled' and 'troublesome'.[24]

Thus current typologies should be expanded to include two other aspects of client-related violence type 2 – that of vicarious trauma to staff, and violence and abuse by staff against those in their care or for whom they are supplying a service.

Type 3: relationship violence

During the 1970s and 1980s it began to be recognized that in some situations staff themselves were the instigators of aggression and violence against other staff through bullying and harassment. This phenomenon was probably first investigated systematically amongst nurses and was referred to as horizontal violence.[25]

In this historical context there has been a growing interest and concern about workplace bullying,[26] or mobbing as it is called in the European context. Such individual and group violence is not particularly new but seems to be growing in the current economic rationalist climate of decreasing job security, individual work contracts, massive retrenchments and expanding unemployment that pits workers and unions against employers and other workers.

However, this relationship violence can also involve aggressive acts by former employees or other persons with an employment-based relationship with an organization. These could include an employee's current or former spouse, family members or significant others. It could also include cases of stalking, domestic violence occurring at work or former employees seeking justice for perceived previous wrongs against them by the organization.

One ongoing debate has been around to what extent are sexual harassment (including stalking) and domestic violence considered to be workplace violence and treated as such or as a related but separate issue to be dealt with in a unique manner. In a response to this issue, more recent expansions of this OSHA typology[27] have divided this classification into two separate types: 1) worker on worker; and 2) personal relationships violence. Whether personal relationships that include domestic violence should be made separate categories is open to debate, as both classifications are based on some type of actual, assumed or desired relationship. Regardless of where it is placed as a category, domestic violence spilling over into the workplace it is an increasing concern that needs to be built into any comprehensive workplace violence typology.

A related key issue raised in this book by Santana and Fisher, Mayhew, Hopkins and others, is the relationship between gender and the experience of types of workplace violence. As these contributors clearly demonstrate, there is a relationship between gender and the types of workplace violence experienced by women and men. This gender relationship could extend to types 1, 2 and 3 workplace violence.

There is a need, then, for workplace bullying and its various manifestations to be taken much more seriously and for the gendered nature of this interaction to be more closely researched. Thus any comprehensive response to workplace violence and bullying needs to incorporate insights gained from such current and future investigation.

Type 4: organizational violence

Many earlier responses to workplace violence by employers deflected attention from a potential key contributor to workplace violence – the ways organizations are structured and managed. Common early employer responses to workplace violence, often at the request of their workers, were to provide training in violence and aggression management, including self-defence and restraint techniques. However such training by implication often blamed the workers, identifying their skill shortfall as the primary 'cause' of client/customer/patient dissatisfaction and aggression.

Another early employer response was to 'harden' the target, making it more difficult for attackers to gain access to staff by reducing opportunities to offend. This target-hardening approach in a broader sense also began to involve the use of psychological testing or 'profiling' to eliminate potentially aggressive job applicants. In some instances the profiling approach, like training, proved to be an extension of blame the (potential) worker, diverting attention from an aggression-producing climate within the organisation and projecting blame for violent incidents back on to the individual.[28]

Many of the contributors to this book, especially Mayhew and Braverman, refer to the growing awareness of the role organizations may play in creating an oppressive and violent climate that may in turn trigger violence amongst staff, by clients and by external intruders. Greenberg and Barling (p. 898)[29] comment on the lack of research into such structural determinants of workplace violence as organizational factors:

> To date, the majority of studies addressing workplace aggression and violence has taken one of three approaches....First, there are those addressing customer or client-perpetrated violence, describing elements of jobs, or characteristics of employees, which increase susceptibility to violence by non-employees...The second approach to workplace aggression investigates demographic and psychological correlates, attempting to isolate employee attitudes, and/or personal characteristics associated with perpetrators of workplace violence (eg., history of violent behaviour, domestic disputes, alcohol or substance abuse)...A third area of research focuses on situational determinants/correlates of employee violence. However this area has attracted little attention.

Diamond[30] further supports such an analysis: 'Beyond the statistics, most reports and studies of violence in the workplace provide little to no insight into the relationship between organizational cultures and the production of aggression and hostility between fellow workers and between employers and employees.' Such a realization has been hindered by the still current focus on the personality or pathology of the individual worker, client or intruder as the main contributor to workplace violence. Thus to types 1, 2 and 3, Bowie[31] has suggested that a new category, type 4 organizational violence, should be added, emphasizing the role an organization can play in triggering workplace violence. Type 4 violence involves organizations knowingly placing their workers or clients in dangerous or violent situations or allowing a climate of abuse, bullying or harassment to thrive in the workplace. Such a climate can also include the threat or reality of downsizing or layoffs.

This phenomenon is referred to in the research literature by a number of names, including 'structural violence', 'systemic violence or abuse' and 'institutional abuse'.[32] This most important category not specifically noted in the OSHA classification should include organizational violence against both workers and clients. Southerland et al.[33] use evocative language, describing such organizations themselves as murderers where they knowingly put employees in risky situations without making employees aware of the potentially lethal situations or doing anything to protect them. Macarthy[34] also expresses these trends in equally graphic terms: 'The widespread exercise of economic rationalism through the restructuring in these conditions does have the potential to carry forward a kind of ritual "sacrificial violence", with the ongoing offering up, through downsizing, of those deemed less useful to the venture.'

Catalano and his colleagues (p. 12),[35] in examining the personal impact of job loss on workers in the USA found that:

> job loss was associated with a higher risk of violent behaviour than many of the characteristics cited as the leading predictors of violence. In our study losing a job increased the odds of a violent episode more than having a history of psychiatric disorder (including alcohol disorder) or of being male, young or of low socioeconomic status. In fact, the estimated odds ratio for the effect of job loss on violent behaviour was greater than that for a history of violent behaviour.

Catalano et al. make the conclusion that job loss is a better predictor of future violent behaviour than any other of the usual key indicators, even the most 'reliable' one of past violent behaviour. They were careful in this study to control for previous violent behaviour – that is, those who showed violent behaviour after layoffs had not shown recent violent behaviour prior to the layoffs.

If this conclusion is supported by future more detailed research, it should have major implications for the way organizations should approach or even contemplate downsizing and job layoffs.[36] A number of well publicized mass shootings within American workplaces, such as the post office, have been to some extent triggered by an individual's perception of being unjustly disciplined or layed off. Thus violent actions which may have been seen as purely the acts of an unstable individual may be in fact the interaction of personal and organizational factors.

Bensimon (p. 52)[37] comments: 'time and time again, disgruntled workers who have become violent have said that what impelled them was not the fact that they were demoted, fired or laid off, but the dehumanizing way the action was carried out.'

A number of researchers have suggested that such rapid and ruthless organizational change may be a key trigger in what is often perceived and explained as violence that stems from individual worker pathology. Williams,[38] for example, notes that: 'The issue of workplace violence becomes a response or reaction to an unexpected, unexplained, unwarranted change in a policy, procedure or practice that creates trauma among employees and in the organization itself'.

In a similar fashion, Baron and Neuman (p. 448)[39] hypothesize that 'The greater the extent to which changes have occurred recently in a given workplace (changes likely to induce anxiety, frustration, and negative effect amongst employees), the higher incidence of aggression in that workplace'.

Though no type of workplace violence is acceptable, of particular concern is a potential increase in type 4 violence – that of organizational violence partly fuelled by economic rationalism. Ironically such negative consequences have continued in a climate in which the supposed benefits to organizations and the world economy of downsizing are being increasingly challenged and often discredited.[40]

Thus the organizational climate may be an important factor in influencing the types of workplace violence experienced within the organization. A strong emphasis by Braverman in this book is the impact that the context, especially in type 4 organizational violence, can play in the sorts of aggression and violence displayed by staff and clients/customers. Such organizational oppression is often not recognized as being an integral part of what is expressed as types 2 and 3 workplace violence.

Such an organizational climate of rapid and ruthless change may not only provide an environment conducive to types 2 and 3 workplace violence but devalued staff may also collude, directly or indirectly, with external assailants in type 1 violence.[41] Thus staff who are themselves poorly trained, under stress and feeling devalued due to type 4 organizational violence may in turn create an environment that makes it easier for external assailants to gain access to the organization or to capitalize on perceived 'weaknesses' in the organization's security. It may be possible to speculate that such collusion in type 1 violence may be a direct result of the organizational climate.

Therefore it could be posited that a positive management culture could be part of minimizing the impact of internal and external violence upon organizations. Thus this 'trickle down' effect of type 4 violence in stimulating other types of workplace violence needs to be much more closely examined. Denial by management of their role in this trickle-down effect can further inflame the situation. Diamond[42] documents how such denial can polarize the workplace:

> ...workers' reactions to oppressive managerial practices often mirror the aggression of their superiors, closing a vicious circle of dominance and submission that virtually assures the continuation of an oppressive workplace. Workers, managers and executives often polarize into subgroups that view the other as 'all bad' (evil and punishing) and themselves as 'all good' (righteous and victimized).

Is the 'story', however, as simple as the guys in the white hats (us) versus the bad guys in the black hats? Or is it that staff at all levels of organizations have mixed motives for what they do and how they react? Williams[43] reflects this approach in his comments: 'We must recognize that our vested interests are tied to one another and only through recognizing and responding to those interests on multiple levels can we jointly build credibility, security, and accomplishments toward any number of outcomes.'

Such an overall expanded typology is challenging and confronting to all the parties involved in workplace violence. Its implications are that all can potentially contribute to the problem as well as to its solutions. Such issues (though difficult ones) should be faced and not denied by staff, unions and employers. Lets now look at the issue of defining the workplace.

How do we define the workplace?

The second issue raised by Bulatao and VandenBos and by Budd was: where is the workplace?

Bulatao and VandenBos[44] attempt to define the workplace as follows: '...though it has its limits, the most convenient way to identify workplace violence appears to be to refer to crimes of violence that occur in the workplace or while the victim is at work or on duty.' With work being redefined in a much more flexible way in a variety of possible worksites, including the worker's car or home, a definition of work-based violence is now more dependent on the task being undertaken at the time of the attack rather than the specific locale. Though an increasing number of workers are undertaking their work-related duties outside a particular fixed geographic locale, most would still identify some particular site as the base for their work. For taxi drivers it may be the place where they pick up their car; for mobile security guards it may be back at their company's office, where they return after completing their patrols.

As previously outlined, violence can come from outside an organization or have its origin within an organization. External violence is perpetrated by people outside the organization and may be aimed at individual staff or directed at the organization itself. Internal violence may be the result of one person's actions or may be part of an organization's own culture of aggression. The assailant may be known or not known to the target of the violence.

Assuming the worker still has some sort of identification with a work 'base', even if it is his or her home or car, the following combination of locations and participants for workplace violence is possible:

Inside the workplace
- Internal worker; external assailant unknown
  (petrol station attendant robbed by an unknown gunman).

- Internal worker; external assailant known
  (social security officer assaulted by an angry client).

- Internal worker; internal assailant unknown
  (psychiatric nurse attacked by new admission).

- Internal worker; internal assailant known
  (worker sexually harassed by a colleague).

Outside the workplace

- External worker; external assailant unknown
  (mobile security guard confronted by an intruder).

- External worker; external assailant known
  (manager stalked and attacked by a retrenched worker outside the office).

- External worker; internal assailant unknown
  (police officer confronted in a domestic violence situation).

- External worker; internal assailant known
  (mental health worker on home visit to an aggressive patient).

These combinations can be further expanded to include groups of assailants and organizations. Group assaults could include gang attacks on youth workers or internal harassment by a group of workers on some of their colleagues. This is an example of 'mobbing', as previously referred to. Organizational assault by one organization on another could include the hostile take-over of one organization by its competitor, leading to the emotional trauma of downsizing, retrenchment or redeployment. This internal–external dimension of the location of the violence needs to be integrated with the types 1–4 of workplace violence to give a comprehensive checklist for identifying potential workplace violence hazards.

Finally, let us look at the link between violence and the workplace and how that should be reflected in these definitional issues.

What is the link between violence and the workplace?

The third issue raised by Bulatao and VandenBos concerns how closely the violent incident must relate to the employee's work at the time of the incident. In examining the link between violence and the workplace, such issues as the following arise:

- Has the violence arisen because of the staff's particular work activities, or just because of their presence in a particular workplace? For example, when an employee working at home disturbs a burglar and is assaulted, is this workplace violence? Similarly, when an off-duty police officer is attacked by people he has previously arrested, is that violent incident work related?

- How far does the employer's responsibility extend to provide a safe working environment? Does this include the worker's home and/or car? Does it include workers killed in terrorist attacks?

- To what extent are staff covered by insurance and workers' compensation schemes when they are attacked on the way to or from a base but still 'at work'?

- Are domestic disputes or stalking that spill over into the workplace cases of workplace violence, and what is the employer's obligation in such incidents?

Such questions are more than academic, especially when questions of litigation, workers' compensation and employers' responsibilities under health and safety legislation and other legal frameworks are concerned. This link also needs to be clear in the collection and analysis of workplace violence statistics. In some incident report forms the place of injury may be described as on a street but it is not clear that in fact what occurred was an assault on a 'bouncer' outside a club – a definite workplace-related violent incident.

Thus any definition of workplace violence should reflect and make clear the link between these two issues, especially where legal responsibilities are involved. Therefore it may be important to clarify what are the work-related duties that lead to involvement in violence as compared to a worker who just happens to be in a situation where violence occurs. As Perone[45] illustrates, these questions are being addressed, or ignored, in different ways across a number of countries in various occupational health and safety, workers' compensation and other legal frameworks.

Conclusion

There are various trends and issues that have arisen over the last 30 years and that are currently still being debated as regards workplace violence. A number of the key issues identified in this chapter are:

- What is workplace violence?

- How do we define the workplace?

- What is the link between the workplace and violence?

- These issues were closely examined and key themes and principles drawn out and used to inform better the debate around definitions and to develop a more comprehensive typology of workplace violence.

This expanded typology is key in a number of ways. First it identifies the various types of workplace violence, some of which have not been recognized and others of which overlooked or put into the 'too hard basket'. It also stresses the inter-relationship between the various types of workplace violence and the integral role organizational management and structures play in escalating or decreasing such violence within the workplace.

Finally, this typology points out the interconnectedness of a number of these issues in a way that, it is hoped, will allow workers, employers, unions, researchers and practitioners to challenge current assumptions and to increase further their knowledge about these concepts. At the same time it is hoped it will also provide a comprehensive framework to help implement non-violent management practices and to improve workplace safety for staff and those in their care.

Notes

1. See Bowie, V. (2000) Current trends and emerging issues in workplace violence. *Security Journal* 13(3) 7–23, for a more detailed historical overview of workplace violence.
2. See Budd, T. (1999) *Violence at Work: Findings from the British Crime Survey.* London: Health & Safety Executive; VandenBos, G. and Bulatao, E. (1996) *Violence on the Job: Identifying Risks and Developing Solutions.* Washington, DC: American Psychological Association; Harrison, R. (ed.) (1996) Occupational medicine. *Violence in the Workplace: State of the Art Reviews* 11(2); Chappell, D. and Di Martino, V. (1998) *Violence at Work.* Geneva: International Labour Office; Graycar, A. (1998) The cost of occupational violence. Paper presented at the conference 'Conflict and Violence in the Workplace', Canberra, for the Australian Institute of Criminology; Mayhew, C. and Leigh, J. (1999) Occupational violence in Australian workplaces: defining and explaining the problem. Paper presented at the 'Occupational Violence' seminar, Faculty of Law, University of Sydney; Mullen, E. (1997) Workplace violence: cause for concern or the construction of a next category of fear? *Journal of Industrial Relations* 39(1), 21–23; Perone, S. (1999) *Violence in the Workplace. Australian Institute of Criminology Research and Public Policy Series* 22. Canberra: AIC.
3. Diamond, M. (1997) Administrative assault: a contemporary psychoanalytic view of violence in the workplace. *American Review of Public Administration* 27(3), 228–47.
4. Bulatao, E. and VandenBos, R. (1996) Workplace violence: its scope and issues. In

VandenBos, G. and Bulatao, E. (eds) *Violence on the Job: Identifying Risks and Developing Solutions.* Washington, DC: American Psychological Association, 1.

5. Budd op. cit., 1.

6. Ibid., 2.

7. Littlechild, B. (1997) I needed to be told that I hadn't failed: experiences of violence against probation staff and of agency support. *British Journal of Social Work* 27, 219–40.

8. Budd op. cit., vi.

9. Perone op. cit., 18.

10. Ibid., 17.

11. Quoted in Leather, P., Brady. C., Lawrence, C., Beale, D. and Cox, T. (1999) *Work-Related Violence: Assessment and Intervention.* London: Routledge, 4.

12. Russell, B. (1999) Violence in the workplace. Briefing document for the Strategic Operations Group, WorkCover NSW, Australia.

13. Folger, R. and Baron, R. (1996) Violence and hostility at work: a model of reactions to perceived injustice. In VandenBos, G. and Bulatao, E. (eds.) *Violence on the Job: Identifying Risks and Developing Solutions.* Washington, DC: American Psychological Association, 52.

14. Standing, H. and Nicolini, D. (1997) *Review of Workplace-Related Violence.* London: Health & Safety Executive, 6.

15. Bowie, V. (1996) *Coping with Violence: A Guide for the Human Services.* London: Whiting & Birch. xvi

16. California Occupational Safety and Health Administration (Cal/OSHA) (1995) *Cal/OSHA Guidelines for Workplace Security.* San Francisco, CA: State of California Department of Industrial Relations, Californian Division of Occupational Safety and Health.

17. International Federation of Journalists (2001) International code of practice for the safe conduct of journalists (www.ifj.org/publications/press/newsline).

18. Kyle, M. and Hampshire, A. (2000) *The Impact of Working with Survivors of Violence and Abuse.* Sydney: The Benevolent Society, 3.

19. See McMammon, S.L. (1995) Painful pedagogy: teaching about trauma in academic and training settings. In Stamm, B.H. (ed.) *Secondary Traumatic Stress: Self-Care Issues for Clinicians, Researchers and Educators.* Lutterville: Sidran Press.

20. Kinnell, H. (2000) Serial homicide by doctors: Shipman in perspective. *British Medical Journal* 23(321), 1594.

21. Kohnke, M. (1981) Nurse abuse, nurse abusers. *Nursing and Health Care* May, 256–60.

22. Rylance, J. (2001) Bullying in the helping professions. In McCarthy, P. *et al.* (eds.) *Bullying from Backyard to Boardroom.* Sydney: Federation Press, 31.

23. See Braverman's chapter in this book (Chapter 7) for more information on how this dilemma can be addressed.

24. See Williams, L. (1994) *Organizational Violence: Creating a Prescription for Change.* Westport, CT: Quorum Books, for some detailed strategies about how organizations can respond appropriately to this issue.

25. See Smythe, E. (1984) *Surviving Nursing.* Menlo Park, CA: Addison-Wesley; Farrell, G. (2000) Danger! Nurses at work. *Australian Journal of Advanced Nursing*

18(2), 6–7.

26. See Macarthy, P. (1998) Strategies: between managementality and victim-mentality in the pressures of continuous change. Paper presented at the conference 'Conflict and Violence in the Workplace', Canberra, and also Barron in this book (Chapter 9).

27. Injury Prevention Research Center (2001) *Workplace Violence: A Report to the Nation*. Iowa City, IA: The University of Iowa.

28. See Borum, R., Fein, R., Vossekuil, B. and Berglund, J. (1999) Threat assessment: defining an approach for evaluating risk of targeted violence. *Behavioral Sciences and the Law* 17, 323–37, for a detailed critique of the limitations of the profiling approach.

29. Greenberg, L. and Barling, J. (1999) Predicting employee aggression against coworkers, subordinates and supervisors: the roles of perceived workplace factors. *Journal of Organizational Behavior* 20, 897–913.

30. Diamond op. cit., 230.

31. Bowie, V. (1998) Workplace violence. Paper presented at the Australian Institute of Criminology conference 'Crime against Business', Melbourne, June.

32. See Stanley, N., Manthorpe, J. and Penhale, B. (eds.) (1999) *Institutional Abuse: Perspectives across the Life Course*. London: Routledge.

33. Southerland, M., Collins, P. and Scarborough, K. (1997) *Workplace Violence: A Continuum from Threat to Death*. Cincinnati, OH: Anderson Publishing, 97.

34. Macarthy op. cit., 4.

35. Catalano, R., Dooley, D., Novaco, R., Wilson, G. and Hough, R. (1995) Using ECA survey data to examine the effects of job layoffs on violent behaviour. *Journal of Hospital and Community Psychiatry* 44, 874–79.

36. Baron, A.S. (1996) Organisational Factors in Workplace Violence: Developing Effective Programs to Reduce Workplace Violence in Harrison, R. (ed.) *Occupational Violence – Occupational Medine State of the Art Reveiws*, Vol. 11, no. 2 April–June 1996, 334–348.

37. Bensimon, quoted in Karl, K. and Hancock, B. (1999) Expert advice on employment termination: how expert is it? *Public Personnel Management* 28(1), 51–62.

38. Williams op. cit., 7.

39. Baron, R. and Neumen, J.H. (1998) Workplace aggression – the iceberg beneath the tip of workplace violence: evidence of its forms, frequency and targets. *Public Administration Quarterly* 21(4), 446–64.

40. See Wright, L. and Smye, M. (1996) *Corporate Abuse: How 'Lean and Mean' Robs People and Profits*. Toronto: Key Porter Books; Sennett, R. (1998) *The Corrosion of Character: The Personal Consequences of Work in the New Capitalism*. New York: W.W. Norton; Robinson, M. and del Carmel, R. (1999) Re-engineering (downsizing), corporate security and loss prevention. *Security Journal* 12(2), 27–38.

41. See Gill, M. (2000) *Commercial Robbery*. London: Blackstone Press, 158.

42. Diamond op. cit., 10.

43. Williams op. cit., 18.

44. Bulatao and VandenBos op. cit., 3.

45. Perone op. cit.

Chapter 2

Occupational violence in industrialized countries: types, incidence patterns and 'at risk' groups of workers

Claire Mayhew

Introduction

This chapter provides some baseline data about the types, incidence ratios and severity of occupational violence in selected western industrialized countries. Overall, the data indicate that the high-risk jobs are similar across western industrialized countries, although intervening factors can exacerbate or diminish the threats. The seminal international comparative work on violence patterns was conducted by Chappell and Di Martino for the International Labour Office.[1] In this chapter, evidence is presented that indicates there is an emerging 'epidemic' of occupational violence in some jobs. However, the incidence varies across nation-states because patterns of employment (and hence exposure) and other structural factors (such as firearms access) are diverse from one country to another and, indeed, between industry and occupational subgroups. There is also a propensity to report some forms of violence but not others. In general, the level of risk is rising over time, with new 'at risk' groups of workers and new types of threats emerging as job tasks and employment structures alter.

Patterns of reported and non-reported occupational violence in industrialized countries

Accurate information about the true extent of occupational violence is not available, apart from fatal incidents – which represent only the 'tip of the iceberg'. The lack of a uniformly accepted definition for non-fatal incidents prevents identification of clear trends. Some databases and surveys include only physical attacks that result in an injury, while others include sexual harassment, verbal abuse, intimidatory behaviours and obscene phone calls.[2] Further, because routine reporting only began around 1990, long-term trends cannot be unequivocally identified. *Non-reporting* of some incidents contributes to confusion over incidence and severity patterns. The reasons for non-reporting vary and can include embarrassment, the influence of organizational culture, toleration of minor incidents with reporting of only major attacks, and staff may ignore inappropriate behaviours if they are fearful of being blamed for the incident. One widely accepted estimate is that, at best, 1 in 5 incidents are reported.[3]

Nevertheless, there appears to have been a rise in non-fatal incidents over the past decade. This general increase may reflect, to some extent, improved *reporting* as the issue has gained prominence.[4] For example, amongst workers in public agencies (where reporting is likely to be more consistent), an increase has been seen across western industrialized countries, including databases collating workers' compensation claims, internal organizational records, surveys, insurance claims and police records.[5]

In this chapter it is argued that four factors determine levels of reporting/non-reporting:

1. *Injury severity* The more severe incidents are more likely to be reported, for example, those that result in fatalities or hospital admission.

2. *Departmental jurisdictions* Occupational violence 'falls between stools'. While it is clear that violence associated with armed hold-ups at retail establishments is a matter for the criminal justice system and will almost inevitably be recorded in police records, recording requirements following threats to a worker by a client or 'internal' violence are clouded. In these latter two cases, the responsible authorities are located within departments of labour in most western industrialized countries – for example, the Health and Safety Executive (HSE) in the UK, Occupational Safety and Health Administration (OSHA) in the USA, and the occupational health and safety (OHS) authorities in each of the Australian states and territories. That is, police databases, those of OHS authorities and internal organizational records may include quite different events under quite different categories. As a result, collation of data and calculation of incidence ratios within nation-states – let alone across countries – are very difficult.

3. *The different origins of violence significantly influence the propensity to report* Type 1 violence (as described by Bowie in the previous chapter), which originates from a person outside an organization – such as hold-ups – is quite likely to be reported to the police irrespective of whether there were any injuries suffered by workers. Indeed, there is often an insurance requirement to report before a claim for loss of goods or cash can be lodged. With type 2 client-related violence (which originates from a client, customer, detainee or in some rare occasions staff), the propensity to report may be mediated by concern for the perpetrator, such as amongst healthcare workers caring for senile patients. Further, in some caring jobs, staff experience so much lower-level aggression they would never be able to complete their job tasks if they were continually filling in incident report forms.[6] In contrast, type 3 violence (which originates from individuals who have, or have had, some form of employment relationship *within* the organization) is least likely to be formally recorded unless the severity of violence between perpetrator and victim has escalated and intensified to an extreme level. Even in severe cases, the injuries are more often emotional than physical, difficult to define precisely and may manifest as stress-related illnesses.[7] Finally, in type 4 violence (which is more systemic in nature and stems from excessive organizational pressures), individual perpetrators and victims may be difficult to identify unequivocally, the symptoms may be diffuse and there may be an inability to identify solutions because the essential source is frequently economic stress from the broader globalized market. In sum, type 1 violence is most likely to be formally recorded, and type 4 the least.

4. *Job insecurity mediates the propensity to report occupational violence* If employment is insecure, victims may be unwilling formally to report lower-level violence, particularly bullying, because of job loss fears (see evidence below).

The discussion below elaborates on the factors that determine the propensity to report incidents, identifies some 'at risk' jobs and indicates areas where threats are increasing.

Industries and occupations where occupational violence is more common

The consistent pattern evident in data from the UK, the USA and

23

Australia is that jobs where 1) cash is on at hand (type 1 violence) and 2) tasks that involve a lot of face-to-face contact between workers and clients (type 2 violence) are higher risk. Thus the probability and severity of violence vary markedly between these jobs and those where workers have little contact with their clientele and where money does not change hands. The potential for violence may increase at particular times of the day or night, on specific days of the week, at venues where there is excessive alcohol intake, if large amounts of cash and valuables are held in poorly secured premises, in particular geographical areas or if there are long client waiting periods. Close examination of the contexts of violent incidents and of minutiae in data patterns is necessary to identify particular risk factors.

There are also gender variations in exposure to occupational violence.[8] While the international evidence is patchy, it appears consistent. Females tend to experience higher levels of verbal abuse, while males tend to receive more overt threats and physical assaults.[9] This variation in risk can be partially explained by the gender division of labour, with women concentrated in lower-status and 'caring' jobs with greater face-to-face contact. For example, homicides are now the leading cause of death for US women workers because females are frequently employed in convenience stores – which are higher risk.[10] Interestingly, aggression against a woman may be more restrained if she is perceived to be attractive.[11] While one study found younger workers may be particularly at risk,[12] others have identified an increased risk for older females who may be perceived to be 'easy targets' in hold-ups as they are unlikely to fight back.[13, 14]

Off-site or isolated work environments are also higher risk. One UK study of 800 women and 200 men found that 1 in 3 professionals who went out to meet their clients had been threatened, and 1 in 7 male professionals working away from their office had been attacked.[15] Unfortunately there are a number of jobs that require off-site visits, many with clients in their car – and transporting a stranger in a car is a particularly high-risk activity.

Type I violent incidents: external threats

The jobs at highest risk of armed hold-up and robbery-related violence are similar across the industrialized world, and have remained relatively constant over time. There are four core risk factors: the business exchanges money with customers; there are few workers on site; the business trades in the evening or at night; and workers have face-to-face communication with customers.[16] Any site where money transactions occur is at higher risk of instrumental (or type 1) violence, especially banks, post offices, gambling outlets, armoured vehicles that transport cash, convenience stores, drive-through hotel sales and off-licences, video stores, service stations and chemist shops for those with addictions.[17] In both Canada and the UK, bank workers, retail sales staff, those in take-away food outlets, bar and off-licence staff, milkmen and transport and taxi drivers are at increased risk.[18] In the USA, bar, liquor store, service station, hotel and motel, grocery shop, eating and drinking establishment, and jewellery and convenience store workers were at very high risk of robbery-related violence.[19] A five-year study of one town in Florida found 96% of all convenience stores had been robbed, 36% of fast-food outlets, 21% of service stations and 16% of liquor stores, with robbers frequently assuming the identity of a customer as a pretext to entry.[20]

Workers in the transport industry are at particular risk of type 1 violence because they work alone, carry money, are on the job in the evening and night, drive on comparatively deserted streets and carry inebriated passengers. Taxi drivers have one of the highest levels of work-related homicide and severe assaults across all industrialized countries.[21] One explanation for the higher levels of risk in taxi driving is that they are now seen to be comparatively 'easy' targets as banks, all-night chemists, service stations and 'convenience' stores have progressively tightened security.[22]

Repeat and multiple victimization is common in some areas ('hot spots'), and little crime at all is reported in others.[23] Bellamy explained this phenomenon in terms of 'attractive' or 'unattractive' targets, with those that were perceived to be more difficult passed over and 'easier' victims robbed repeatedly.[24] 'Attractive' targets are situated in high-crime areas, have minimum protection for workers, limited observation from passers-by, allow ready access to highways for get-away, and have a number of possible exits from the site.[25] Nevertheless, rewards can be small – in half of all US convenience store robberies, less than $50 was stolen.[26] Thus convenience stores have been called the 'poor man's ATM' (automatic teller machine).[27]

Yet the Fisher and Looye[28] study found that 9% of burglaries, 33% of vandalism acts and all employee thefts went unreported to police. Other forms of violence are also likely to be under-reported; for example a customer murdered in a US retail shop would not be counted, nor would the homicide of an off-duty employee on-site to pick up a pay cheque.[29] The desire to prevent similar future events and the claiming of insurance were the most common reasons for formally reporting type 1 incidents, with minor robberies that did not result in injuries or loss of goods more likely to go unreported.[30]

The *severity* of violent incidents may be increasing over time. In the UK, bank robberies where firearms were used increased by 59% over 1990–91.[31] Similar rapid increases in the use of weapons during violent robberies have been reported in Scandinavia.[32] Robberies and other criminal activity account for almost 80% of all US work-related homicides and at least 30% of non-fatal assaults.[33] The increased level of homicide during robberies in the USA compared with other industrialized countries is undoubtedly related to weaker gun control laws and increased levels of gun ownership with over three quarters of homicides committed with firearms.[34]

Self-employed owner/managers were over-represented amongst victims; for example in California, 34.8% of 147 assault-related fatality victims were self-employed.[35] As Thomas[36] identifies, difficulties in accessing baseline employment data make calculation of incidence ratios for the self-employed very difficult. Similarly, Fisher and Looye[37] found in their study of 400 US small businesses that 1 in 8 had been victims of burglary or vandalism, with repeat victimization common.

In Australia, in contrast to the US pattern, only 2.8% of traumatic work-related fatalities are due to homicide – taxi drivers and security guards were at highest risk of type 1 violence.[38] As in the USA, access to weapons was an important influence on severity – 49% of workplace homicide victims were shot, 22% stabbed with a knife, and 18% assaulted with another weapon.[39] Most assailants, and most homicide victims, were male. Yet the occupational pattern is quite different for violence-related *injuries.* For example, in the state of Western Australia, female employees in service stations, chemist shops and video outlets, and pizza delivery and taxi driving were at higher risk than males.[40]

There are other forms of robbery-related violence that remain, as yet, largely unexplored but which may be increasingly common in particular parts of the world. For example, in the maritime industry (which is predominantly staffed by an international labour-force), robbery-related violence associated with piracy at sea is growing: ' ... violent attacks on ships and their crews are occurring with increasing frequency and intensity. In 1997 some 229 vessels were attacked ... 631 crew members suffered violence in these attacks, with 51 crew members reported killed.'[41]

Type 2 violent incidents: client initiated

Client-related violence is very common in western industrialized countries. This category includes client, patient, customer and prisoner-initiated violence. It can also include violence by staff against those they 'serve'. In both the USA and the UK, the jobs at high risk of client-initiated violence were the police, security and prison guards, the fire service, teachers, and welfare, healthcare and social security workers.[42] In Australia, 38% of all work-related homicides were committed by clients, customers or patients of the murdered worker.[43] A similar pattern of risk exists for assaults: in the Australian state of New South Wales, 85% of all violence-related workers' compensation insurance claims were from health, welfare and community services; education; property and business services; retail trade; public administration; and road and rail transport.[44] By occupation, the most 'at risk' jobs were miscellaneous labourers, registered nurses, miscellaneous para-professionals (such as welfare, community and prison workers), personal services (refugee, home companion, enrolled nurse and family aid), police, road and rail transport, and schoolteachers.[45] In Australia, as elsewhere, prostitution is a very high-risk job – but one for which the violence data are notoriously under-reported.[46]

Healthcare workers in the UK had a 1 in 10 chance of a minor injury, and 1 in 6 were verbally abused.[47] Other UK studies have found that 1 in 200 healthcare workers suffer a major injury from violent clients each year, and 1 in 10 need first aid.[48] One survey of general practitioners in the UK found 10% had been assaulted and 5% threatened with a weapon; and another study found 11% had been assaulted and 91% experienced verbal abuse.[49] A study in Ireland found 44.4% of male and 32.5% of female physicians were the victim of some form of violence in the year studied.[50] In a study co-ordinated by the UK HSE, variations by healthcare subsectors were collated: accident and emergency department and psychiatric hospital workers were at greatest risk, followed by those working with people with a mental handicap and ambulance staff.[51] The higher levels of risk in emergency admission departments can be exacerbated by other problems. For example, one US study found that 25% of major trauma patients treated in emergency rooms carried weapons.[52] A Swedish study of violence in healthcare workplaces found many perpetrators were mentally ill (44%), senile (37%) or under the influence of alcohol or narcotics (12%).[53] Between 46 and 100% of nurses, psychiatrists and therapists in psychiatric facilities in the USA are estimated to have been assaulted during their career.[54] *Some* people with psychiatric disorders pose an increased risk.[55] Younger male patients suffering psychosis with active impaired thinking or neurological abnormality and with a history of violence are most likely to assault staff.[56] Thus, patients with psychosis may present a far higher risk to staff than do those with schizophrenia.[57] Nevertheless, clients with paranoid schizophrenia may be quite dysfunctional, may have delusions of persecution or grandeur, unrealistic perceptions of events, live in both real and fantasy worlds at the same time and, when they strike out, they may do so in 'righteous' self-defence.[58] Specific events may also trigger unprovoked assaults, such as too much ward activity at one time, denial of services, overcrowding or inadequate facilities, or negative staff attitudes.[59]

Community welfare and social workers are at increased risk when they visit clients in their homes or take children into care, and housekeepers in hostels are at increased risk.[60] An important risk factor is the availability and carrying of weapons by clients. For example, many homeless people carry weapons such as screwdrivers to protect themselves on the street.[61] Thus clients who have been on leave from hostels, psychiatric support units or community homes should be screened for weapons on their return.[62]

The education sector is increasingly risky for workers. There have been several major incidents in US schools, as well as the much publicized multiple homicide at Dunblane in Scotland. Evidence suggests that violence in schools is greatest in geographical areas with higher crime rates and street gangs.[63] This pattern (logically) suggests that school populations and risks mirror the community in which they are situated. Highest rates are found in schools with lax discipline, lackadaisical or arbitrary enforcement of rules, a weak principal and where students did not aspire to high grades.[64] Most assaults involve one student attacking another, although around 10% of secondary teachers are abused by pupils each week, and many are attacked by ex-pupils or the parents of pupils.[65] As a result, the New South Wales education department has taken out a series of apprehended violence orders since late 1996 following the stabbing of a teacher.[66]

Law enforcement officers are at risk when making arrests, conducting drug raids, serving warrants, investigating suspicious vehicles or during high-speed chases or random alcohol or drug testing.[67] Robberies and domestic disputes are particularly high risk. In the USA over 100 police officers are killed in the line of duty each year. This has significant costs on surviving officers and the public purse, as 70% of those involved in shootings leave the force within 5 years, and untreated post-traumatic stress disorder is a serious problem.[68] Correctional and juvenile detention workers face similar risks. One Canadian study found that most assaults and homicides occurred in high-security cellblocks during the day shift, with officers with less than 1 year of experience at greatest risk. Incarcerated assailants were usually young males with a history of violence, and the incident usually occurred when few potential witnesses were around.[69] Correctional and juvenile detention workers also face the potential risk of being taken hostage in institutional riots.

The other major type of client-related violence, that by staff against those in their 'care' as identified by Bowie in Chapter 1, is a largely hidden but emerging concern which needs to be addressed in more detail elsewhere.

Type 3 violent incidents: 'internal' or bullying

Internal violence is committed by individuals who have, or have had, some form of employment relationship within the organization. The incident(s) may occur between supervisor/employee or employee/ employee. The direction of violence is not always a simple abuse of power from supervisors to subordinates: employees can harass their supervisors, older workers can intimidate apprentices or males can terrorize young females. Covert malicious intent distinguishes internal violence from normal workforce interactions.

The incident may involve a 'one-off' physical act of violence or, more commonly, repeated bullying or harassment. In this latter case, multiple perpetrators may be involved (for example, mobbing where groups of workers 'gang-up' on a victim) and more than one recipient, and the events may be repeated over time (such as during violent initiation rites). While some bullying activities are obvious, others are subtle and covert. Incidents may involve verbal abuse, threats, 'behaviours that create an environment of fear', activities that lead to stress or avoidance behaviour in the recipient, stalking, initiation rites or actual physical assault.[70] An important feature is that bullying is usually *repeated* and *escalates in intensity* over time.

Management style and organizational culture can influence levels of internal violence as the origins may lie in 'bad management' rather than malicious intent. A highly competitive business environment with increased competition can elevate stress levels and increase the potential for violence. Quasi-military hierarchical and rigid management styles, and marked supervisor/employee divisions, exacerbate a 'them and us' culture, foster resentment and anger and also increase the probability of violence. 'High-risk' scenarios include management toleration of bully-ing, job insecurity, workers facing unemployment with little chance of re-employment, workers with a strong sense of entitlement who feel cheated, vengeful workers, a loss of self-esteem and stability amongst workers and disciplinary suspensions.[71] The advancement of female workers may further contribute to the resentment felt by some males who perceive they have been passed over unfairly.[72] Numerous studies have suggested that violence rarely 'comes out of the blue', but is commonly preceded by behaviour that indicates a potential for violence.[73] Supervisors or employees with a history of assaults, or who have exhibited belligerent, intimidating or threatening behaviours, are higher risk.[74] White males in the age range 30–50, who are married with families and who have been employed with the organization for some time, may be more common perpetrators.[75] Improper behaviours such as horseplay, scuffling or practical jokes may add to a culture where intimidation is tolerated.[76]

If inappropriate behaviours have been tolerated or ignored for some time, the perpetrator may have come to believe bullying is acceptable and normal, or that this is the only way to get the 'best' out of employees or fellow workers. Sometimes, the inappropriate behaviour has evolved slowly over time, and perpetrators may not even be aware of the impact of their conduct. Thus a 'culture of denial' of lower-level violence may develop. Similar denials have been documented in other areas of occupational health and safety when new diseases first emerged – for example, with repetition strain injury (RSI) disbelief was frequently expressed through an attitude now known as 'blame the victim'.

The perpetrators of violence (or bullies) act as they do because of envy, fear of their own inadequacy, experiences of childhood bullying, provocation and an inability to manage their own aggression.[77]

If their employment is insecure, victims may be unwilling to report less severe forms of violence because of job loss fears. Frequent turnover of staff in an area, particularly those who are distinctive in some way (for example gender, ethnicity or youth), may be a warning sign that bullying is occurring. Victims of bullying are likely to have at least twice the rate of stress-related illness compared with non-victims, and the impact will be exacerbated by non-supportive colleagues who wish to avoid involvement and protect their own jobs, and so they ignore the pain experienced by recipients, and may even 'blame the victim'.[78] Potential consequences from bullying include high levels of anxiety, absenteeism and turnover; diminished productivity; poor industrial relations; difficulties in recruiting and retaining valued staff; and a poor organizational reputation.[79]

A range of strategies has been tried to stamp out bullying. Demonstrated top management commitment to non-violence appears to be of central importance. Many other strategies are counterproductive (for example, the use of mediation meetings where victims are forced to confront perpetrators is often extremely painful for the victims). The impact of such confrontations, even with the best of counsellors present, can be compared with the logic of placing rapists into mediation meetings with their victims. Effective strategies may also be informed by domestic violence and stalking-reduction prevention programmes.

Type 4 violent incidents: organizationally based or systemic

Type 4 violence occurs where the organization, by commission or omission, creates an environment where fear is rampant, bullying is tolerated, overwork is expected and yet worker attributes are blamed for any problems.[80] Arguably, this is another variation of 'blame the victim' ideologies. Bowie has discussed this form of violence in depth in the previous chapter. Suffice to state that this form of violence is essentially *systemic* across an organization, is highly unlikely to be the influence of individual workers and broader market forces may limit the capacity of organizations to reform themselves quickly.

It is proposed here that a broader focus should be used when analyzing type 4 violence. It is argued that wider societal forces, structural preconditions and a marked shift to short-term precarious work contracts contribute to work environments where bullying, fear and violence can grow unchecked and remain relatively unrecognized. Enhanced modern management practices and a broadening of employment opportunities have generally accompanied the efficiencies, improved competitiveness and opening up of markets through globalization. However, on occasions, increased pressure, long hours of work, loss of traditional market share, changing skill requirements, work overload and demand fluctuations can contribute to stress and the emergence of non-productive behaviours such as bullying. That is, a fundamental contradiction can arise between the imperatives of efficiency and competitiveness and 'good' management practices. This contradiction can manifest as overt or covert violence against employees (as in type 3 violence) or, in the case of precariously employed workers, as veiled threats against continued or future contracts. The underlying *causal* factor is economic stress. Thus type 4 violence is usually systemic across whole sectors of the economy and concentrated within particular industry subgroups and/or geographical areas where threats of unemployment are greatest.

Empirical evidence gathered by the author over the past decade in Australia indicates that (allowing for type 1 and 2 risk factors) violence appears to be more common amongst precariously employed workers, for example, those employed under casual, subcontract or very short-term contracts. In a series of studies involving face-to-face interviews using a detailed questionnaire (which was marginally altered between studies to pick up specific features), 1,738 workers evaluated their experiences of violence under the categories of abuse, threats, assaults, road rage (for truck drivers) and hold-ups. Findings from these studies about violence and other occupational health and safety problems have been reported in detail elsewhere.[81] Three direct quotations are provided below to illustrate the economic contexts within which precariously employed workers are subject to violence or excessive work demands:

> A clothing manufacture outworker: *'Contractor yelled and abused me like I was an animal; then didn't pay me.'*[82]

> A building subcontractor: *'Economically we are in terrible times. Technically it is too hard for us to perform correctly...People cutting corners to get the job. Few big developers say to subbie [subcontractor] "you will do this for XX dollars", killing the industry.'*[83]

> A long-haul truckdriver in a small economically vulnerable fleet: *'1.45pm, checking the load restraints in a yard and load binder snapped shut on my hand. Smashed my hand and for four days he kept me away from home. Hand was as big as a balloon when I finally got home after 4 days...I was given six weeks off work but the following Sunday (3 days later) was told "here's another job to do and if you don't do it, you haven't got a job".'*[84]

In Table 2.1 summarized data are shown, broken down by: 1) the industry/occupation/job task of the worker groups in the left-hand column; 2) in the second column by security of employment; and 3) by type of violence experienced. (The 'road-rage' and 'held-up' categories were used only once in recent studies.) The studies summarized in Table 2.1 found that experiences of occupational violence varied markedly by industry. The primary high-risk factors were as follows:

- First, cash on hand (as expected).

- Second, amount of face-to-face contact with customers (as expected).

- Third, risks varied by gender – primarily because of the marked sexual division of labour in Australia. However in jobs where males and females did similar jobs, there was a tendency for females to suffer proportionately more verbal abuse and for males to experience a disproportionate number of threats and assaults.

- Fourth, employment status was an important subsidiary factor: those with less job security tended to experience more occupational

Table 2.1 Job task and gender variations in experiences of violence amongst 1,738 Australian workers

Job task	Employment status	Abuse (male) (%)	Abuse (female) (%)	Threats (male) (%)	Threats (female) (%)	Assault (male) (%)	Assault (female) (%)	Other (male) (%)	Other (female) (%)
Long-haul trucking n = 300								Road rage	Road rage
Owner/drivers	Precarious	36.4	*	10.1	*	1.0	*	21.2	*
Small fleet	Precarious	35.6		6.7		–		19.2	
Large fleet	Secure	25.9		5.9		1.2		21.2	
								Held up	Held up
Young casual n = 304	Precarious	35.2	59.9	12.3	5.8	3.3	–	4.1	1.7
Clothing mfg n = 200									
Factory based	Secure	6.2	3.6	6.2	–	–	2.4		
Outworkers	Precarious	60.0	43.0	40.0	25.8	20.0	5.4		
Small business owner managers n = 248									
Garage	Precarious	9.9	–	4.2	–	–	–		
Café	Precarious	51.1	40.9	23.4	–	2.1	–		
Newsagent	Precarious	67.6	57.6	16.2	6.1	2.7	–		
Printing	Precarious	34.6	44.4	3.8	–	3.8	–		
Building n = 331									
Contractors	Semi-prec.	12.7	–	5.3	–	2.7	–		
Cabinet-makers	Precarious	14.7	–	4.7	–	2.0	–		
Demolishers	Precarious	29.0	–	6.4	–	3.2	–		
Outsourced n = 255									
Childcare	Secure/prec.	50.0	32.0	–	8.0	–	6.7		
Hospitality	Precarious	64.7	50.0	52.9	16.7	17.6	3.3		
Transport	Secure/prec.	31.2	–	9.4	–	6.2	–		
Building	Precarious	38.7	–	9.7	–	–	–		
Taxi drivers	Precarious	81.0	*	17.0	*	10	*		

Note: Abuse, threats and assaults in the previous 12-month period on one female truck driver and three female taxi drivers interviewed have been combined with those for males in these two studies.

violence. However, competition for work, limited bargaining power, reduced job control and a fear of 'speaking out' compounded tendencies to non-reporting. Thus the vast majority of incidents were never formally reported and, as a result, the official databases significantly understated the extent.

This means that industry sector is the primary determinant of occupational violence because of levels of exposure to type 1 'external' violence through cash on hand, and type 2 'client-initiated' violence through levels of face-to-face contact with clients. Gender may mediate the severity of these incidents. However, employment status is another important, but usually overlooked, mediating variable. Of concern is the fact that the industry sectors within which precariously employed workers are most commonly employed are 'growth' areas for job (e.g. service sector work in the fast-food and hospitality areas). Simultaneously, the very insecure nature of these jobs means the proportion of under-reporting is likely to increase. Thus, over time, a greater proportion of the workforce is likely to be exposed to occupational violence, but this will not be reflected in official violence statistics. Hence the rush to increased precarious employment may reinforce a situation within which systemic violence can flourish without recognition.

Conclusion

This chapter began by elaborating part of the typology of violence described by Bowie. The incidence patterns and 'at risk' groups of workers in a number of western industrialized countries were identified within the framework of this typology. The data indicate that occupational violence is a predictable accompaniment to work in some jobs, and is in epidemic proportions in a few.

Type 1 violence originates from outside to the worksite and is predictably common in jobs where cash is at hand. Type 2 violence originates from clients, patients, customers, detainees and sometimes staff and is commonly experienced by workers who have a lot of face-to-face contact with their clientele – particularly those who are distressed, inebriated or angry. Type 3 violence has a quite different profile and originates within organizations, particularly those where dominant/ subordinate relationships are strongly enforced or under challenge. In contrast, type 4 violence has a systemic nature. In this chapter it has been argued that the type 4 violence categorization developed by Bowie should be expanded further to emphasize broader national and international economic pressures that can enhance a workplace culture where violence arises and is sustained. That is, a fundamental contradiction can arise between 1) the benefits from enhanced efficiency, competitiveness and productivity associated with globalization, which are antithetical to 2) the non-productive outcomes associated with occupational violence. For example, the rush to embrace globalization tacitly incorporates acceptance of employment practice such as increased casualization. Of seminal importance to the focus of this book, recent evidence suggests the probability of exposure to occupational violence is mediated by employment status, with those employed under precarious arrangements (casual, short-term contract, subcontractor, outworker, etc.) facing increased threats – although these are irregularly formally reported.

In sum, those working within the criminal justice system have long been concerned to reduce the incidence of type 1 violence. Similarly occupational health and safety authorities have focused much attention on the reduction of type 2 client-initiated violence. Some organizations have now begun to examine the causes of, and control strategies for, type 3 violence. However, the causative variables, effective control strategies, formal data collection strategies and authorities responsible for controlling type 4 occupational violence have yet to be identified. These challenges will be picked up in some of the following chapters.

Notes

1. Chappell, D. and Di Martino, V. (1998) *Violence at Work*. Geneva: International Labour Office.
2. Wynne, R., Clarkin, N., Cox, T. and Griffiths, A. (1996) *Guidance on the Prevention of Violence at Work*. Brussels: European Commission, 5; National Occupational Health and Safety Commission (NOHSC) (1999) *Program One Report: Occupational Violence. 51st Meeting of NOHSC, 10 March 1999*. Hobart: NOHSC.
3. Turnbull, J. and Paterson, B. (eds.) (1999) *Aggression and Violence: Approaches to Effective Management*. London: Macmillan; Barling, J. (1996) The prediction, experience, and consequences of workplace violence. In VandenBos, G. and Bulatao, E. (eds.) *Violence on the Job: Identifying Risks and Developing Solutions*. Washington, DC: American Psychological Association; Warshaw, L. and Messite, J. (1996) Workplace violence: preventive and interventive strategies. *Journal of Occupational and Environmental Medicine* 38(10), 993–1005; Wynne *et al*. op. cit., 10; Cox, T. and Leather, P. (1994) The prevention of violence at work: application of a cognitive behavioural theory. In Cooper, C. and Robertson, I. (eds.) *International Review of Industrial and Organizational Psychology* 9. Chichester: Wiley.
4. Long Island Coalition for Workplace Violence Awareness and Prevention (1996) *Workplace Violence Awareness and Prevention: An Information and Instructional Package for use by Employers and Employees*. New York: Long Island Coalition, 2; Reynolds, P. (1994) *Dealing with Crime and Aggression at Work: A Handbook for Organizational Action*. London: McGraw-Hill, 18; Leather, P., Cox, T. and Farnsworth, B. (1990) Editorial comment: violence at work: an issue for the 1990s. *Work and Stress* 4(1), 3–5.
5. Perrone, S. (1999) *Violence in the Workplace. Research and Public Policy Series Report* 22. Canberra: Australian Institute of Criminology, 82; Standing, H. and Nicolini, D. (1997) *Review of Workplace-Related Violence. Report for the Health & Safety*

Executive 143/1997. London: Tavistock Institute, 26; Heskett, S. (1996) *Workplace Violence: Before, During and After*. Boston, MA: Butterworth-Heinemann, 1718; Nelson, N. and Kaufman, J. (1996) Fatal and nonfatal injuries related to violence in Washington workplaces, 1992. *American Journal of Industrial Medicine* 30, 438–46; Cal/OSHA (1994) *Injury and Illness Prevention Model Program for Workplace Security*. San Francisco, CA: Division of Occupational Safety and Health, Department of Industrial Relations; Cardy, C. (1992) *Training for Personal Safety at Work*. Aldershot: Gower, 25, 32.

6. Turnbull and Paterson op. cit., 9.
7. Chappell and Di Martino op. cit., 44; McCarthy, P., Sheehan, M. and Wilkie, W. (eds.) (1996) *Bullying: From Backyard to Boardroom*. Alexandria, NSW: Millennium Books.
8. Chappell and Di Martino op. cit., 44–46.
9. Chappell and Di Martino op. cit., 44; Mayhew, C. and Quinlan, M. (1999) The relationship between precarious employment and patterns of occupational violence: survey evidence from thirteen occupations. In Isaksson, K. *et al.* (eds.) *Health Effects of the New Labour Market*. New York: Kluwer Academic/Plenum.
10. OSHA (1998) *Recommendation for Workplace Violence Prevention Programs in Late-Night Retail Establishments*. Washington, DC: US Department of Labor, Occupational Safety and Health Administration, 1; Reiss, A. and Roth, J. (1993) *Understanding and Preventing Violence*. Washington, DC: National Academy Press, 151; Thomas, J. (1992) Occupational violent crime: research on an emerging issue. *Journal of Safety Research* 23(2), 55–62.
11. Cox and Leather op. cit., 226.
12. Fitzgerald, S. (1998) Games people play: the high cost of bullying and harassment in the workplace. *Occupational Health and Safety Magazine, Sydney* December, 10–14.
13. Nelson and Kaufman op. cit.
14. Indermaur, D. (1995) *Violent Property Crime*. Sydney: Federation Press, 186.
15. Phillips, C., Stockdale, J. and Joeman, L. (1989) *The Risks in Going to Work: The Nature of People's Work, the Risks they Encounter and the Incidence of Sexual Harassment, Physical Attack and Threatening Behaviour*. London: Suzy Lamplugh Trust, 11; VandenBos, G. and Bulatao, E. (eds.) (1996) *Violence on the Job: Identifying Risks and Developing Solutions*. Washington, DC: American Psychological Association.
16. Heskett op. cit., 16.
17. Chappell and Di Martino op. cit., 8; Mayhew, C. (2000a) *Violence in the Workplace Preventing Armed Robbery. A Practical Handbook*. Research and Public Policy Series 33. Canberra: Australian Institute of Criminology.
18. Willis, A., Beck, A. and Gill, M. (1999) Violent victimization of staff in the retail sector. *Journal of Security Administration* 22(2), 23–30; Trades Union Congress (1999) *Protect Us from Harm: Preventing Violence at Work. A TUC Health and Safety Report by Julia Gallagher*. London: TUC Health and Safety Unit, 6–9; Standing and Nicolini op. cit., 7–9; Hancock, M. (1995) Violence in the retail workplace. *Accident Prevention* May/June, 16–21.
19. OSHA op. cit., 1; Department of Justice (1998) About 2 million people attacked or

threatened in the workplace every year. Press release 26 July; US Bureau of Justice Statistics (1998) *Workplace Violence, 1992–96: National Crime Victimization Survey*. Washington, DC: US Department of Justice, 2; Wilkinson, C. (ed.) (1998) *Violence in the Workplace: Preventing, Assessing and Managing Threats at Work*. Washington, DC: Government Institutes Publications, 3–9; NIOSH (1996) Violence in the workplace: risk factors and prevention strategies. Current Intelligence Bulletin 57, 2–3; Myers, D. (1996) A workplace violence prevention planning model. Journal of Security Administration 19(2), 1–19; Cal/OSHA (1995) *Guidelines for Workplace Security*. San Francisco, CA: Division of Occupational Safety and Health, Department of Industrial Relations, 4.

20. Reiss and Roth op. cit., 151.
21. Mayhew, C. (2000b) *Violent Assaults on Taxi Drivers: Incidence Patterns and Risk Factors*. Trends and Issues in Crime and Criminal Justice 178. Canberra: Australian Institute of Criminology; Chappell and Di Martino op. cit., 68.
22. Mayhew (2000b) op. cit.; Chappell and Di Martino op. cit., 68.
23. Fisher, B. and Looye, J. (2000) Crime and small businesses in the Midwest: an examination of overlooked issues in the United States. *Security Journal* 13(1), 45–72.
24. Bellamy, L. (1996) Situational crime prevention and convenience store robbery. *Security Journal* 7, 41–52; National Association of Convenience Stores (1991) *Convenience Store Security: Report and Recommendations*. Alexandria, VA: NACS, 4.
25. OSHA op. cit., 4; Heskett op. cit., 142.
26. National Association of Convenience Stores op. cit., 4; Malcan (1993) cited in Bellamy op. cit., 42.
27. Malcan op. cit.
28. Fisher and Looye op. cit., 58.
29. Nalla, M., Morash, M., Vitoratos, B. and O'Connell, T. (1996) Benchmarking study of workplace violence prevention and response: forty-two components from leading-edge programs. *Security Journal* 7, 89–99; Myers op. cit.; Wynne *et al.* op. cit., 9–10; Cox and Leather op. cit., 214.
30. Fisher and Looye op. cit., 58; Cook, B., David, F. and Grant, A. (1999) *Victims' Needs, Victims' Rights: Policies and Programs for Victims of Crime in Australia*. Research and Public Policy Series 19. Canberra: Australian Institute of Criminology, 5; Thomas op. cit., 58.
31. Reynolds op. cit., 18–19.
32. Wynne *et al.* op. cit., 13–14, 21.
33. Kposowa, A. (1999) The effects of occupation and industry on the risk of homicide victimization in the United States. *Homicide Studies* 3(1), 47–77; OSHA op. cit., 1; Reiss and Roth op. cit., 151; Thomas op. cit., 60.
34. Kposowa op. cit.; OSHA op. cit., 1; Reiss and Roth op. cit., 151; Thomas op. cit., 60.
35. Nelson and Kaufman op. cit., 43840; Cal/OSHA (1995) op. cit., 4; Thomas op. cit., 57.
36. Thomas op. cit., 57.
37. Fisher and Looye op. cit., 45.
38. Driscoll, T., Mitchell, R., Mandryk, J., Healey, S. and Hendrie, L. (1999) *Work-*

Related Traumatic Fatalities in Australia, 1989 to 1992. Canberra: Ausinfo/National Occupational Health and Safety Commission, vii.

39. Ibid., 9.
40. WorkSafe Western Australia (1999) Violence in the Workplace. Perth: WorkSafe Western Australia, 2. Details of this can be obtained from http://www.safetyline.wa.gov.au.
41. House of Representatives Standing Committee (1998) *Ship Safe: An Inquiry into the Australian Maritime Safety Authority. House of Representatives Standing Committee on Communications, Transport and Microeconomic Reform*. Canberra: The Parliament of the Commonwealth of Australia, 49.
42. Chappell and Di Martino op. cit., 72-74; Department of Justice op. cit., 2; Wilkinson op. cit., 3–9; NIOSH op. cit., 2; Mayhew, C. (2000c) *Preventing Client-Initiated Violence: A Practical Handbook*. Research and Public Policy Series 30. Canberra: Australian Institute of Criminology (some of this paragraph is based on this earlier publication); Standing and Nicolini op. cit., 7–9; Trades Union Congress op. cit., 6–9, 18.
43. Driscoll *et al*. op. cit., 7.
44. Estreich, P. (1999) The management of violence in the workplace: a best practice approach. Paper presented at the 'Occupational Violence' seminar, 26 August, University of Sydney Faculty of Law.
45. Ibid., 4.
46. Sex Workers Outreach Program (1999) *Sex Industry Legal Kit and also 9 Lives: Surviving Sexual Assault in the Sex Industry. Sex Workers Outreach Project*. Sydney: Darlinghurst.
47. HSE (1987) cited in Cox and Leather op. cit., 215.
48. Wykes, T. (ed.) (1994) *Violence and Health Care Professionals*. London: Chapman & Hall, 1.
49. Cembrowicz, S. and Ritter, S. (1994) Attacks on doctors and nurses. In Shepherd, J. (ed.) *Violence in Health Care: A Practical Guide to Coping with Violence and Caring for Victims*. Oxford: Oxford University Press.
50. Cited in Wynne *et al*. op. cit., 13.
51. Cardwell cited in Standing and Nicolini op. cit., 13–14; Turnbull and Paterson op. cit., 14–15.
52. Reich, R. and Dear, J. (1996) Guidelines for preventing workplace violence for health care and social service workers. In VandenBos, G. and Bulatao, E. (eds.) *Violence on the Job: Identifying Risks and Developing Solutions*. Washington, DC: American Psychological Association.
53. Arnetz, J. (1998) The Violent Incident Form (VIF): a practical instrument for the registration of violent incidents in the health care workplace. *Work and Stress* 12(1), 17–28.
54. Cited in Cal/OSHA (1998) *Guidelines for Security and Safety of Health Care and Community Service Workers*. San Francisco, CA: Division of Occupational Safety and Health, Department of Industrial Relations, 1–2.
55. Flannery, R. (1996) Violence in the workplace, 1970–1995: a review of the literature. *Aggression and Violent Behavior* 1(1), 57–68.
56. Flannery, R., Hanson, M. and Penk, W. (1994) Risk factors for psychiatric

inpatient assaults on staff. *Journal of Mental Health Administration* 21, 24–31.

57. Turnbull and Paterson op. cit., 17.

58. Capozzoli, T. and McVey, R. (1996) *Managing Violence in the Workplace*. Delray Beach, FA: St Lucie Press, 66.

59. Flannery *et al*. op. cit., 25.

60. Cal/OSHA (1998) op. cit., 3.

61. Ibid., 10.

62. Ibid.

63. Reiss and Roth op. cit., 155.

64. Ibid., 156.

65. Gill, M., Hearnshaw, S. and Turbin, V. (1998) Violence in schools: quantifying and responding to the problem. *Educational Management and Administration* 26(4), 429–42; Redmond, F. (2000) Increasing threats alarm United Kingdom teachers. *The Weekend Australian* 25–26 March, 12.

66. Patty, A. (1998) Teachers get help in seeking protection. *Sun Herald Sydney* 23 August, 34.

67. Cal/OSHA (1995) op. cit., 5; Mayhew, C. (2001) Occupational health and safety risks faced by police officers. *Trends and Issues in Crime and Criminal Justice* 196. Canberra: Australian Institute of Criminology.

68. Flannery op. cit., 60.

69. Ibid.

70. Workers' Health Centre (1999) *Health and Safety Fact Sheet: Violence at Work*. Sydney: Workers' Health Centre, 1; Chappell and Di Martino op. cit., 11, 104; McCarthy *et al*. op. cit.; Neales, S. (1997) When rites go wrong. *Sydney Morning Herald* (Good Weekend section) 6 September, 32–35; UNISON (1996) *Bullying at Work: Guidance for Safety Representatives and Members on Bullying at Work and How to Prevent it*. London: UNISON; Spiers, C. (1995) Strategies for harassment counselling. *Occupational Health* 47(11), 381–82.

71. Randall, P. (1997) *Adult Bullying: Perpetrators and Victims*. London: Routledge, 50–53; Mullen, E. (1997) Workplace violence: cause for concern or the construction of a new category of fear? *Journal of Industrial Relations* 39(1), 21–32; Witkowski, M. (1995) Workplace violence: problems and prevention suggested by Cal/OSHA workplace security guidelines. *Security Journal* 6, 213–18; Seger, K. (1993) Violence in the workplace: an assessment of the problem based on responses from 32 large corporations. Security Journal 4(3), 139–49; Myers op. cit., 3; Mayhew, C. (2000d) *Preventing Violence within Organisations: A Practical Handbook*. Research and Public Policy Series 29. Canberra: Australian Institute of Criminology (some of this paragraph is based on this publication).

72. Mullen op. cit.

73. Speer, R. (1997) Workplace violence: moving beyond the headlines. *Women Lawyers Journal* 83(1), 6–12.

74. Chappell and Di Martino op. cit., 56; Cherry, D. and Upston, B. (1997) *Managing Violence and Potentially Violent Situations: A Guide for Workers and Organizations*. Heidelberg West, Victoria: Centre for Social Health, 12.

75. Dale, R., Tobin, W. and Wilson, B. (1997) Workplace violence: another dimension of precarious employment. *Just Policy* 10, 312; Capozzoli and McVey op. cit., 50;

Heskett op. cit., 43.

76. Workers' Compensation Board of British Columbia (1995) *Take Care: How to Develop and Implement a Workplace Violence Program: A Guide for Small Business*. Vancouver: Workers' Compensation Board of British Columbia, 8.

77. Gaymer, J. (1999) Assault course. *Occupational Health* 51(2), 12–13.

78. Speer op. cit., 10.

79. Randall op. cit., 57; Wynne *et al.* op. cit., 16; UNISON op. cit.; Reynolds op. cit., 35–36; Cardy op. cit., 32.

80. See Bowie's chapter in this volume (Chapter 1).

81. Mayhew and Quinlan (1999) op. cit.; Mayhew, C. (2000e) OHS in Australian 'micro' small businesses: evidence from nine research studies. *Journal of Occupational Health and Safety, Australia and New Zealand* 16(4), 297–305.

82. Mayhew, C. and Quinlan, M. (1998) *Outsourcing and Occupational Health and Safety: A Comparative Study of Factory-Based and Outworkers in the Australian TCF Industry*. Sydney: Industrial Relations Research Centre, University of New South Wales (outworker 102), 110.

83. Mayhew, C., Young, C., Ferris, R. and Harnett, C. (1997) *An Evaluation of the Impact of Targeted Interventions on the OHS Behaviours of Small Business Building Industry Owners/Managers/Contractors*. Canberra: AGPS (interviewee B66), 198.

84. Mayhew, C. and Quinlan, M. (2000) Occupational health and safety amongst 300 truck drivers. Unpublished research report from the Industrial Relations Research Centre, University of New South Wales, conducted as part of the Motor Accident Authority of New South Wales Safety Inquiry into the Long Haul Trucking Industry, Sydney (interviewee 213).

Chapter 3

Causal factors of violence in the workplace: a human resource professional's perspective

A. Giles Arway

Introduction

Problem Background

Workplace violence has been on a steady increase over the past decade.[1] Nearly every form of media has carried stories of violence in the workplace. They range from simple arguments, to one of the most recent horrifying acts of a stock day-trader who took out his frustration on market loses by killing 11 people in two separate locations.[2]

The US Bureau of Justice Statistics (BJS)[3] reports that there were 1,063 workplace homicides reported in 1992. Homicide in the workplace has become the second leading cause of death in the USA and the highest cause of death for women while at work. On the surface, this information looked at in total is misleading. Of these 1,063 deaths in a workplace, only 59 workplace homicides involved co-workers. That is, only 5% of the total reported deaths.[4] The vast majority of the incidents were committed by persons other than employees of the company. Being a victim of workplace violence, in most cases therefore, is most often a result of an outsider preying upon an employee of a company such as in a robbery or in the instance of a dissatisfied customer. The relationship between the aggressor and the victim is often merely one of convenience. In other words, the person in the workplace was not the true target of the act.[5] The act was to rob or steal or commit some other crime. The injury or death of the company employee was incidental to the act. This does not diminish the severity of the act. It merely points out that the occupation or related activities of the organization itself may draw in the aggressor for that person's own extrinsic gain.

For employers, keeping workers safe is extremely important. In dangerous occupations or where crimes may occur against the employee for monetary gain, protection usually centres on physical barriers and security methods. The company endeavours to prevent the intrusion or victimization of the employee in order to prevent injury and/or loss of company assets. Other forms of assault and aggression received by workers occur at the hands of mentally disturbed or severely angered or irritated persons. In this instance, the workers are viewed as outlets for the venting of anger or frustration. The assault is not a direct result of an interpersonal or even a business relationship. The worker represents the establishment, or source, of his or her anger or frustration.[6]

The remaining aspect of workplace violence is that the company actually employs the potential aggressor and that the victims of the offence are co-workers exposed to the potential wrath on a daily basis. In most cases they are unaware of their peril. Of course it is imperative for organizations to provide maximum protection for their employees. One way to do that is to minimize the possibility of hiring people who could potentially harm or kill members of the same organization. This chapter investigates what human resource (HR) professionals feel are contribution causes or catalysts for aggression in the workplace. Once identified, organizations may be able to recognize potential aggressors before they are hired by the organization.

Literature review

But what is at the roots of aggression in the offender, and what are the relationships between aggressive acts and the workplace? Aggression has been studied extensively and certain theories have surfaced. One is that aggressive tendencies may be socially developed. Work on aggression by some social learning theorists suggests that social forces in the emotional development stages of life encourage potential aggression as a means of settling conflict, release of frustration or exertion of power.[7] The influence of the family unit, and its members, in the formative years of emotional development has an impact on the means and ability of a person to interact with life's events.

What may baffle most of us is not why persons commit the violence. What truly perplexes the investigator is what kind of person commits these acts, and how can we identify potential aggressors beforehand.[8] Continuous study of the sources of aggressive behaviour in human beings is furthering our understanding of the violent offender in the workplace. One difficulty arises when the workplace itself is introduced as an intervening variable. One has to wonder, for instance, what role the work environment may play in the development of aggressive behaviour. In addition, since the definition of what exactly the workplace is can be problematic, being able to draw significant correlations between violence, behaviour, work tasks and other occupational-related independent variables is extremely difficult.[9]

Social learning theory
Social learning theory (imitation of behaviour derived from social interactions) has been linked to a variety of settings and a variety of human behaviours. In these studies, it was found that four elements associated with social learning theory were supported and may be related to workplace violence in one of two ways.[10] The first is internal to the organization, where social learning may be associated with the culture or environment of the organization. The other is external, where the subject is influenced through family, society and other environments outside the organization. In both instances, the four major components of social learning and differential association (learnt behaviours from deviant social groups) are present: imitation of admired models, individual definition regarding deviant behaviour, extent of differential association and the extent of differential reinforcement.[11]

Whether in or outside the workplace, potential aggressors initiate violence for acceptance or rewards through their perception of what they see as acceptable or rewarded behaviour. Systemized desensitization towards violent behaviour may also be occurring. If aggressiveness, then, permeates much of the workplace, it seems likely that only members of the work group may begin to assimilate that behaviour. In similar fashion they may also bring those negative behaviours into the workplace from their personal contacts with society as a whole.[12] Differential association in and of itself is not negative. Differential association only means that a person will align him or herself with a group that controls the majority of the desired individual reinforcers. These reinforcers are predominantly peer acceptance, power, security and nurturing. In a negative context, violent behaviour becomes a method of satisfying these needs.[13] Frustration is believed to derive from unsatisfied feelings of incongruence and/or contradiction with one's environment, whether that is at home or at work.[14] Studies focusing on the relationship between frustration and violence have suggested strong relationships between frustration and aggressive behaviour. Frustrations cultivated on the job, at home, within relationships and other environments may influence a person to be violent.[15]

Interpersonal functioning

Numerous studies have attempted to identify elements and aspects of relationships between a person's ability to interact and causes of aggression. There seem to be some contributing factors such as family structures and interactions, child abuse and drug and alcohol abuse, to name a few.[16] The research also suggests that increased diversity among the workforce may cause tension in the workforce. Mixes of gender, ethnicity, races and even religion may result in aggravation for some co-workers whose personal preferences are subject to violation by that diversity.[17]

Working environment

One has to wonder what aspects the work environment may add to aggression. Adding to this question is the complexity of comparing working environments. The physical condition of the facility, exposure to toxic waste, polluted air and water or merely less than sanitary conditions have been found to influence negative attitudes and behaviours in the workplace.[18] The sick building syndrome (SBS) has also been linked to illnesses and poor productivity due to poor internal air quality (IAQ) and the presence of contaminants.[19] There is a lack of a clear empirical study on relationships between SBS and workplace violence, although many environmentalists suggest that our environment can sometimes shape our attitudes.[20] Workplace violence does not seem to be segregated to certain work settings. Incidents have occurred in industrial settings, office complexes and educational institutions.[21]

Stress

Certainly shared stressors are present in any company or business. It is believed that a person's reaction to those daily stresses may instigate aggression.[22] Three factors seem to be related to personal stress reactions. They are tolerance for ambiguity, locus of control and self-esteem.[23] It is the cognitive and affective differences among people on these factors that may heighten an individual's anxiety and overload his or her coping mechanisms. Persons with low tolerance for role ambiguity, with feelings of being controlled by external forces or those suffering from low self-esteem are more prone to negative stress reactions, anxiety and feelings of anguish.[24] Further, personal stress may result from interference with an employee's goal attainment or obstruction of other desirable organizational outcomes. It is believed these events may manifest themselves, depending upon the emotional makeup of the employee, into aggressive behaviour or hostility.[25]

Other stressors in the workplace have certainly been related to aggression in the workplace. Many of these are situational and dependent, of course, upon the individual's perceptions and interpretations. However, several of these have been isolated with some levels of predictability. They include role conflict, role ambiguity, workload and interpersonal conflict.[26] In a study by Chen and Spector, employee stress and frustration were also linked to theft, substance abuse and increased intentions to leave.[27]

Management style

Interactions between management and employees are, of course, an important factor relating to workplace violence.[28] Management styles and/or leadership abilities play a major role in employees' opinions and attitudes towards companies and their members. A manager's style of leadership has often been found to be incongruent with the employee's perception of that style.[29] This misalignment and miscommunication of intentions can cause mistrust, confusion and resentment.[30] In addition, managers are often called upon to direct people to perform unpleasant or disagreeable tasks. These may include administering discipline or even withholding employee benefits. These work environment transactions certainly increase tensions. A manager who is adept at communicating and skilled in interpersonal relations may minimize or divert aggressive behaviours from employees.

Co-worker relationships

Another source of agitation is inter-employee relationships. These are the daily interactions necessary for conducting business and involve the necessity of co-workers to interact, understand and share in transactions. Personality styles, conflicts, ethnic, racial or gender biases, along with differences in personal work habits, may combine to cause aggravations among co-workers. People who operate from a need to control relationships, or those who suffer from self-esteem problems, often tend to develop dysfunctional views of working relationships.[31]

Romantic obsessions

These are different from the close interpersonal relationships that may develop between employees. Unwelcome interpersonal relationships or attractions can heighten the emotional context of work relationships and can be negative in nature. Romantic obsessions with other employees have been cited as significant motives for violence in the workplace.[32] An analysis of this study reveals a modest increase in the amount of co-worker obsession in the last 10 years. The difficulty with these obsessions is that when they occur in a private or social setting, one member of the 'relationship' can back away. In the workplace, however, many workers can be helpless in removing themselves from the proximity of the stalker.[33] Uncontrolled obsessions can affect the rational thought processes. The rejection of romantic notions can build feelings of abandonment and anxiety within a person and may be expressed through anger, aggression, assault and/or murder.[34] The microcosm-like community of the workplace contributes to potential violence through the close interaction of its members. Like any other society, there is always a small percentage of employees who act outside accepted norms of behaviour.[35] Like society in general, the workplace will possess its share of persons who view relationships in abnormal ways. Situations of romantic obsessions are difficult to handle and extremely sensitive, and they exist in just about any workplace setting. Aggressiveness due to rejection, jealousy or rebuffs is always a possibility.

Purpose of the study

The purpose of this study is to determine what factors HR professionals feel are salient as causal factors of violence in the workplace. Much has been written, mostly anecdotal evidence, supporting the determinations of causes of workplace violence. HR managers and professionals view the organization from the inside out, and most work side by side with the daily worker at all levels of the organization. This affords the HR professional a qualified and unique perspective for understanding and identifying those elements of the organization, the workers and the external influences that may affect the organization and its members with respect to workplace violence.

Research hypotheses

Aggression that occurs in the workplace is not derived from a sole source or prompted from a single factor.[36] It is felt that a combination of circumstances, psychological and emotional conditions, organizational elements and external social or environmental factors forms the basis for the expression of the aggressive actions:

- *Hypothesis 1* The role that interpersonal relationships play between members of the organization is strongly related to the exhibition of aggression in the workplace; the more interpersonal problems exist, the more aggressive the workplace.

- *Hypothesis 2*   Social and financial conditions of the employee strongly related to expressions of aggression in the workplace.

- *Hypothesis 3*   Organizational structure and supervisor/subordinate interactions are strongly related to aggression in the workplace.

- *Hypothesis 4*   Drug and/or alcohol abuse is strongly related to aggression in the workplace.

- *Hypothesis 5*   Situations of romantic involvement with co-workers are strongly related to workplace violence.

- *Hypothesis 6*   Environmental working conditions are strongly related to situations of aggression in the workplace.

Limitations/delimitations

This study asked for opinions from HR managers concerning causal factors of workplace violence. These opinions are solely subjective and without empirical or quantifiable supporting evidence. This subjective and qualitative format may not only reflect actual conditions of the organization and the subject matter of this study but it may also include the subjective and personal feelings and attitudes of the respondent.[37] In a qualitative survey, it is important to recognize the ability of the respondent to compartmentalize the salient information from personal or intuitive feelings, which can affect the validity of the results.[38]

Reliability

An additional limitation that may impact reliability is the fact that the researcher represents a single coder. It is recommended that more than one person instructed in the method of analytical coding reviews the results. The individual codings are then compared for consistency. The greater the agreement of meaning for categories and units among the coders, the greater the degree of reliability of the study.[39]

Definitions

For the purposes of this chapter, there are several key words and phrases that need to be aligned with this topic. The phrase 'workplace violence' is so broadly used it loses meaning and clarity as to the relationship between the aggressor and the workplace. The statement of the problem touched upon the fact that workplace violence encompasses all types of violence that occurs against employees of any business enterprise. However, a distinction must be made between what appear to be two types of workplace violence. One type is strictly violence against an employee because of the employment relationship the employee has with the business. This means bank tellers, taxi drivers, police officers and others are targets of violent actions simply because they are between the criminal and the object desired, mostly money or other valuables.

The other type of workplace violence (the nucleus this chapter focuses upon) is the explanation of why a person turns against fellow workers. Here workplace violence is defined as an assault or aggression between co-workers or persons who are employees. Also included in this definition are persons who are innocent by-standers of workplace violence, such as customers, vendors, etc. These people are in the unfortunate circumstance of being in the proximity of violence and are harmed due to their mere presence.

Another important term is aggression. The most pronounced form of workplace violence is homicide. It gains the most recognition due to its horrendous characteristics. The reality, however, is that of the approximately 225,000 workplace incidents that occur each year, only a small percentage result in homicide.[40] However, aggression is thought of in a more general nature here. It includes the obvious connotation of physical harm to another. It also includes intimidation, harassment, sabotage and vandalism.[41] It is important to note that people need not experience physical pain to be harmed by an aggressive act towards a company or its members. There are associated losses and harm through these acts. In cost alone, companies experience over US$6.4 billion a year in lost assets due to violence in the workplace.[42]

Importance of the study

This study provides further insight and support with respect to previously published aspects of casual factors of workplace violence. Though not a rigorously quantitative study, it certainly does reveal actual conditions that effect the workplace and its members. This is also important to HR managers and professions in developing corporate strategies for prevention and responses to workplace violence. This understanding is important to the financial health of an organization and its ability to function at optimum efficiency. There are devastating short-term and long-range effects from these violent actions that impact the workplace, the business, the employee, and the surrounding community.

Methodology

Research design

This is a content analysis study that utilized an open-ended questionnaire to elicit responses from a select group of HR professionals. The HR managers were asked to respond in their own words and terms to an abstract question concerning the causes of workplace violence and what factors are in such situations, including the influences of the workplace itself.

According to Holsi,[43] content analysis is a technique for making references '...through systematic and objectively identifying special characteristics of messages'.

It provides a particular means of describing the contents of a variety of types of communication, such as news reports, written documents and verbal exchanges.[44] In studies where verbal or written content is examined, the analysis is broken down into categories and units. Categories represent the broader basis of interpretation of the statements. Units define the intent of those statements.[45] The interpretation of results has two components: manifest or latent content. Manifest content is the more superficial, observable content of statements, words or representations that are obviously present and countable. Latent content refers to the meaning of such words or phrases.[46] Supporting this differentiation of content method was an investigation by Strauss[47] who described the differences as in vivo codes and *sociological* constructs.

The *in vivo* codes are the literal terms used by the individual. As reported by Strauss:[48] '*in vivo* codes tend to be the behaviors or the processes which will explain to the analyst how the basic problem of the actors is resolved or processed'. The sociological constructs are formulated by the analyst based on the meaning of the *in vivo* codes. This study performed both manifest and latent content analysis. The researcher feels that, in this way, interpretation of the findings will be comprehensive and more meaningful for HR professionals.

Procedures

Sample
For generalization purposes, this study focused upon the population of all HR professions in private manufacturing business. A convenience sample of 25 HR managers and professionals were selected from a major US consumer paper products manufacturing corporation. The sample represents both manufacturing and corporate operations of the corporation. The HR personnel surveyed each represent the facility to which

they are assigned and for which they are solely responsible. No facility or person selected shared responsibilities with another person selected. The facilities are dispersed throughout the contiguous USA. No other states, territory or foreign country facility is involved. The respondents were not given forewarning of the questionnaire.

Each manager was contacted and sent the questionnaire via email. While the researcher was aware of the identity of the individuals within the target group, steps were developed and implemented to ensure the responses were anonymous (see the appendix A to this chapter).

Questionnaire
The questionnaire was in the form a single interrogatory statement that requested the respondents to identify six areas that may influence workplace violence, bearing in mind what aspects the workplace itself may influence that aggression. The researcher's choice of six responses was determined so as to provide sufficient data sampling but still maintain project manageability. The questionnaire also included instructions for the return of the responses.

Collection
The studied paper products corporation has a total of 32 facilities in the contiguous USA. Of those, 25 were assigned an HR manager. The remaining were either assigned an HR assistant or were combined with another facility. It was these 25 who were asked to complete the questionnaire. Of those, 20 responses were received. Of the 20, one was eliminated because the HR manager's name and location were printed in a corner of the sheet of paper.

Data processing and analysis

Category coding
The characteristics of the content of responses were examined for the purposes of classification into categories. These categories reflect the significant factors of workplace violence supported in the review of literature. These groupings were analyzed for fit with existing theory and assumptions in the literature. Further, the categories were developed to be consistent with the question asked and the objective of the investigation.[49] Additionally, the categories were subjected to open coding.[50] Based on the replies, each subcategory was fashioned to be consistent with the initial response category and the original question, and also so that they would provide subtle and distinct differences of descriptions of that particular category.[51]

Unit coding

The initial results were defined into six basic units. These were developed to be more specific in their explanation of the elements and character-istics of workplace violence. Though similar to characteristics established in the literature, these units were defined by the respondents as their interpretations and experiences, as related to the identification of the factors of aggression in the workplace.

Findings

Responses to questionnaire

Out of the 32 available facilities, only 25 had a full-time HR manager assigned. Each of these managers was sent the questionnaire. Twenty responses, for an 80% response rate, were returned. This rate far exceeds the normal rate or return. This may be due to the nature of the topic, since it is extremely important and contemporary and well represented in the media. Also, the corporation used for the study has a well established zero-tolerance workplace violence policy and an active workplace violence prevention and response programme.

As mentioned, of the 20 replies, one questionnaire was eliminated due to a violation of the procedure for anonymity. The remaining 19 questionnaires represent an adjusted usable rate of 76%.

Of the 19 questionnaires, 36% (or 7 replies) had incomplete data. This was because these respondents provided less than the six responses requested. The amounts of workplace violence factors in the incomplete responses are; 3 in 1, 4 indicators in 4 incomplete responses, and 5 factors in 2 incomplete responses. The information offered in these incomplete responses was, however, still included in the analysis. However, the effects of the missing data are unknown due to the inability to follow up with the surveyed individuals for explanation of the missing data or the reasoning behind the incomplete response.

Categories identified

Three distinct latent sociological categories emerged from the responses: organizational issues, interpersonal conflict issues and external issues. The responses showed a clear differentiation between the categories, with organizational issues receiving 44.1% of the total responses, followed by interpersonal issues at 29.4% and then external issues at 26.4 %. Manifest words and phrases that represented organizational issues were:

- terminations
- work recognition
- working hours
- supervision
- downsizing/job elimination
- working environment
- tasks assigned.

Manifest words and phrases that represent interpersonal issues were:

- romantic/love interests
- affairs
- supervisor interactions
- co-worker conflicts
- inability to communicate
- frustration.

Manifest words and phrases that represented external issues were:

- home finance/money problems
- stressful events at home (accidents, illnesses, etc.)
- domestic situations
- psychological dysfunction
- drug/alcohol abuse.

The aforementioned terms were analyzed for more explicit content and meaning. The units were, again, identified through open coding of the *in vivo* responses. The HR manager's responses were examined further and 21 separate terms were identified that either were literally repeated by the sample of the managers, or were similar terms used by the managers in their identification of workplace violence elements. After identifying these terms, the words and phrases were examined for content and latent meaning and grouped into six units. Each unit is followed by the percentage of responses that were grouped into that particular response unit. That is, the percentages reflect what portion of the total amount of responses fit into each unit:

- love/romantic interests: 23.5%
- terminations/job eliminations: 21.1%
- interpersonal conflicts: 16.4%
- emotional/psychological: 15.2%

- discipline/performance issues: 14.1%
- drug/alcohol abuse: 9.4%.

Research hypothesis

Based on the review of literature, six research hypotheses were developed for this study. Hypothesis 1 stated that interpersonal relationships were possibly related to aggression in the workplace. It appears that this hypothesis was supported by the information revealed by the HR managers. It is further supported by the identification of *interpersonal conflicts* as consisting of 16.4% of the total responses to the survey.

Hypothesis 2 stated that social and financial conditions of the employee would be related to workplace violence. This appears to not be supported by the information provided by the HR professionals. It is neither identified as one of the categories nor included in one of the six coding units. There is the possibility that social and/or financial conditions may affect the workers' emotional or psychological condition. However, the data did not support them as an identifiable entity related to workplace violence. Hypothesis 3 stated that organizational structure and supervisor/subordinate interactions were strongly related to aggression in the workplace. The data support this hypothesis in that one of the categories identified was *organizational,* and two of the coded units were terminations/job eliminations and discipline/performance issues. Hypothesis 4 stated that drug and/or alcohol abuse was correlated to aggression in the workplace. This is also supported by the information provided by the HR professionals in that 9.4% of the total responses related to drug/alcohol abuse. Hypothesis 5 stated that romantic relationships are connected to expressions of aggression in the workplace. A significant showing of 23.5% of responses in the unit coding measures supported this hypothesis. Lastly, hypothesis 6 stated that environmental working conditions were associated with aggression in the workplace. This hypothesis was not supported by the survey responses. Though it may be remotely considered an organizational issue, it is not one of structure or of design but rather a health and safety category, one which was not expressed by the HR managers nor identified in the coding units.

Discussion

When asked for catalysts or causal conditions of aggression in the workplace, the HR professionals of a major US manufacturing corporation seemed to agree on several important issues. The first is that interpersonal relationships either between co-workers or supervisory members of the organization hold the potential for negative interactions that could escalate into aggression. Another significant area identified by the professionals was in the manner in which the organization operates. The task of doing business occasionally requires layoffs, task modification, job elimination and other operational changes. Some HR managers feel these conditions are a source of friction and difficulty with the employee; that when exacerbated may evolve into violence at work. Further, the baggage the employee may bring into work is an element that interacts with organizational, operational and interpersonal conditions. Drug abuse, domestic situations, personal responsibility involving romantic notions, emotional control ability, psychological neurosis and stress and/or frustration coping abilities are associated with the workplace violence phenomenon by the professionals. They may be derived from numerous social, family, even genetic foundations. However, according to the surveyed HR managers, the individual's reaction to conditions and transactions in the workplace may be further complicated when being filtered by a myriad of personal circumstances.

Based on the results of this research, HR professionals may wish to develop strategies that monitor the conditions and operations that confront workers, along with how these mix with personal violent indicators. These should be examined for appropriateness, reasonableness, respect and value to both the worker and the organization. Further, the present study reveals that HR managers feel that the employee brings unnecessary and unwelcome detrimental personal conditions into the workplace. More effective and exacting pre-employee procedures may help to reduce the organization's vulnerability to these negative and potentially violent tendencies.

Recommendations

Information derived from this study may be generalized to other similar organizations. To increase the validity and reliability of the data, empirical research is required to substantiate further each of the elements identified by the professionals. In addition, other companies of other industries should be surveyed and the results compared. This study is clearly just a beginning, but it does point the researcher in some direction. In particular, these perceptions of the factors of workplace violence should be compared with studies of actual instances of workplace violence to see if the trends match.

Appendix: questionnaire for determining causal factors of aggression in the workplace

Workplace violence is a serious and acute national issue for business. Much has been written concerning violence in the workplace, but the majority of that information is anecdotal. Few empirical studies have been performed on the topic.

For this reason I am asking for your professional [human resources] opinion on the topic to develop data for analysis. Please take a few minutes and give me six areas that you feel would be possible causal factors for a person to become aggressive in the workplace. Please keep in mind that I am also looking for the potential relationship between these events and the workplace. That is, how does the work environment, if at all, contribute to the aggression. The responses need only be in a word or two. If an explanation is required, please keep it brief.

I wish all responses to be anonymous. Any responses that have identifying features of the author or the facility from which it originated, will be dropped from the survey. For this reason please do not identify yourself in the reply. Simply write your responses on a sheet of plain paper and return via plant mail in a plain white business envelope. My address is *Art Arway, RiverPark #3X1*. If you do wish to identify yourself, send along the reply first, then contact me by email after January 31, 2000. I am in the corporate email directory. Also, if you wish to be notified of the results of this study, you may email me after January 31, 2000 to request those results.

I thank you for your assistance in this endeavor. Your response may help the HR professional to better understand workplace violence and develop more appropriate prevention and incident solution strategies.

Notes

1. Cannon, S., Florence, E., Speakman, W., Rice, M. and Breitman, L. (1995) Workplace violence: analysis of the issues and recommendations to reduce the exposure. *CPCU Journal* 48(40), 208–36.
2. Atlanta Journal Constitution (1999) Anatomy or a massacre: the day Atlanta can't

forget (http://www.accessatlanta.com/partners/ajc/).

3. Bureau of Justice Statistics (1998) *Workplace Violence, 1992–1996 (Special Report, July)*. Washington, DC: Bureau of Justice.

4. Bureau of Labor Statistics (1999) Employment status of the civilian population by race, sex, and age, 1999. Table A-2 (http://BLS.gov.news.release/empsit.t02.htm).

5. Bureau of Labor Statistics (1994) *Violence in the Workplace Comes under Close Scrutiny. Issues in Labor Statistics*. Washington, DC: US Department of Labor, Bureau of Labor Statistics; Kinney, J. (1995) *Violence in the Workplace: How to Make your Company Safer for Employees and Customers*. New York: Prentice-Hall.

6. Kreiger, G. (1996) Waste, rage, and frustration. *American Medical News* 39(47), 17–19.

7. Bandura, A. (1985) *Social Foundation of Thought and Action: A Social Cognitive Theory*. New York: Prentice-Hall; Akers, R. (1998) *Social Learning and Social Structure: A General Theory of Crime and Deviance*. Chicago, IL: Northwestern University Press.

8. Ward, A. and Dockerill, J. (1999) The Predictive Accuracy of Violent Offender Treatment Program Risk Assessment Scale. *Criminal Justice and Behavior* 26(1), 125–41.

9. Kiem, J. (1999) Workplace violence and trauma. *Journal of Rehabilitation* 65(1), 16–21.

10. Alexander, R. and Langford, L. (1992) Throwing down: a social learning test of students fighting. *Social Work in Education* 14(2), 114–25; Rimm, D. and Masters, J. (1979) *Behavior Therapy: Techniques and Empirical Findings*. New York: New York Academic Press; Schultz, D. (1976) *Theories of Personality*. Monterey, CA: Brooks & Cole.

11. Akers, R. (1973) *Deviant Behavior: A Social Learning Approach*. Belmont, CA: Wadsworth; Sutherland, H. (1947) *Sanctions and Social Deviance: The Question of Deterrence*. New York: Praeger; Akers, R. (1985) *Deviant Behavior: A Social Learning Approach* (3rd edn). Belmont, CA: Wadsworth.

12. Gadon, K., Sprafkin, J. and Ficarrotto, T. (1987) Effects of viewing aggression-laden cartoons on preschool-aged emotionally disturbed children. *Child Psychiatry and Human Development* 17(3), 257–74; Krohn, M., Lanza-Kaduce, L. and Akers, R. (1984) Community context and theories of deviant behavior: an examination of social learning and social bonding theories. *Sociology Quarterly* 25(2), 353–71.

13. Garofalo, J., Siegal, L. and Laub, J. (1987) School-related victimization among adolescents: an analysis of National Crime Survey narratives. *Journal of Quantitative Criminology* 3(1), 321–38.

14. Holland, J. (1973) *Making Vocational Choices: A Theory of Careers*. New York: Prentice-Hall; Mantell, M. and Albrecht, S. (1994) *Ticking Bombs: Diffusing Violence in the Workplace*. Burridge, IL: Irwin Professional.

15. Rich, M. and Woods, E. (1985) Aggressors or victims: gender and race in music videos. *Pediatrics* 101(4), 669–75. Cannon *et al.* op. cit.

16. Metha, A. (1999) Embodied discourse: on gender and fear of violence. *Gender, Place and Culture: A Journal of Feminist Geography* 6(1), 67–85; Julian, T., McKenry, P., Gavazzi, S. and Law, J. (1999) Test of family of origin structure models of male

verbal and physical aggression. *Journal of Family Issues* 20(3), 397–434; Mills, J. and Kroner, D. (1998) Measuring alcohol abuse and the incidence of serious misconduct in violent offenders. *Prison Journal* 78(1), 45–55.

17. Suzuki, B. (1991) Unity with diversity. *Liberal Education Journal* 77(1), 30–35.

18. Bower, B. (1992) Sick buildings exert stressful impact. *Science News* 141(17), 260–63; Altman, I. (1993) Dialectics, physical environments, and personal relationships. *Communication Monographs* 60(1), 26–35.

19. Odom, J. and Barr, C. (1997) Sick building litigation: the role that occupant outrage plays. *Journal of Environmental Law and Practice* 4(6), 21–26; Boyles, S. and Key, S. (1999) Could ultraviolet lights solve sick buildings? *Tuberculosis and Airborne Disease Weekly* 26 July, 10–12.

20. Chappell, D. and Di Martino, V. (1998) *Violence at Work*. New York: FAO United Nations International Labor Office Publications; Wilkinson, C. (1996) *Violence in the Workplace: Preventing, Assessing, and Managing Threats at Work*. Washington, DC: Government Institutes Publications.

21. Chenier, E. (1998) The workplace: a battleground for violence. *Public Personnel Management* 27(4), 557–69; Weisberg, D. (1994) Preparing for the unthinkable. *Management Review* 83(3), 58–61.

22. Chen, P. and Spector, P. (1992) Relationships of work stressors with aggression, withdrawal, theft and substance use. *Journal of Occupational and Organizational Psychology* 65(4), 177–85; Kinney, J. (1994) *Preventing Violence at Work: A Step by Step Program to Protect your Employees, Company and Assets*. New York: Prentice-Hall.

23. Abel, M. (1996) Self-esteem: moderator or mediator between perceived stress and expectancy of success? *Psychological Reports* 79(2), 635–42; Shepard, D. and Fine, L. (1994) Role conflict and role ambiguity reconsidered. *Journal of Personal Selling and Sales Management* 14(2), 57–66.

24. Matteson, M. and Ivancevich, J. (1987) *Controlling Work Stress: Effective Human Resource and Management Strategies*. San Francisco, CA: Jossey-Bass.

25. Spector, P. (1975) Relationships of organizational frustration with reported behavioral reactions of employees. *Journal of Applied Psychology* 60(1), 635–37; Keenan, A. and Newtown, T. (1984) Frustration in organizations: relationships to role stress, climate and psychological strain. *Journal of Occupational Psychology* 57(4), 57–65.

26. Chen, P. and Spector, P. (1991) Negative affectivity as the underlying cause of correlations between stressors and strains. *Journal of Applied Psychology* 76(2), 398–407.

27. Chen and Spector (1992) op. cit.

28. Bacharach, S. (1998) *Dysfunctional Behavior in Organizations: Violent and Deviant Behavior in Organizations*. Stamford, CA: JAI Press.

29. Minor, M. and Henry, C. (1995) *Preventing Workplace Violence: Positive Management Strategies*. New York: Crisp Publications.

30. Leo, J. (1995) Just too much rage. *US News and World Report* 118(18), 22–23.

31. Ford, M. and Linney, J. (1995) Comparative analysis of juvenile sexual offenders, violent nonsexual offenders, and status offenders. *Journal of Interpersonal Violence* 10(1), 56–71.

32. Bureau of Labor Statistics (1994) op. cit.; Barnett, O. and Martinez, T. (1995) Jealousy and romantic attachment in maritally violent and nonviolent men. *Journal of Interpersonal Violence* 10(4), 473–87.
33. Dietz, P. (1995) A stalker could be anyone. *USA Today* 11 January, A11.
34. Marble, M. (1996) Early family experiences linked to abusive male personality. *Women's Health Weekly* 15 July, 9–11; Raine, A. (1994) Links between early rejection and violence. *Brown University Child and Adolescent Behavior Letter* 9(10), 3–4.
35. Koonce, R. (1996) Workplace as a community. *Training and Development* 50(5), 25–26.
36. Johnson, P. and Indvik, J. (1994) Workplace violence: an issue of the nineties. *Public Personnel Management* 23(4), 515–614.
37. Careny, T. (1972) *Content Analysis*. Winnipeg: University of Manitoba Press; Chadwick, B., Bahr, H. and Albrecht, A. (1984) *Social Science Research Methods*. Englewood Cliffs, NJ: Prentice-Hall.
38. Berg, B. (1989) *Qualitative Research Methods for the Social Sciences*. Needham Heights, MA: Allyn & Bacon; Lasswell, H. and Leites, N. (1949) *The Language of Politics: Studies in Quantitative Semantics*. New York: George W. Stewart.
39. Lasswell and Leites op. cit.
40. Bureau of Labor Statistics (1994) op. cit.
41. McClure, L. (1999) Address workplace anger early and fend off sabotage before it becomes a problem. *Workforce* 7897, 39–40.
42. Chenier op. cit.
43. Holsi, O. (1968) *The Handbook of Social Psychology*. Reading, MA: Addison-Wesley, 608.
44. Janis, I. (1943) Meaning and the study of symbolic behavior. *Psychiatry Journal* 6(4), 425–39.
45. Holsi (1968) op. cit.
46. Holsi, O. (1969) *Content Analysis for the Social Sciences and Humanities*. Reading, MA: Addison-Wesley.
47. Strauss, A. (1987) *Qualitative Analysis for Social Scientists*. New York: Cambridge University Press.
48. Ibid., 33.
49. Schatzman, L. and Strauss, A. (1973) *Field Research: Strategies for a Natural Sociology*. Englewood Cliffs, NJ: Prentice-Hall.
50. Berg op. cit.
51. Strauss op. cit.

Chapter 4

Developing a framework for understanding patterns of abuse and violence against businesses

Matt Hopkins

Introduction

There has been little attempt to develop a theoretical framework for understanding patterns of abuse and violence against businesses. Despite this, a number of theoretical frameworks have been developed that attempt to explain why crime occurs in specific locations against specific targets. These theories have postulated a link between the lifestyle characteristics of victims of crime, the routine activities of the community and locational factors that generate and attract crime. This chapter considers how Hindelang *et al.*'s lifestyle theory of personal victimization[1] and Cohen and Felson's routine activity theory[2] can be utilized to develop a framework for understanding abuse and violence against businesses. The chapter begins by outlining the major tenets of these theories. We then consider some of the lifestyle characteristics of businesses that promote abuse/violence, and how staff and customers converge to generate incidents. Finally, the implications of this framework for preventing abuse and violence will be considered.

Lifestyle theory, routine activities and abuse and violence against businesses

Hindelang *et al.*'s lifestyle theory of personal victimization conjectures that some individuals develop lifestyles that are more conducive to victimization than others. Empirical data are used to establish a relationship between such lifestyle characteristics as age, martial status, gender and the risk of victimization. Whilst lifestyle theory establishes a link between demographic characteristics and victimization, it could also be postulated that businesses have 'lifestyles' that make them more or less likely to become victims of crime. We can postulate that abuse and violence against businesses are dependent upon clearly distinguishable 'lifestyle' characteristics such as the location of the business, the type of business or the service offered by the business, the risk of experiencing crime types such as shop theft and demographic characteristics of staff.

However, a criticism of the lifestyle theory of personal victimization is that it fails to address how or why certain types of people are victims of crime. The theory only establishes correlations between empirical data and lifestyle characteristics and does not pay any attention to how victims and offenders converge in time and space. A theory that does take these factors into account is routine activity theory.[4] This hypothesizes that, for a direct contact predatory violation to occur, there has to be a convergence in time and space of an offender, suitable target and an absence of capable guardianship.[5] This simple framework has been applied to a number of crime types such as burglary, robbery and shop theft, and it can also be applied to abuse and violence against businesses. Therefore, this theory would prompt us to ask questions about the target suitability of business types to abuse and violence (similar to lifestyle theory), though it also begins to ask why there is a *convergence* of suitable targets and motivated offenders in time and space.

Table 4.1 outlines the key underpinnings of lifestyle and routine activity theory and how they can be developed in relation to abuse and violence against businesses. Through utilizing these theories we can begin to hypothesize which lifestyle features and routine activity patterns of businesses generate the contexts that are conducive to abuse and violence. Previous research indicates that there are variations in the rates of abuse and violence according to business sector. For example, the Commercial Victimization Survey highlights that retail premises experience higher rates of assaults than manufacturing premises.[6] Therefore, it is apparent that retail premises have certain lifestyle characteristics that generate higher rates of assaults than manufacturing premises. If we consider what lifestyle theory and routine activity theory tell us about victimization, then it would be expected that factors such as demographic characteristics of staff, the location of the business, the opening times of businesses, the types of people attracted to the business and levels of guardianship in the premises would all be important in generating abuse and violence against premises.

Table 4.1   Lifestyle theory, routine activity theory and abuse and violence against businesses

	Lifestyle theory of victimization	Routine activities theory
Key underpinnings of the theory	There is a correlation between individual lifestyles and victimization	For direct predatory violation to occur, there has to be a convergence in time and space of a suitable target and motivated offender in the absence of capable guardianship
Development in relation to abuse and violence against businesses	Highlights the possibility that businesses have definable lifestyles that promote the risk victimization	Some business (with life-styles that promote abuse/violence) will have a convergence of victims/offenders in time and space

The lifestyles of victims of abuse and violence: the target suitability of victims

Abuse and violence within business premises may be generated in one of two ways. First, if the business has lifestyle characteristics and routine activity patterns that are conducive to abuse/violence, employees would be vulnerable as the nature of the business increases their risk of abuse and violence. Secondly, employees may possess lifestyle characteristics that make them vulnerable to abuse/violence. For example, certain demographic characteristics could increase vulnerability to abuse and violence.

Here we begin to identify some of the lifestyle characteristics that will create contexts suitable for abuse and violence.

Location of the business

Previous research has considered how criminal victimization concentrates in certain types of communities and how these communities develop. For example, Skogan, Hope and Foster[7] have all considered how the demographic characters of residents on housing estates may lead to high crime. Wilson and Kelling[8] considered how relatively trivial incidents in a community (if unchecked) will help the community to spiral into general decline and become a high crime area, and Reiss[9] hypothesized that certain types of communities can have careers in crime.

As with households, the victimization of business premises will be dependent upon their location. Though there are few data linking rates of abuse/violence against businesses to location, the Scottish Business Crime (SBC) survey[10] made comparisons of such nature and found variations in overall crime risks according to location. It was noted that the highest prevalence risk of crime was for businesses in poorest council housing areas, on council estates with older residents and in areas with private tenements and flats (Scottish ACORN areas H – poorest council estates; G – council estates with older residents; and D – private tenements and flats, respectively). It would be expected that similar geographical patterns would be observed for abuse and violence.

Business type/service offered

Some businesses possess lifestyle characteristics that will generate high rates of abuse and violence. We can test this hypothesis by using data from a survey of crime against small business.[11] The survey was conducted in September 1995 to help develop a strategy to reduce crime against small businesses in the Belgrave and West End areas of Leicester. In total, 894 businesses were interviewed.

The SBC survey established that retail and service sector premises experienced higher prevalence and concentration rates of abuse and violence over the 12-month recall period than wholesale and manufacturing premises.[12] This suggests that business in the retail and service sector have 'lifestyle' characteristics that are more likely to generate abuse and violence than those in the wholesale and manufacturing sector. These may include factors such as having a high turnover of customers (which increases the risk of a convergence of victims and offenders) or having a high risk of shop theft (which may generate disputes when apprehending offenders). However, of particular interest here are the intra-sector variations in risk. Tables 4.2 and 4.3 outline the prevalence, average incidents per 100 businesses and average number of incidents per victim for the highest-risk business types in the retail and service sector. The highest prevalence rates for abuse were recorded for off-licences, motor vehicle parts/fuels and food shops (the lowest prevalence rates for business types in this sector were for photo/art dealers, car dealers, repair shops, video rental and florists). The highest average number of incidents per 100 premises was for off-licences and the highest

Table 4.2   Businesses identified as at the highest risk in retail sector (sample size in brackets)

	% Victims		Average incidents per 100 businesses		Average incidents per victim	
	Abuse	Violence	Abuse	Violence	Abuse	Violence
Off-licence (53)	34	21.0	155	26.0	4.5	1.3
Motor fuels/ parts (19)	32	21.0	152	26.0	1.4*	12.5*
Food shops (62)	32	6.5	93	14.5	3.0	2.2
Clothing/ footwear (51)	22	6.0	94	6.0	4.4	1.0

Note: *One business claimed to have experienced 99 incidents of abuse and violence; there this outlier is removed.

Table 4.3   Businesses in the service sector with highest risks of abuse and violence (sample size in brackets[13])

	% Victims		Average incidents per 100 businesses		Average incidents per victim	
	Abuse	Violence	Abuse	Violence	Abuse	Violence
Bookmakers (4)	75	25.0	200	50.0	2.0	2.0
Postal services (5)	60	20.0	220	20.0	3.7	1.0
Public houses (21)	43	38.0	200* (580)	200.0	4.7	5.3
Hotels (4)	25	50.0	150	125.0	6.0	2.5
Eating places (57)	21	3.5	47 (221)*	3.5	2.3	1.0

Note: *The figures in brackets include the outliers.

average number of incidents per victim was also in this category at 4.5 incidents per victim. This was followed closely by clothing (4.4), food (3) and motor fuels/parts (1.4).

There were also four business categories within the retail sector that experienced at least one incident of violence. All these businesses had also experienced abuse. The business categories where incidents of violence were recorded were off-licences (21%), motor fuels/parts (21%), food shops (6.5%) and clothing/footwear (6%).

If we turn to the service sector, Table 4.3 outlines the prevalence, incidence and concentration for the 'high-risk' victims. Here, the highest prevalence risks for abuse in the service sector were against bookmakers (75%), postal services (60%), public houses (43%), hotels (25%) and eating places (21%) (the lowest was for road haulage firms, care homes, education offices, public administration offices and doctors' surgeries). Public houses and eating-places experienced the highest average number of incidents per 100 businesses at 580 and 221 per 100, respectively. However, both these categories included victims who reported incident counts of 80 and 99. If these are removed the average per 100 businesses are 200 and 47, respectively. The public house sector and eating categories also had an average number of 13.5 and 10.5 incidents per victim, respectively, if the outliers are included. If the outliers are removed the figure becomes 4.7 and 2.3 incidents per victim. The hotel sector also experienced a high rate of repeat abuse (6 incidents per victim), though the highest average number of incidents per victim was 11 in the hair/beauty sector. This was a result of this sector having only two victims experiencing a high number of incidents.

A number of businesses experienced a much lower prevalence rate of violence than abuse, the most noticeable being for the postal services, eating places and bookmakers. This indicates that businesses in these categories may have a risk of abuse, but these incidents are unlikely to develop into violence. Generally the risks of repeat violence were low. The only significant number of repeat incidents were against public houses. Here, a victim of an incident of violence experienced an average of 5.3 incidents over a 12-month period.

From this evidence, it is apparent that a number of business types have distinctive lifestyle characteristics that generate the risk of abuse and violence. The high-risk businesses are those that generally have a high number of customer visits that maximizes the potential for a convergence of targets and offenders. A number of high-risk businesses attract motivated offenders (for example, public houses, off-licences); they constantly handle cash and credit cards, which increases the risk of disputes over cash, change and service; and many have alcohol on the business, which can generate drunken violence in public houses and disputes over service in off-licences.

Victimization by gender of staff

There has been only little research that has considered the demographic variables of victims of abuse and violence within businesses. Of the research that has been conducted, high rates of assaults have been recorded for females,[14] and Asian shopkeepers.[15]

If patterns recorded in these surveys of personal victimization replicate themselves here, one would also expect to find high rates of abuse and violence against females and ethnic minority employees. Figure 4.1 outlines the ratio of incidents of abuse/violence for males and females for sweep 1 of the SBC survey.[16] In total, 362 incidents of abuse and violence were recorded where the gender of the victim was known. The proportion of staff in the businesses where the incidents occurred was 44% male and 56% female. The proportion of incidents against males was 71% (230 per thousand male employees); 19% were against females (74 per thousand female employees); and 10% were against both gender groups (see Figure 4.1). This tells us that the proportion of incidents that males suffer is slightly higher than expected.

We may draw the conclusion from these data that males experience higher risks of abuse and violence than females (and are thus deemed more suitable targets than females). There may be a number of reasons why females have lower risks of abuse and violence than males. These may be broadly divided into situational and behavioural factors. If we

Figure 4.1 Abuse and violence by gender

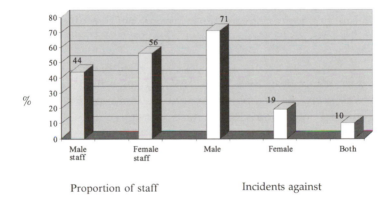

consider situational factors first, many businesses employ a high proportion of females who have little contact with the public. For example, 60% of the female workforce were employed in the 'low risk' manufacturing and wholesale sectors, compared to 50% of the male workforce.[17] As a consequence, females may have a slightly lower risk of contact with assailants. Secondly, females who work in the 'high risk' sectors may take steps to avoid becoming targets for abuse/violence. For example, they may not allow themselves to work until late at night or to be left alone on the premises at vulnerable times. Finally, it may also be apparent that if confronted by a potentially violent situation, males may be less likely to 'back down' from conflict than females.

Victimization by ethnicity of staff

Here we will consider both the distribution of abuse and violence by ethnic group. The SBC survey recorded the ethnic group of the majority of staff in businesses. These were recorded as 'white', 'Asian', 'black' or 'mixed'. This section considers the study population by area due to the differing ethnic compositions of businesses in the West End and Belgrave communities.

Table 4.4   Ethnicity of business staff and risk of abuse (%)

Area	Proportion of businesses: white	Proportion of incidents: against white	Proportion of businesses: Asian	Proportion of incidents: against Asian
West End	65	47	19	53
Belgrave	35	25	57	72

Note: Afro-Caribbean omitted due to the small numbers of businesses.

In the West End area, 65% of businesses had predominately white staff and 19% Asian (Table 4.4). In Belgrave, 57% of businesses had predominately Asian staff and 35% white. In 273 incidents of abuse, the SBC was able to record the ethnicity of the victim and in both areas. In the West End, 53% of incidents of abuse were against Asian businesses (despite constituting only 19% of the business population) and in Belgrave 72% of incidents of abuse were against Asian businesses (despite constituting 57% of the business population).

From this evidence we can conclude that Asian businesses are more likely targets of abuse than white businesses. The most obvious explanation for the high proportion of abuse against Asian businesses is racial motivation. However, it should be noted that there were a high number of Asian businesses in high-risk groups. In total, 153 businesses that could be defined as 'high risk' (see Figure 4.2) were able to describe the ethnicity of the majority of staff. Of these businesses, 57.5% (88) were 'Asian' and 42.5% (65) were 'white'. Therefore, Asian staff experience increased risks as they are employed in businesses with a high risk of abuse.

In total, 161 incidents of violence were recorded where the ethnicity of the business could be identified (Table 4.5). Of these incidents, 102 (63%)

Figure 4.2   High-risk businesses and ethnicity (bookmakers, hotels and postal services ommited due to low numbers)

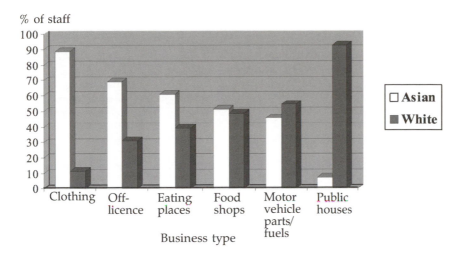

were in the West End and 59 (37%) in Belgrave. In both the West End and Belgrave, white businesses were victims of a higher proportion of violence than may be expected. In the West End, 83% of violence was against the 65% of white businesses. In Belgrave, 44% of violence was against the 35% of white businesses. In both areas, Asian businesses were subject to less violence than one may expect, though in Belgrave the proportion of incidents against Asian businesses is higher than in the West End because of the high proportion of Asian businesses in that area. It is difficult to ascertain here why Asians appear to be victims of a higher proportion of abuse and whites a higher proportion of violence than one may expect. One explanation may be that whites are more likely to precipitate incidents than Asians. However, this is hard to verify. A more likely explanation is found when considering the distribution of Asian and white businesses within the 'high risk' business types.

Table 4.5   Ethnicity of business staff and risks of violence (%)

Area	Proportion of businesses: white	Proportion of incidents: against white	Proportion of businesses: Asian	Proportion of incidents: against Asian
West End	65	83	19	3
Belgrave	35	44	57	31

Figure 4.2 considers the distribution of staff by ethnic group within the 'high risk' business types.[18] Two key observations can be made from this figure. First, the types of businesses where Asians form the majority of the workforce are those such as clothing shops and off-licences. Secondly, whites-only form a clear majority of staff in public houses. Businesses such as clothing and off-licences have a high risk of abuse (and in some circumstances violence), though public houses will often be settings for violence. Therefore, the high proportion of white members of staff working in public houses may have higher risks of experiencing violence than their Asian counterparts in other 'high risk' businesses.

The triggers and processes of abuse and violence: how do victims and offenders converge in time and space?

The previous section identified that some businesses have routine activity/lifestyles that generate contexts suitable for abuse and violence. However, it is also important to understand how victims and offenders convergence in time and space (or how an incident of abuse and violence is triggered).

Here it is hypothesized that there are norms that govern business transactions. These 'norms of business transaction' regulate and define the way we are expected to behave within the business environment. It is only when these norms are violated that an incident of abuse or violence will be triggered. The norms of business transaction can be violated either by a customer (motivated offender) or by the business (suitable target). A customer will violate these norms in three main ways. First, by engaging in criminality such as a robbery or shop theft. These criminal acts clearly violate norms that customers pay for goods and services from the business. Secondly, under-age customers may also violate the norms of business transaction by attempting to buy drink or cigarettes from the premises (which also violates a norm-written in law). Finally, customers may act in an 'anti-social manner' on the premises. This may include being deliberately rude to staff, moving goods around and creating a disturbance on the premises.

Businesses may also violate the norms of businesses transaction. Businesses can do this in three ways. First, by selling substandard or overpriced goods to customers; secondly, by offering a substandard service to customers; and, thirdly, by giving customers the wrong change. All these violations will cause customers to complain and potentially trigger abuse.

In addition to an initial trigger, there will also be a number of de-escalating and escalating events that are a response to triggers that determine the final result of the incident. These processes will vary according to the perceptions and outcome aims of the participants (for example, participants may want to engage in violence). The escalating acts constitute a verbal or physical act that will intensify the incident or provoke an aggressive response from the person the act is directed against. Escalating acts that may intensify an incident include refusals by either party in the exchange to comply with certain requests or orders from the other, making identity attacks on the other in the exchange (such as name calling, swearing or racist taunts), making threats against the person or business and attempting to remove the offender(s) from premises, detain them or stop them from engaging in criminal activity.

De-escalating acts will defuse a situation and reduce the risk of the incident developing into violence. De-escalating acts will include complying with certain requests or orders, making apologies, explanations and reasoning with the other person in the exchange and third parties de-escalating incidents by encouraging assailants to back down from conflict.

Here we can begin to identify the triggers and process of incidents by considering two case studies of incidents of abuse and violence. These case studies are taken from qualitative interviews with victims identified through SBC data and are presented here as vignettes. The interviews highlight how refusals to serve customers and customer complaints can trigger incidents.

Case study I: abuse, violence and refusals to serve to those under age

This guy came in, who was obviously under age at the time of the incident and he wanted alcohol and I refused to serve him. So anyway he goes over to the freezer (he points to the freezer) and he opens it and starts to mess all the ice-cream around. My wife was here and he was telling her to fuck off and called her 'a Paki bitch' and all this so I called the police. They say that it's my shop so if I want I can just push him out. So I tell him to get out and I grabbed hold of him and pushed him out, it was a nice day like today and I stood at the door. He went down near the factory (he points over the road) and he got a piece of wood, came and threw it at my face whilst I was outside. He knocked all these teeth out see, (he shows me where he now has false teeth on one side of his face) you can see here what he did. The police came, but I don't know what happened after that, the guy was in a detention centre, but I'm not sure why, they never kept me informed. Now the guy is over age and he can come and buy what he wants (*off-licence owner, Belgrave*).

The context, trigger (T) and process events of case study 1 are all outlined in table 4.6. Here violence is generated as an under-age customer trying to purchase alcohol breaks the norms of business transaction. Staff refuse to serve the customer and an incident is triggered. The assailant begins to act anti-socially by messing goods around whilst also subjecting staff to racist and sexist identity attacks (escalation – ES1). Staff attempt to de-escalate the situation by calling the police, who advise the staff to throw the customer out of the shop (ES2). However, removing the offender acts as a major escalating mechanism as the offender then resorts to physical violence (as a form of punishment or retribution).

Table 4.6   The context, trigger, process events and result of case study 1

Context	Trigger (norm-breaking behaviour)	Process events	Result (R)
Small off-licence on quiet terraced street is the suitable target. The motivated offender is a teenager. Two staff are present	Teenager refused alchohol (T)	Offender starts to mess goods around in shop and there are racist and sexist identity attacks against staff (ES1). Police are called. On their advice assailant is thrown out of shop (ES2)	Offender returns with piece of wood and causes injury to shop owner (R)

T + ES1 + ES2 = R

Three additional features can be noted about case study 1. First, whilst the refusals to serve the under-age customer generated violence, there was a time lapse between the first and second incident. Therefore, the incident of violence could be classified as 'event dependent' repeat victimization. Secondly, the offender is obviously frustrated and angry, though he resorts to a serious act of violence that is triggered by a trivial matter (a refusal to serve alcohol). The violence is used as retribution against the member of staff who refused to serve the customer alcohol and because the offender was eventually thrown out of the shop. Thirdly, the advice given to the victim by the police (to remove the offender) helped to propel the incident from abuse to violence. Therefore, an action expected to de-escalate the incident actually escalated it from one of abuse to violence.

Case study 2: abuse, violence and complaints over pricing

> It started when this guy came in effin and blindin. He'd had a cleaner repaired and said I'd overcharged him for it. I looked over the counter, over the partition to say to him you know, aye up calm down chap that's enough in here. He says 'and you yer long fucker he says, I'll have you as well'. That puts my hackles up straight away, so I put the phone down and went round the corner on to the counter. I tried to passify the chap, but I still got a lot of verbal abuse so I told the lad (the other member of staff present) to put out a three 9's call. Anyway he (the assailant) says 'you can get them fuckers here'. Then he carries on and I don't know if I should tell you about the bar (laughs). Well, I got the bar (shows me long bar of iron about two feet long) from the door and banged it on the counter. That shut him up. I felt the shudder go up my arm (laughs). Anyway, then he left. The police came about three hours later at about five o' clock. They said he was threatening to take me to trading standards (*electrical shop owner, Belgrave*).

The context, trigger and process events of case study 2 are outlined in Table 4.7 below. Here, the incident is triggered before the assailant enters the business. He is unhappy over the pricing of a repair. Therefore, the norms of business transactions are broken in two ways. First by the business not making the customer clear regarding the cost of the repair and, secondly, by the customer complaining to the business in an overtly aggressive manner (T).

The incident is of particular interest as, throughout, there are a number of attempts made by the staff to de-escalate (D) the incident that fail. For example, on two occasions staff attempted to calm the customer by reasoning with him. Calling the police fails to calm the customer (as he believes he is correct) and finally it takes an act of violence to de-escalate the conflict. Therefore, within this incident there are a number of process events one might expect to de-escalate a conflict and are intended to do so, but fail to have this effect.

Table 4.7   The context, trigger, process events and result of case study 2

Context	Trigger (norm-breaking behaviour)	Process events	Result (R)
Shop selling electrical items located on busy main road is the suitable target. A customer is the motivated offender. Two members of staff are present	Customer unhappy over price charged for a job. He comes into shop and is abusive (T)	Member of staff tries to calm customer (D1) Customer abusive and makes identity attacks (ES1). Member of staff again tries to calm the situation (D2). The customer is still abusive (ES2). Police called (D3). More abuse from customer (ES3). Staff use weapon to make threats against customer (D4)	After being abusive the threat of violence from staff leads to customer leaving (R)

T + D1 + ES1 + D2 + ES2 + D3 + ES3 + D4 = R

Whilst the accounts given in the case studies may be slightly 'one-sided' (as they are victims' accounts of events and not the offenders'), they do highlight how the triggers and processes of incidents of abuse and violence unfold within the business environment. Some of the major features of the case studies are summarized below:

1. It is apparent from the SBC data and the case studies that we can identify clear contexts, triggers and processes of incidents.

2. Often verbal or physical actions that one would expect to escalate incidents actually de-escalate them. For example, in case study 2 the member of staff bangs an iron bar against the counter in an attempt to scare off the assailant. In many instances, this would have escalated the incident though in this case it led to a de-escalation of the incident.

3. Incident processes consisted of a number of threats and identity attacks. It appears that assailants will often make identity attacks against staff to make them comply with requests. Commonly used identity attacks refer to ethnicity, gender or some obvious physical feature of the victim, such as his or her height.

4. Though incidents were relatively short, quick events, sometimes the repercussions of incidents would continue over a period of time. These could be classified as event-dependent repeats. For example, in case study 1 the violent result occurs some time after the initial trigger.

Summary

This chapter has shown that we can begin to develop a framework for understanding abuse and violence against business premises by considering the lifestyle and routine activity characteristics that promote abuse/violence, the triggers of incidents and incident processes. The key elements of the theory are presented in Figure 4.3. It is acknowledged that the key 'lifestyle' features that promote contexts conducive to abuse/violence highlighted here are not exhaustive. However, by using empirical data, correlations can be established between such lifestyle characteristics as business sector/type, demographic characteristics of staff and the risk of victimization.

Figure 4.3   Lifestyles, routine activites, triggers and processes of abuse and violence

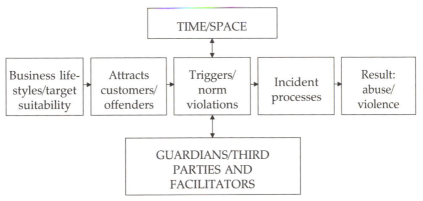

The chapter also highlights how violations of the norms of business transaction trigger incidents and how incident processes can be classified into escalating and de-escalating acts. Whilst the triggers of incidents can often be clearly identified, it can be difficult to determine the final result of the incidents through simply identifying escalating and de-escalating acts. This is because the final result of the incident is highly dependent upon the intentions of both the offender and victim and how far they are prepared to take the incident.

This has clear implications for crime prevention. The lifestyle theory of business victimization shows that we can identify high-risk businesses; therefore we should be able to predict where incidents will tend to occur. We are also able to identify how incidents are triggered. Therefore if businesses could prevent the triggers of incidents from occurring (for example, by reducing the risk of shop theft and complaints from customers), then a reduction in abuse/violence would logically follow. What is more difficult to predict is the final result of an incident when it is in progress. The case studies show that incidents triggered over trivial matters can potentially generate serious assault. This suggests that it would be impossible accurately to predict the final result of an incident already in progress. However, this should not deter either academics or practitioners from identifying the contexts in which abuse and violence are likely to be generated and the triggers of these incidents. Identifying these contexts and triggers would still help to develop prevention strategies and would potentially yield dividends in reducing abuse and violence against staff.

Notes

1. Hindelang, M.J., Gottfredson, M.R. and Garofalo, J. (1978) *Victims of Personal Crime: An Empirical Foundation for a Theory of Personal Victimization*. Cambridge, MA: Ballinger.
2. Cohen, L.E. and Felson, M. (1979) Social change and crime rate trends: a routine activity approach. *American Sociological Review* 44, 588–607.
3. Hindelang *et al.* op. cit.
4. Cohen and Felson op. cit.
5. It should also be noted that 'crime facilitators' could also be important here. These are facilitators (such as drugs or alcohol) that help to generate crime – see Clarke, R.V. (1995) Situational crime prevention. In Tonry, M. and Farrington, D. (eds.) *Building a Safer Society: Strategic Approaches to Crime Prevention*. Chicago, IL: University of Chicago Press.
6. See Mirrlees-Black, C. and Ross, A. (1995) *Crime against Retail and Manufacturing Premises: Findings from the 1994 Commercial Victimisation Survey. Home Office*

Research Study 146. London: Home Office.

7. See Skogan, W. (1990) *Disorder and Decline: Crime and the Spiral of Decay in American Neighborhoods*. New York: Free Press; Hope, T. (1998) Community safety, crime and disorder. In Marlow, A. and Pitts, J. (eds.) *Planning Safer Communities*. Russell House; Foster, J. (1995) Informal social control and community crime prevention. *British Journal of Criminology* 35, 563–83.

8. Wilson, J. and Kelling, G. (1982) Broken windows: the police and community safety. *Atlantic Monthly* March, 29–38.

9. Reiss, J. (1986) Why are communities important in understanding crime? In Reiss, J. and Tonry, M. (eds.) *Communities and Crime. Crime and Justice: A Review of Research. Vol. 8*. Chicago, IL: University of Chicago Press.

10. Burrows, J., Anderson, S., Bamfield, J., Hopkins, M. and Ingram, D. (1999) *Counting the Cost: Crime against Business in Scotland*. Edinburgh: Scottish Executive.

11. See Wood, J., Wheelwright, G. and Burrows, J. (1996) *Crime against Small Business: Facing the Challenge*. Swindon: Crime Concern.

12. For example, in sweep 1, 9.4% of service sector premises and 7% of retail premises were victims of violence in one year, compared to 1.1% of wholesalers and 2.5% of manufacturers.

13. It is acknowledged that bookmakers and postal services had a low sample size. However, these businesses did experience high prevalence rates. It should also be noted here that hotels experienced a prevalence rate of 25%, though there was a sample size of only 4 businesses.

14. Beck, A., Gill, M. and Willis, A. (1994) Violence in retailing: physical and verbal victimization of staff. In Gill, M. (ed.) *Crime at Work: Studies in Security and Crime Prevention*. Leicester: Perpetuity Press.

15. Ekblom, P. and Simon, F. (1988) *Crime and Racial Harassment in Asian-Run Small Shops. Police Research Group Crime Prevention Paper Series* 15. London: Home Office.

16. Here, the data for abuse and violence are aggregated as the ratio of incidents experienced by males and females is similar for both abuse and violence.

17. The full breakdown was males: 31% (987) employed in the service sector; 29% (911) in retailing; 27% (864) in manufacturing; 13% (439) in wholesaling. For females: 42% (1,351) in manufacturing; 31% (1,004) in services; 19% (610) in retailing; 8% (264) in wholesaling.

18. The sample sizes were as follows: clothing/footwear 26 (3 white; 23 Asian); off-licences 32 (10 white, 22 Asian); eating places 28 (11 white, 17 Asian); food shops 35 (17 white, 18 Asian); motor vehicle parts 11 (6 white, 5 Asian); public houses 15 (14 white, 1 Asian).

Chapter 5

The process of employee violence: the building of a workplace explosion

James F. Kenny

Introduction

We expect violence from gang members, career criminals or drug dealers, but not from co-workers. When violence 'punches in' at work, the unfocused eye sees it as 'random', 'senseless', 'sudden' and 'crazy'. The deaf ear does not hear the message being communicated by the violent act. The casual observer does not question the motive of the perpetrator or have knowledge of the events that preceded the violence.

The post-incident interviews of co-workers, victims and offenders reveal the true context of workplace violence. The perpetrators will tell us their purpose, how they have been harmed and the reason for specific targets. Those who had lived through the violence process acknowledge they had seen, experienced and complained of bizarre behaviours that had progressively grown to a dangerous stage. They had hoped something would be done; they had hoped their worst fears were wrong.

Workplace violence has become too common, too dangerous for us to be surprised and unprepared. The Bureau of Labor Statistics reported that there were over 23,225 workers injured due to assaults and violence during the year 1999.[1] Estimates from the 1992–96 National Crime Victimization Survey (NCVS), carried out by the Bureau of Justice Statistics, show that there are over 2 million workplace incidents yearly involving homicides, sexual assaults, robberies, aggravated assaults and simple assaults.[2] Various studies suggest that the overwhelming amount of workplace violence results from threats, harassment, stalking and relationship assaults.[3] While over 50% of the NCVS crimes were committed by strangers, the great majority of threats, harassment, stalking and relationship violence is committed by co-workers and others known to the victims.

In these dangerous times we cannot accept workplace violence as a cost of doing business, and we do not have to limit our intervention to post-incident clean-up. Workplace violence can be prevented by effective interventions in the early stages of the process. The process approach to workplace violence looks to identify elements in the escalating stages of violence and to dismantle various parts of the employee time bomb before the fuse is lit. It acknowledges that behaviours are not senseless, but are driven by purpose. Even an assembled bomb can be diffused if we know what is causing to tick.

Purpose: the driver of the violence process

'The human violence we abhor and fear the most, that which we call random and senseless, is neither. It always has purpose and meaning, to the perpetrator, at least. We may not choose to explore or understand that purpose, but it is there, and as long as we label it senseless, we'll not make sense of it.'[4]

The process of workplace violence starts with a purpose, a need the employee must have satisfied. Violence is just one of the tools he or she may utilize to satisfy that need. It is usually the tool of last resort, used when the employee sees no other way to resolve his or her problem.[5] Understanding the employee's purpose increases the ability of decision-makers to identify early warning signs, predict future conduct and develop effective strategies to address potential violence. It also provides an opportunity to provide the employee with alternatives and inappropriate behaviours before they escalate to violence.

Understanding the motives of troubled or violent individuals is difficult, but they are always there. They may be hard to detect as these employees are oriented to expressing their thoughts in the form of actions rather than words.[6] We must learn to listen, observe and translate their words and actions. We listen as they attempt to communicate their problems. We observe as they interact in the workplace. We translate our observations after those closest to the employees tell us what they have heard and what they have seen.

At the heart of almost all aggressive and bizarre behaviours is an attempt to achieve or maintain justice, or correct or prevent some wrong.[7]

Violence may be used in response to some perceived attacks to their person, property or self-esteem. Violent individuals may see themselves as victims, powerless to protect themselves through conventional means. While most of those who perceive themselves to be victims of injustice do not become violent, those with weak social learning skills and internal control systems pose higher risks.[8]

Once the employee's purpose is uncovered, the ability to predict future behaviours is enhanced. His or her actions no longer seem senseless and random, but rather, are seen as pieces in identifiable patterns that follow logical sequences. Each violent event is preceded and influenced by those actions that came before it. Pre-incident indicators cannot tell the exact times or places of violent events, but they do warn us to prepare for them.

Too many major tragedies have been triggered by seemingly minor and unrelated events. It is not the magnitude of the event that triggers a violent response, but its significance to the employee and the stage in the violence process that it takes place. Employee explosions are usually consistent with the urgency of his or her needs and his or her level of frustration. They often follow seemingly harmless events that had not been defused but allowed to escalate to the crisis level.

Extreme violence becomes a viable option when the perpetrator places blame externally and believes that all means to resolve the injustice are blocked or exhausted.[9] There are always options to violence, and sometimes the employee's needs can be satisfied. Some employee demands or needs can never be met, but others addressed with minor concessions. These concessions may be an option that management would have never considered without the employee's input, but something that it deems entirely appropriate. Often mixed among all the bizarre behaviours and inconsistent language is the employee's need to be understood – his or her desire for respect. In some cases, that may be all the employee really wanted.

The stages of employee violence

Extreme violence is rarely an isolated event but, rather, the last link in a chain of a series of purposeful behaviours.[10] Employee violence is the final stage of a process of progressively dangerous, interdependent and highly visible behaviours. Troubling behaviours in their early stages are largely correctable and minimally volatile. When these behaviours are allowed to progress over time to more aggressive acts, the employee becomes increasing frustrated, committed to and confident of his or her ability to deliver violence.

The employee who commits extreme violence does not snap without warning and may even tell people explicitly what he or she plans to do.[11] These details are usually known by those physically and emotionally closest to him or her. Co-workers may perceive these revelations as threats but, initially, they reflect the employee's desperation and his or her desire to influence events.[12] The act of extreme violence eventually substitutes for the thoughts or statements previously communicated.[13]

The process of violence is usually not linear. Periods of bizarre behaviour or aggression are followed by periods of compliance and calm. A period of calm may fool the observer into believing that the employee's inappropriate behaviour will not be repeated. The failure to address these behaviours timely and effectively strengthens the employee's resolve as he or she perceives minimal consequences for his or her actions.[14]

Stage 1 behaviours serve as early warning signs the individual needs monitoring (Table 5.1). The presence of these actions does not necessarily mean that violence will occur. They can identify an employee with personal or professional problems who is signalling for help.[15] In fact, in most cases these behaviours will desist without intervention or incident. It is when they do not stop or increase in intensity and frequency that careful observation and thoughtful intervention are needed.

Table 5.1   The stages of violence

Stage 1: early warning signs
- Consistently argues with co-workers and customers
- Extreme paranoia
- Refuses to co-operate with management
- Frequently angry, easily frustrated
- Veiled threats
- Harmful graffiti and gossip

Stage 2: impact and intervention
- Stalking
- Destruction of personal and corporate property
- Persistent verbal attacks, bullying or intimidation of co-workers
- Sexual harassment, employee/customer harassment
- Specific threats to harm an employee/manager
- Consistently challenges authority, corporate policies

Stage 3: crisis response
- Unauthorized weapon at work
- Sexual assault
- Physical assault
- Suicide attempts
- Bombings
- Murder

Stage 1 offences are very difficult for managers to address. It is difficult to choose a course of action when no laws or company policies have been clearly broken. Management may feel paralysed by fear, by not wanting to set the employee off. They may blindly hope his or her behaviour will not repeat itself, or they may not know where to go for help.

The offensive, annoying or disruptive stage 1 conduct can serve as the building blocks for more serious offences when they are not effectively addressed. When behaviours escalate to stage 2 (Table 5.1), the workplace will usually suffer some significant impact that requires prompt intervention. Should the management response be ineffective or untimely it can fuel the offender's anger and lessen his or her fear of consequences for his or her actions.

Behaviours unchecked at stage 2 can grow into acts that set off a crisis. The acts of violence in stage 3 (Table 5.1) demand immediate and planned responses. Usually these events are triggered when the perpetrator believes he or she is the victim of some extreme unfairness. A study of 125 workplace homicides found that half of the offenders had been laid off or terminated.[16] The loss of a job to a long-time employee can be as traumatic as the loss of a loved one. The greater his or her sense of entitlement and victimization, the more likely he or she will feel justified in his or her use of violence.

By the time the process has reached the crisis stage, employee violence is more difficult to prevent and often it can only be contained. The employee who has reached the point of experiencing severe humiliation, disrespect or shame may see violence as the only way to regain some pride.[18] There are more opportunities to resolve the issue and protect the employee's dignity when the problem behaviours are recognized early. Co-workers and first-line managers are in the best position to recognize these behaviours, but they must know where to report them and be confident that upper management will provide appropriate professional, legal and emotional support to those involved. As unresolved problems can escalate to violence, early and effective intervention can reverse the process and lead to peaceable solutions.

The building of a violent workplace time bomb

Most explosions are not spontaneous; they are manufactured. The building of a bomb involves the assembly of several essential ingredients, such as dynamite, cap, fuse and a match. The building of the workplace explosion involves a series of risk factors that come together over time. They include employee at-risk behaviours and traits, workplace stressors, co-worker instigation and triggering events. It is the combination of these factors, not solely the existence of an unstable employee, that will set off the explosion.

Employee at-risk behaviours/traits: the dynamite

The dynamite is the critical ingredient in the building of a bomb. Left undisturbed, its risk of exploding is minimal. Individuals with volatile tendencies are low risks until agitated or disturbed. When they feel overwhelmed by some threatening force, violence becomes a viable instrument to achieve relief. It becomes the behaviour outlet of their paranoia.[19]

Violence profiles have become a popular tool to identify potentially aggressive employees.[20] They list various personality traits and behaviours associated with employees who have used extreme workplace violence in the past (Table 5.2). Identifying at-risk behaviours can signal that the process of manufacturing violence has begun. While at-risk traits can identify a troubled employee, they could also be attributed to millions of workers who are entirely peaceable.

Table 5.2   Employee at-risk behaviours/traits (the dynamite)

Behaviours
- History of violence, police encounters
- Frequently angry, easily frustrated, inflexible
- Recent talk of or suicide attempts
- Frequent acts of insubordination or violations of company policy
- Prior personal threats, interpersonal conflicts
- Recent attempts to obtain or secured weapons

Traits
- Drug/alcohol abuse
- Personality disorders, psychiatric problems, paranoia
- Socially isolated

- Frustration over ignored or dismissed complaints and grievances
- Defensive and believes others are out to get him or her
- Low self-esteem, feelings of hopelessness
- Lacks self-control

The improper use of profiles can do more harm than good. Attempts to single out potentially violent employees can stigmatize, traumatize and encourage an already-troubled employee to act out a self-fulfilling prophecy. Profiles will produce many false positives in predicting extreme violence as it is not a common event. Violence does not result from isolated behaviours or personality traits alone but, rather, from a process that combines various factors that play on each other and become more serious over time.

Despite the limitations of the profile, it can alert the user that an individual needs help and monitoring. The frequency, intensity and immediacy of the at-risk behaviours should dictate the type of management intervention. In the less serious cases we should not focus on the employee as potentially violent but rather as an individual in need of assistance. When managers identify and help troubled employees early in the process, they can prevent them from becoming violent ones.

Workplace stressors: the fuse

Corporate downsizing, reorganizations and outsourcing have caused many employees to be faced with the prospect of layoffs, reduced pay and benefits and uncertainty about their futures. Many long-time employees feeling a lack of control, employment insecurity and victimized by unfair workplace policies experience higher levels of stress. A study by Northwestern National Life Insurance Company[21] suggested a link between job stress and workplace violence.

Workplace violence is usually the final incident in a predictable sequence of events involving the individual and the workplace.[22] The process usually begins with a traumatic event that produces extreme anger and anxiety, such as a termination or a negative performance appraisal. The employee who becomes obsessed by this event may blame others for this failure. The internal stress may build over time as the consequences of the event eventually become a reality. Finally, the employee sees no other option but to use violence to achieve justice.

It is not a coincidence that some companies have more incidents of employee violence than others. Kinney[23] identifies 'sick companies' that are more likely to be crisis prone (Table 5.3). Corporate climates that are characterized by chronic and severe personnel problems contribute additional stresses to workplaces that may already be unstable. The interaction of a poor corporate climate and a toxic work group climate (Table 5.4) combined with an at-risk employee can put the violence process on a fast track.

Table 5.3   Workplace stressors (the fuse – 'the sick company')

- Labour/management conflict
- Reorganization, restructuring, downsizing
- Ineffective grievance process
- Threatened benefits
- Inconsistent application of company practices
- Ethnic tensions

Table 5.4   Workplace stressors (the fuse – 'the toxic work group')

- Authoritarian, insensitive management
- Poor communications
- Double standards
- Poor working conditions
- Frequent personal conflicts
- Shifting work priorities

Companies must find ways to turn sick workplaces into healthy ones. Managers should be encouraged to improve their coaching and counselling skills, rather than being authoritarian and unresponsive. Companies need to develop procedures to resolve labour/management disputes as quickly and as fairly as possible. Employees should be made knowledgeable of their companies' grievance procedures, and their claims should be investigated promptly. Workforces must be maintained at reasonable levels so that employees are not stressed by constant demands 'to do more with less'. When employees do become stressed, efforts should be made to change their work assignments, to provide counselling and to encourage them to attend stress, anger and life-management classes.

Co-worker instigators: the cap

Co-workers can play an active or passive role in contributing to the building of the bomb. They can directly factor into their victimizations (Table 5.5) or they can be unwitting accomplices. Often, victims initiate the social interactions that lead to violent responses.[24] These interactions can take the form of physical force, verbal incitements or insinuation. Should the other employee be sufficiently agitated, an aggressive movement or tone can trigger an explosive response.

Table 5.5   Co-worker instigators (the cap)

- Using challenging/threatening behaviour
- Bullying, belittling or insulting the employee
- Pushing or other unauthorized touching
- Aggressive movement or tone of speech
- Intimidating employee with a weapon
- Invading another's personal space
- Threatening another's economic or emotional security

Sometimes, the contribution of the co-worker can be subtle. He or she can ignore, frustrate or disrespect the agitated co-worker. The co-worker may not initiate the insult that causes the co-worker emotional pain, but he or she may laugh at it. He or she may look the other way when bizarre behaviours need to be reported. Sometimes managers go by the book when the situation calls for an understanding or innovative solutions.

Triggering events: the match

When the bomb is fully assembled, an explosion can be set off by an untimely and unplanned spark. A performance action, a perceived poor performance review or termination can push an already-agitated at-risk employee towards violence. Denial of or ignored grievances and complaints can be just as problematic. Sudden changes in job status (downgrade, layoff, transfer) can serve as the match that ignites the dynamite.

Once the fuse is lit, it is important to put it out as quickly as possible and to take steps to dismantle the bomb. Termination interviews do not have to be volatile when they are well planned and administrative details such as final pay, employee benefits, references and return of company property are researched. The interview should be conducted in a private place with security nearby. The interviewer should never argue, negotiate, respond back to threats or say anything further to damage the employee's self-esteem. He or she should be direct, honest, should summarize the reason for termination and focus on the future.[25] The employee should be advised of services that are available to help ease the transition and offered help in using those services.

Stopping the process: disarming the bomb

As extreme employee violence is the end product of a progressively dangerous process, employers who recognize inappropriate behaviours in their early stages will have both the time and opportunity to prevent and de-escalate potential violence. Violence prevention is best accomplished by stopping the process before it gets started. Maintaining a healthy work environment and addressing minor violations of corporate policy lower the risk of aggressive responses and increase the possibility of peaceful solutions. Recognizing the early warning signs alerts us that the process has begun and provides opportunities to intervene before the employee becomes committed to violence. When violence has progressed to the crisis level, management must be prepared to diffuse and contain the problem.

Strategies to maintain a healthy work environment include securing a management commitment, employee involvement, effective hiring practices, target hardening and safety training. The Occupational Safety and Health Administration contends that the success of any programme is dependent on getting the endorsement and visible involvement of top management.[26] Written policy statements communicating the types of inappropriate behaviours, the consequences and contact sources should be drafted and sent to all employees.[27] When issues are reported, a prompt and effective response will show management is serious about reducing workplace stress. Employees and unions can partner in reviewing safety practices and in making recommendations for corrective strategies.

The hiring process permits employers to screen out many of their potential mistakes. This can be accomplished through effective background checks, reference verification and interviewing.[28] Background checks should usually include review of criminal records, credit reports, military discharges, motor vehicle records, education and employment backgrounds. References can confirm or explain employee reasons for leaving previous employment, confusing job titles and gaps in employment. The interview process can help to clear up inconsistencies in the applicant's background and to reveal how the applicant deals with conflict, frustration, anger and disappointment.

The National Institute for Occupational Safety and the National Safe Workplace Institute suggest that companies can make their workplaces hardened targets through the use of environmental designs[29] and safety strategies[30]. The goal is to deter attacks by increasing the probability of identification and apprehension of the perpetrator. Some of these environmental designs include the use of silent alarms, metal detectors, card-key access systems, video surveillance equipment and panic-bar doors with outside locks. Some safety strategies include providing photographs of the suspect to security, seeking restraining orders, relocating work stations, altering employees' work schedules and providing threatened employees with mobile phones with pre-programmed numbers.

Training and education should ensure all employees are aware of the warning signs of co-worker violence and of strategies to protect themselves.[31] The training should involve all employees and be conducted annually. It should include topics such as the company policy, risk factors, recognition of escalating behaviours, strategies to diffuse volatile situations and where to report violent behaviours. It should communicate the location of security phones, alarms and other safety devices, and procedures for getting assistance after a violent incident.

The workplace should be evaluated periodically to identify potential and existing hazards.[32] This evaluation should include analysis of incidents, physical risk factors (lighting, access control, security devices) and the effectiveness of current security measures. Companies should consider using threat assessment teams to direct employee education and to undertake threat tracking, post-incident analysis, incident intervention, referrals to employee assistance programmes and workplace assessment.[33] The team can serve as a liaison between the company and local law enforcement, provide counsel to corporate executives and serve as a sounding board for first-line managers.

When the workplace time bomb has been assembled and is ticking, managers and co-workers need to engage in crisis management responses that de-escalate the situation. Suggestions to 'defuse' the situation can be found in Table 5.6.[34] In dealing with the angry co-worker, the co-worker must refrain from hostile, threatening, apathetic or cold communications. Rejecting demands from the start, showing disrespect, trivializing the situation, challenging or invading the individual's personal space can set off an explosion.

Table 5.6   Defusing an explosive situation

Do stay calm and control your anger

Encourage the individual to express his or her emotions; be an empathic listener

Find out what he or she wants; repeat back what you feel he or she has requested

Understand the individual's feelings; show empathy and respect

Suggest several alternatives to fix the problem

End the interview/conversation on a positive and futuristic note.

The process approach to employee violence: implications and conclusions

It is sad to account for the human suffering during the aftermath of a violent event. It is tragic when warning signs were unnoticed or ignored and opportunities missed to stop the escalation of violence. The process approach helps to identify, understand and address troubling behaviours before they become violent ones. It defines violence not as senseless, random and sudden but, rather the final product of a long series of highly visible, purposeful, interdependent and progressively dangerous events. It is an empowering approach as inappropriate behaviours identified and addressed early are largely correctable and minimally volatile. Employee frustration and anger allowed to build to an explosive level are both risky and difficult to defuse.

The process approach to employee violence encourages a comprehensive corporate strategy that includes crisis management planning, pre-crisis intervention and prevention. Employee violence prevention practices include a strong and unambiguous policy communicating inappropriate behaviours, target hardening, thorough hiring practices and maintenance of a healthy work environment. Pre-crisis intervention is enhanced by early identification of the warning signs, trained personnel and responsive professional, legal and emotional support systems. A crisis management plan would include prompt mobilization guidelines, specific procedures and assignments, conflict management strategies and a co-ordinated team approach. None of this is possible without top management commitment, involvement and vision of a violence-free workplace.

Notes

1. Bureau of Labor Statistics (2001) *Number of Nonfatal Occupational Injuries and Illnesses Involving Days away from Work, Assaults and Violent Acts by Selected Worker and Case Characteristics, 1999*. Washington, DC: US Department of Labor.
2. Warchol, G. (1998) *Workplace Violence, 1992–1996*. Washington, DC: US Justice Department.
3. Northwestern National Life Insurance Company (1993) *Fear and Violence in the Workplace*. Minneapolis, MN: Northwestern National Life Insurance Company; Tjaden, P. and Thoennes, N. (1998) *Stalking in America: Findings from the National Violence against Women Survey*. Washington, DC: National Institute of Justice and Centers for Disease Control and Prevention; Kenny, J. (1999) Stalking in the workplace: the enemy among us. In Webber, P. (ed.) *Leaders Digest* (fall). Washington, DC: IRS Communications; Kenny, J. (2001) When domestic violence punches in at work: how to help a friend. In Webber, P. (ed.) *Leaders Digest* (spring). Washington, DC: IRS Communications Division.
4. de Becker, G. (1997) *The Gift of Fear: Survival Signals that Protect us from Violence*. Boston, MA: Little, Brown & Co., 15.
5. Gilligan, J. (1997) *Violence*. New York: Random House.
6. Ibid.
7. de Becker op. cit.; Gilligan op. cit.
8. Englander, E. (1997) *Understanding Violence*. Mahwah, NJ: Lawrence Erlbaum Associates; Gilligan op. cit.
9. Kinney, J. (1995) *Violence at Work: How to Make your Company Safer for Employees and Customers*. New York: Prentice-Hall.
10. Baron, S. (1993) *Violence in the Workplace: A Prevention and Management Guide for Business*. Ventura, CA: Pathfinder Publishing; de Becker op. cit.; Government Training Institute (1998) *National Symposium on Workplace Violence*. Washington, DC: GTI.
11. Fessenden, F. (2000) They threaten, seethe and unhinge, then kill in quantity. *The New York Times*, 9 April.
12. de Becker op. cit.
13. Gilligan op. cit.
14. de Becker op. cit.
15. Meadows, R. (2001) *Understanding Violence and Victimization* (2nd edn). New York: Prentice-Hall.
16. Johnson, D. (1994) Breaking point: the workplace violence epidemic and what to do about it. *Corporate Security* 20, 26.
17. de Becker op. cit.
18. Gilligan op. cit.
19. Ibid.
20. Kinney op. cit.; Maxey, B. (1996) *Violence in the Workplace is a Serious Problem*. San Diego, CA: Greenhaven Press; Southerland, M., Collins, P. and Scarborough, K. (1997) *A Continuum from Threat to Death*. Cincinnati, OH: Anderson Publishing; Government Training Institute op. cit.; Fessenden op. cit.; Meadows op. cit.
21. Northwestern National Life Insurance Company op. cit.

22. Johnson op. cit.; Kinney op. cit.; National Safe Workplace Institute (1995) *The Essentials of Managing Workplace Violence*. Charlotte, NC: Pinkerton Services Group; Meadows op. cit.

23. Kinney op. cit.

24. Wolfgang, M. (1967) *Studies in Homicide*. New York: Harper & Row.

25. de Becker op. cit.

26. Occupational Safety and Health Administration (1996) *Guidelines for Preventing Workplace Violence for Health and Social Service Workers*. Washington, DC: US Department of Labor.

27. International Association of Chiefs of Police (1995) *Combating Workplace Violence: Guidelines for Employers and Law Enforcement*. Alexandria, VA: US Department of Justice; National Institute for Occupational Safety (1996) *Violence in the Workplace: Risk Factors and Prevention Strategies. Bulletin 57*. Washington, DC: US Department of Health and Human Services; US Office of Personnel Management (1998) *Dealing with Workplace Violence: A Guide for Agency Planners*. Washington, DC: US Office of Personnel Management.

28. Kinney op. cit.; National Workplace Safe Institute op. cit.; US Department of Health and Human Services (1997) *Understanding and Responding to Violence in the Workplace*. Washington, DC: US Department of Health and Human Services; Southerland *et al.* op. cit.

29. National Institute for Occupational Safety op. cit.

30. National Safe Workplace Institute op. cit.

31. National Institute for Occupational Safety op. cit.; Occupational Safety and Health Administration op. cit.; Government Training Institute op. cit.

32. National Institute for Occupational Safety op. cit.; Occupational Safety and Health Administration op. cit.

33. National Safe Workplace Institute op. cit.; Occupational Safety and Health Administration op. cit.; US Postal Service (1997) *Threat Assessment Team Guide. Publication* 108. Washington, DC: US Postal Service; US Office of Personnel Management op. cit.

34. International Association of Chiefs of Police op. cit.; Center for Conflict Management (1996) *Conflict Management Skills. Publication* 9952-106. Washington, DC: IRS; Southerland *et al.* op. cit.; Agry, B. (1998) *Taming Anger: Theirs and Yours*. Chicago, IL: Dartnell Corporation; Government Training Institute op. cit.

Chapter 6

Workplace violence in the USA: are there gender differences?

Shannon A. Santana and Bonnie S. Fisher

Introduction

Victimization research has consistently reported that gender differences exist with respect to the types of crimes women and men experience and with respect to the victim–offender relationship. Several recent national-level studies illustrate this point. First, the Bureau of Justice Statistics reported that although the violent crime rate[1] from 1972 to 1999 for men in the USA was higher than the rate for women, the rate has been getting closer over time. In 1999, for example, there was only an 8.2 percentage point difference between the violent crime rates for men and women compared to a 36.6 percentage point difference in 1973.[2] Secondly, results from the 1999 National Crime Victimization Survey (NCVS) indicated that males were victimized at rates 22% higher than females. Rape and sexual assault were the exception to the gender pattern: females were raped or sexually assaulted at a rate about eight times that of males in 1999.[3] Thirdly, closer examination of the 1993–98 NCVS results revealed that women were victims of intimate partner violence at a rate of about 5 times that of males (766.8 per 100,000 persons compared to 146.2 per 100,000, respectively), while men were victims of stranger violence at a higher rate than women (31.8 per 100,000 compared to 12.9 per 100,000, respectively).[4] Supportive of these gender differences, results from the National Violence Against Women Survey found that women are significantly more likely to report being victims of intimate partner rape and physical assault, whether the estimates are based on a person's lifetime or the previous 12 months.[5] Fourthly, women are also more likely than men to be stalked. Results from the National Violence Against Women Survey reported that 8.1% of women in their sample were stalked in their lifetime compared to 2.2% of men.[6]

In light of these gender differences in victimization patterns in general and the large number of people who are employed outside the home in the USA, questions concerning gender differences with respect to violence in the workplace naturally arise. Despite the volumes devoted to discussing workplace violence and security issues, few, if any, of these books address differences in workplace violence patterns between female and male employees.[7] Consequently, there are many fundamental questions that remain unanswered. For instance, are males and females equally likely to be victims of workplace violence? Are females in the workplace more likely to be attacked by people they know (e.g. ex-intimates) than males? Are females at work more at risk for certain types of violence (e.g. rape and sexual assault) than males? Are the economic costs of workplace violence the same for males and females or are there gender differences? While a few researchers have begun to examine several of these questions, there has been little systematic research designed explicitly to focus on gender differences in workplace violence.[8]

This lack of attention given to gender differences (and even similarities) is somewhat surprising, for several reasons. First, various women and victim advocacy groups and federal, state and local agencies recognize violence against women as a national problem in need of research attention, prevention strategies and accountability mechanisms. During the 1990s, governments at all levels responded with increased funding for research, educational materials and for efforts to address its prevention and prosecution. To illustrate, the US Congress acknowledged the importance of violence against women in its 1994 passage of the Violence Against Women Act as part of the Violent Crime Control and Law Enforcement Act and by President Clinton's establishment of an Office of Violence Against Women in the US Department of Justice.[9]

Secondly, the number of women working outside the home has increased over the last several decades and there is reason to believe this number will steadily increase during this decade as well.[10] In fact, statistics from the Bureau of Labor Statistics reveal that, as of February 2001, there were 66 million women in the labour-force, comprising almost 47% of the USA's workforce.[11] In addition, the statistics reveal that almost 58% of females in the USA aged 16 years and older were employed in the workforce.

Thirdly, evidence indicates that homicide is the leading cause of work-related deaths for females in the USA.[12] Research suggests that the reason for this is related to the types of occupations in which females typically work. Females are concentrated in many of the high-risk occupations: teachers, social workers, nurses and other healthcare workers, and bank and retail workers.[13] In other words, there are certain job characteristics and occupations that put females more at risk than males for experiencing workplace violence.

This chapter provides an overview of what we know about gender-related workplace violence issues in the USA.[14,15] First, we describe the extent and nature of workplace violence incidents committed against male and female employees. Secondly, we compare and contrast workplace violence committed against female and male employees in terms of its motives and impacts. And, thirdly, in light of our analysis, we conclude with a discussion of the implications for security and violence prevention efforts, including current efforts to prevent violence in the workplace, and offer suggestions for future research in this area.

Workplace violence patterns and gender

Workplace violence is a salient issue for women and men who are employed outside the home. A recent Gallup Poll[16] reported that American employees are not optimistic about the safety and security of their respective workplaces. To illustrate, 41% of the respondents indicated they were worried about possible violence in their respective workplace by a co-worker or other employee.[17] Twenty-three per cent said they personally knew someone who they believe is capable of committing an act of violence at their respective place of work. Forty per cent indicated they were not confident the security measures where they work were sufficient to prevent acts of violence similar to the ones that have been reported by the news media. Their perceptions may be justified given the extent and nature of workplace violence in the USA.

National-level estimates of the extent of workplace violence come from data collection efforts by several federal government agencies, including the Bureau of Labor Statistics (BLS), the National Institute for Occupational Safety and Health (NIOSH) and the Bureau of Justice Statistics (BJS). Although these agencies use different data sources and different definitions of workplace and violence, overall, all their reports indicate that a substantial number of employees have experienced an act of violence.[18] For instance, data from the 1992–96 NCVS indicated that each year US residents experienced more than 2 million acts of violence while they were working or on duty.[19] Other researchers who have examined workplace violence across occupations or within a specific organization or occupation have drawn similar conclusions.[20] Specifically, retail sales and law enforcement were the two occupations with the largest number of average violent victimizations in the workplace for 1992–96.[21] As we highlight below, research results also reveal noteworthy gender-based victimization patterns in the workplace.

The extent of violent incidents in the workplace committed against males and females

Three studies using the data from the 1987–92, 1992–94, and 1992–96 BJS's NCVS[22] reveal a similar pattern with respect to the extent of workplace violence: on average, violent *incidents* committed against male employees outnumbered violent *incidents* committed against female employees.[23] For example, between 1992 and 1994, on average, the number of violent incidents committed against males outnumbered those committed against females 2 to 1 (1,239,499 incidents compared to 615,204 incidents).[24] This is to be expected as males outnumber females in the labour market.

Consider for a moment that we previously cited that females comprise 47% of the total labour market. Fisher and Gunnison[25] argue that it would appear that relative to their size in the labour market, females are disproportionately 'under-victimized' with respect to certain types of violence because females who work part time comprise 25% of the total labour market as compared to males who comprise 8%.[26] They point out that females are actually spending much less time at work than males and, therefore, they are less 'exposed' to the risks of being a violent workplace victim than males but yet one-third of violent workplace incidents are committed against females.

Recent research also suggests these incident counts may be masking gender differences in terms of the pattern of workplace violence. Fisher and Gunnison[27] examined these incidents more closely over time and found a pattern somewhat contrary to the overall decline in workplace violence that Warchol[28] reported. For example, Fisher and Gunnison report that from 1992 to 1996, the number of violent incidents committed against females in the workplace increased by 17%. In comparison, the number of violent incidents against males over this time period decreased by 34%. Fisher and Gunnison point out that a five-year time frame is a relatively 'short' time and may reflect year-to-year variation. The divergent pattern, however, does suggest that further examination of data over time is needed to fully understand and appreciate a pattern of the extent of workplace violence committed against male and female employees.

The nature of workplace violence committed against males and females

To compare and contrast the extent of different types of workplace violence committed against females and males, we examine different types of violence in the workplace.

Homicides

Several studies that have examined the extent of homicide in the workplace among males and females have reached noteworthy conclusions. First, four studies came to a similar conclusion: males are more likely than females to be the victim of a homicide in the workplace. For instance, Jenkins,[29] using the death certificate-based National Traumatic Occupational Fatalities (NTOF)[30] surveillance system data, reported that 80% of the workplace homicides between 1980 and 1982 involved male victims. Kraus et al.,[31] in their review of nine peer-reviewed journal articles published from 1980 onwards, reported that work-related homicide rates were 3.0 to 5.6 times higher for males than for females. Likewise, Castillo and Jenkins,[32] using the NTOF data from 1980 to 1989, reported that the homicide rate for male workers was 1.02 per 100,000 workers compared to 0.33 per 100,000 workers for female workers. Their results suggested that the male homicide rate was three times higher than the homicide rate for females. Finally, using data from the BLS's Census of Fatal Occupational Injuries (CFOI), Sygnatur and Toscano[33] found that males were the victims of 81% of the workplace homicides between 1992 and 1998, while females were the victims of 19% of the workplace homicides during this period.

There are some notable twists in these findings, however. First, although males have higher rates of workplace homicide than females, homicide is the leading cause of death for females in the workplace but not for males.[34] Studies have found that homicides range from 10 to 30% of the work-related injury deaths for males compared to 40–57% of such deaths for women.[35]

Another line of research has examined the *nature* of work-related homicides. Results from the BLS's national CFOI[36] presented by Toscano and Weber[37] reveal that most homicide victims were males who were shot during a robbery. In his study of work-related homicides in California from 1979 to 1981, Kraus[38] found that while firearms accounted for 77% of all work-related homicides during this time period, females were more likely to have been killed by cutting or stabbing instruments. In addition, Howe,[39] using data from the 1993 CFOI, found that female homicide victims were more likely to have been fatally assaulted with a tool than male homicide victims. Noteworthy, Howe also found that differences occurred in which part of the body homicide victims were fatally shot. Most of the male homicide victims died from gunshot wounds to the torso, whereas most females died from gunshot wounds to the head. Overall, however, Howe found that most workplace homicide victims, both male and female, died of gunshot wounds and not from injuries caused by bombs, tools, vehicles or other people.

Rape and sexual assaults

Data from the NCVSs for 1992–96 reveal that approximately 42,000 rapes and sexual assaults were reported during each of these years as having occurred to females while they were working or on duty.[40] A much larger percentage of females experienced a rape or sexual assault in the workplace compared to males. Warchol[41] reported that 83.3% of the rape and sexual assault *victims* were females compared to 16.7% who were males.

Incident-level NCVS data reveal a similar pattern among females and males: rape and sexual assault *incidents* are, by far, committed more frequently against females than males. Between 1992 and 1996, on average, 6.3% of the workplace incidents committed against females were rapes or sexual assaults compared to 0.6% of the incidents committed against males.[42]

Using 1992–96 NCVS data, Fisher[43] reports that sexual assaults were the third most frequently occurring violent incident that females experienced in the workplace; 5% of the incidents, on average, were sexual assaults. A little over 2 per cent of the incidents against females were rapes. For males, on average, both sexual assault and rape incidents were infrequent; less than a half of a per cent of the total number of violent incidents committed against males in the workplace were rapes and sexual assaults.

Research indicates there may be certain factors that increase the likelihood of being raped in the workplace. One such study was conducted by Alexander *et al.*,[44] who used workers' compensation claims to examine work-related sexual assaults in Washington State between 1980 and 1989. They found that the isolation of workers from co-workers and from the public increased one's risk of being raped at work. In fact, 85% of the rapes in their study happened to victims who were working alone at the time of the incident.

Robberies

Results from the NCVS show that males were more likely than females to be *victims* of robbery while at work or on duty. Seventy-two per cent of the workplace robbery victims were males, while 28% of the victims were females.[45] Examining the number of *incidents* from the NCVS, Fisher and Gunnison[46] found that the percentages of robberies committed against males and females were almost equal: 4.5% compared to 4.2% of their respective total number of incidents.

Stalking

Little is known about stalking in the workplace, as stalking was not criminalized throughout the USA until the early 1990s.[47] Chenier[48] reports there is an increase in the number of women who are stalked in the workplace.[49] She suggests this increase may be due to the fact that increasing numbers of women are working and are thus able to leave abusive situations. Although these women may be able to change their place of residence, they are often unable to change their work location, which is known to the perpetrator.

To our knowledge, only one published study has examined stalking among co-workers. Using data from the National Violence Against Women Survey, Tjaden and Thoennes[50] found that respondents who indicated they had been stalked by co-workers were more likely to be female than male. Specifically, 73.9% of the victims who reported they had been stalked by co-workers were female. Thus, the data do suggest that females are more likely to be stalked by co-workers than are males.

Cyberaggression

Electronic communication via the Internet is a relatively new technology that is widely used by employees to perform their required tasks. To our knowledge, there have been no systematic studies conducted on the extent or nature of cyberaggression in the workplace.[51] Although there is no standard definition of cyberaggression, Tjaden[52] provided the following examples of news media reports of cyberaggression:

1. Sending racially or sexually offensive jokes through company email.

2. Posting another person's photograph or private information on a highly accessible electronic bulletin board.

3. Mail bombing (i.e. sending repeated messages which cause a computer to shut down).

4. Flaming (i.e. sending abusive email or news group messages that attack the victim in overly harsh, often personal tones).

5. Posting unsolicited or abusive messages in a target's web page guest book.

6. Depicting a victim as a prostitute or someone who enjoys kinky or sado-masochistic sex.

7. Direct threats to harm the victim or someone close to the victim.

Known as cyberstalking, stalking as previously discussed can also be perpetuated through the Internet.

To our knowledge, one study of cyberaggression has been published. A survey of 500 members of Systers, an electronic mailing list for women employed in the computer science field, was administered in 1993. The results indicated that 20% of the respondents reported being targets of sexual harassment on-line.[53]

It seems reasonable to believe that cyberaggression does occur and will continue to thrive in the workplace as electronic means of communication play an integral role in many different types of jobs. Given the number of women in the labour-force, there are many women who can be potential targets of threatening and harassing email in the workplace. The emergence of cyberaggression means that females and males in the workplace may be vulnerable to a new type of victimization. Unlike more 'traditional' types of victimization, cyberaggression and cyberstalking are ones that do not necessarily require the perpetrator to actually be present in the workplace in order to victimize the target; the perpetrator can be virtually anywhere. This characteristic of cyberaggression and cyberstalking alone poses new challenges to the safety and security of employees.

Aggravated and simple assaults

Using data from the NCVS, Warchol[54] reports that the percentage of males who had experienced an aggravated assault while working or on duty was three times greater than the percentage of females who did: 74.4% compared to 25.6% of the aggravated assault victims. He also reports a similar pattern for simple assaults: 66.1% of males reported being simple assault victims compared to 33.9% of females who reported being simple assault victims.

Results from the BLS's Survey of Occupational Injuries and Illness (SOII)[55] indicate that women were the victims in 56% of non-fatal assaults in the workplace.[56] These acts usually took the form of 'hitting, kicking, and beating'. There is at least one methodological explanation for the difference in the BLS's SOII–based results and the BJS's NCVS-based results. The SOII is an injury and illness survey based on a sample of businesses (excluding the self-employed and government workers), whereas the NCVS is a victimization survey based on a sample of households. Also, the definition of assault differs across the two surveys.[57]

Other researchers, using NCVS data, have examined the number of assault *incidents* committed in the workplace and the ranking of the frequency of the different types of violence. As to the extent of assaults, Fisher and Gunnison[58] report that 75.1% of the incidents committed against females in the workplace were simple assault incidents. Similarly, 73% of the incidents committed against males were simple assaults. A slightly different pattern emerges with respect to aggravated assault incidents in the workplace. A smaller percentage of aggravated assault incidents were committed against females compared to males: 15.1% and 21.9%, respectively.

Shedding further insight on the extent of workplace violence among males and females, overall, the studies report a similar pattern with respect to the ranking of frequency of workplace violence incidents: by far, simple assault was the most frequently occurring type of workplace violence among males and females, followed by aggravated assaults.[59]

In sum, while a larger percentage of males were simple assault *victims* while working or on duty, simple assault *incidents* were the most frequently occurring type of violence for both sexes.

After reviewing these studies that have examined workplace violence committed against males and females, a theme becomes apparent: there are differences across gender in terms of the extent and nature of workplace violence. There also appears to be a difference between males and females in terms of the sociodemographic factors related to robbery and assault. Warren *et al.*[60] cite a study by Klien and associates, using data from the NCVS, that reports for males, the risk of experiencing a work-related robbery and assault was higher for those under the age of 45 years with a family income of less than US$40,000 but with more than a high-school education. For females, the risk was higher for younger women (i.e. 18–34 years old) and for those who were not married.

Gender differences in work-related deaths

Despite the fact that homicides are the leading cause of death for females, males are still at a greater risk of being murdered in the workplace.[61] Jenkins[62] attributes differential risks of homicide victimization by gender to variations in employment patterns. Males suffer greater risks of accidental death than do women because they are more likely to work in hazardous industries. For example, Jenkins[63] notes that the male-dominated construction, agriculture/forestry/fishing and mining industries pose a greater threat to workers than the retail trade, services and finance/insurance/real estate industries that have a greater gender balance of workers. Thus, even though a greater number of males are murdered in the workplace each year, homicide is the leading cause of death for females in the workplace (and not males) because male workers are more likely to suffer accidental deaths than homicides.

Gender differences in workplace violence by job characteristics and occupation

Results from a number of studies, using a variety of data sources, suggest that certain job characteristics and occupations put females more at risk than males for experiencing workplace violence. Several job characteristics appear to be related to experiencing an incident of workplace violence. First, Mustaine and Tewksbury,[64] using data from the 1983 National Crime Survey (NCS) Victimization Risk Supplement, identify job characteristics that significantly increase the probability of women experiencing an incident of workplace violence. Their multivariate results suggest that males were more likely to be crime victims[65] if they did not have security at work, lived in a metropolitan area, worked in a place that is open to the public and worked in a job that involved the protection of others or property. On the other hand, females were more likely to be victims if they were better educated and if their work involved late hours.

Secondly, Warren et al.[66] cite a study of public service employees by Hurell et al.[67] Hurell et al. report that females and males who were assaulted while on the job had significantly different indices of stress. For example, women who were assaulted on the job had lower mental demands, greater role conflict, more skill underutilization and limited alternative job opportunities as compared to men who were assaulted. These men reported less job-decision control, fewer alternative job opportunities and underutilization of their training and experience.

Thirdly, Alexander et al.[68] found, as mentioned previously, that workers in Washington State who were isolated from fellow employees and the public were more likely to be the victims of work-related sexual assaults. In addition, they found that 'the occupations of the rape victims were similar to occupations identified as high risk for other intentional injuries'.[69]

Other researchers have examined specific occupations and all report gender-related patterns.[70] First, Castillo and Jenkins,[71] analysing data from the National Traumatic Occupational Fatalities (NTOF) surveillance system, found that females had low rates of work-related homicide in three industries that were high-risk for males: justice/public order/safety, hotels and motels, and eating and drinking establishments. Females had high rates of occupational homicide in liquor stores, gasoline stations and grocery stores.

Secondly, Fisher and Gunnison[72] found that a higher percentage of incidents of robbery occurred against women who worked at teaching institutions, in law enforcement, and in retail compared to males who worked in these occupations. Note, however, that Wooldredge et al.,[73] using a sample of faculty from one university, found no gender difference in the likelihood of personal victimization (i.e. robbery, aggravated assault, sexual assault and assault with a deadly weapon). A methodological rationale for this discrepancy may be found in the composition of the two studies' respective samples. Fisher and Gunnison used a nationally representative sample from the population of US residents, while Wooldredge et al. used a single sample of members of one type of occupation from a single university.

In the last two studies, each set of researchers examined violence in a specific type of occupation. Keim[74] cites results from a study done by Harlan in which four times as many females as males in healthcare settings were injured by their patients. And finally, Hurrell et al.[75] conducted a cross-sectional study on job stress among public service employees in a northeastern state in 1989. They found that 9% of the females and 17% of the males in their study reported they had been physically assaulted while on the job during the past year. For females, the largest percentage of assaults occurred among mental health workers (29%), followed by clerks (8%), human services case workers (7%), and nursing personnel (4%). For males, the largest percentage of assaults occurred among state police personnel (21%), mental health workers (11%), guards (8%), and clerks (8%). Within these job categories, 65% of the male mental health workers, 51% of the state police personnel and 35% of the guards reported being assaulted within the previous year. They also found that workers who had direct contact with clients had a higher likelihood of being assaulted while on the job, regardless of gender. According to Hurrell et al., this finding is consistent with other studies that have shown that the greatest risk of physical assault while on the job is from workers outside the organization (e.g. customers, clients, and patients), not from co-workers.[76]

Other evidence indicates that a greater proportion of female work-related homicides occur in the retail and service industries relative to other industries than do male work-related homicides.[77] One reason that females may be more likely to be victimized in retail and service industries than in other occupations is that the nature of retail and service positions puts women at greater risk of victimization. As discussed above, those at greatest risk of becoming a victim of workplace homicide are those who work alone or in small groups, those who work late at night and those who work with cash.[78] These characteristics are typical of the retail positions in which women often work.

Gender differences in the relationship between the victim and offender

The victim-offender relationship in the workplace can take various forms – co-worker, ex-intimate, current intimate, acquaintance, customer/client and stranger. Co-worker violence has been the focus of media accounts of workplace violence. Contrary to these media accounts, Tjaden and Thoennes[79] present findings from the National Violence Against Women Survey (NVAW)[80] that suggest that co-worker violence is relatively rare: 1.7% of the respondents indicated they had been victimized by a co-worker sometime *during their life*, while 0.1% said they had been victimized by a co-worker *during the past year*. They also found that males were the victims of co-worker violence in 68.1% of the cases, while females were victims of co-worker violence in 31.9% of the cases.

Their findings, however, indicate that men and women experienced different types of co-worker violence. Specifically, they found that the majority of victims of co-worker rape (76.7%) and the majority of victims of co-worker stalking (73.9%) were women. However, the majority of victims of co-worker assault (83.4%) and the majority of victims of threats by co-workers (80.6%) were men.

In addition to examining whether there was a working relationship between victims and perpetrators of workplace violence, five studies have also examined whether there was a personal relationship between victims and perpetrators. First, Bachman,[81] using data from the 1987–92 National Crime Survey,[82] found that males who were victimized while working were more likely than females to be attacked by a stranger: 58% of the victimizations compared with 40%, respectively.[83] On the other hand, females were more likely than males to be attacked by someone they knew while at work or on duty. For example, 35% of the workplace victimizations experienced by females were committed by an acquaintance whereas slightly less – 30% – were against males. Bachman found a larger difference with respect to victimizations committed by a person well known to the victim – a well-known person committed 19% of victimisations against females whereas such a person only committed 10% of such victimizations against males. Additionally, Bachman found that husbands, ex-husbands, boyfriends and ex-boyfriends were responsible for 5% of the attacks against females in the workplace compared to 1% of the attacks against males.

Secondly, Howe,[84] using data from the 1993 CFOI, found that female workers were more likely to have been fatally assaulted by relatives than male workers: 10% of the female homicide victims had been assaulted by a relative compared to less than 1% of the male homicide victims.

Thirdly, Warchol,[85] using data from the NCVS, found that in 0.2% of the incidents committed against male workers, the victim and offender were intimates, compared to 2.2% of the incidents committed against female workers. In addition, he also found that 29.9% of male victims of workplace violence reported that their attacker was an acquaintance compared to 46.2% of females. Warchol found that 65.0% of the male victims reported that their attacker was a stranger compared to 47.0% of women.

Fourthly, Toscano and Windau[86] also found that many female victims of workplace violence knew their attacker. Specifically, they found that one-sixth of the female workplace homicides in 1996 were the result of domestic disputes. And, fifthly, according to Lord,[87] the US Department of Justice estimates that domestic partners were responsible for more than 13,000 non-fatal acts of workplace violence against women in 1993. However, in a study of full-time employees in state government agencies and universities in North Carolina, Lord found that few respondents reported they had been victimized at work by domestic partners. Lord argues it is likely that domestic problems do carry over into the workplace but that employees may feel too embarrassed to report such incidents. In addition, it may be that supervisors support employees' reluctance to report these types of incidents.[88]

Given the research results noted above that women are frequently victimized by an ex-intimate and the perpetrator of stalking is most likely to be an ex-intimate, it is not surprising that research supports the notion that domestic violence is often carried over into the workplace. Collins et al.[89] examined two different types of lethal workplace violence: multi-site and single-site. Multi-site workplace violence differs from single-site workplace violence in that multi-site violence is carried out over a short period of time at multiple sites, at least one of which is a workplace to which the offender has a connection. In contrast, single-site workplace violence refers to incidents which occur at a single site: the workplace. Collins et al. examined 220 cases of workplace violence occurring between 1984 and 1993. Twenty-three of these cases were considered multi-site incidents. Collins et al. found gender and age to be significantly related to type of workplace violence. Specifically, they found that women and children were more likely to be victims in multi-site cases while men and individuals over 26 years of age were more likely to be victims in single-site cases. This finding is very important for women since victims of workplace violence are 'much more likely to be killed and somewhat more likely to be seriously injured' in multi-site rather than single-site workplace violence.[90] Collins *et al.* argue that what distinguishes multi-site incidents from single-site incidents is that there is often a 'family connection' between the victims and offender in cases of multi-site workplace violence. Single-site incidents of workplace violence, on the other hand, typically occur between a co-worker and/or a stranger. Thus, many multi-site workplace violence incidents may be characterized as cases where domestic violence has been carried over into the workplace.

Further research supports the notion that many cases of workplace violence are the result of domestic violence, more so for females than for males. For instance, a study of workplace homicides that occurred between 1977 and 1991 in North Carolina found that dispute-related homicides made up a larger proportion of the workplace homicides for women than for men.[91] The authors point out that the nature of the disputes differed for male versus female victims. For male victims, the majority of the dispute-related homicides involved disputes between co-workers, followed by other non-strangers and customers. For female victims, however, the majority of the dispute-related homicides (12 out of 16) involved a dispute with an estranged intimate partner. In all 16 of these cases, the women were living separately from the offenders at the time the homicide occurred. In addition, in 40% of the cases a history of domestic violence was mentioned in the medical examiner case file. Further, two of the female victims had filed domestic violence-related charges against the offender on the very day they were killed. Thus there appears to be evidence that domestic violence is a serious problem for women, not only in the home but in the workplace as well. This is important since research indicates that domestic violence in the workplace can have significant negative effects, such as a loss in productivity and increases in employee absenteeism, turnover, stress and healthcare costs.[92]

Gender differences in motives behind workplace violence

As the research described above indicates, some violence against women in the workplace may be the result of domestic disputes carried over into the workplace. There is also some speculation suggesting that the advancement of women in the workplace may lead to feelings of resentment among men, who feel they were unfairly passed over for jobs or promotions. For instance, an employee of the US Postal Service shot three people and killed one other at work 6 weeks after his complaint to the Equal Opportunity Commission that he had been discriminated against in favour of female employees was dismissed.[93]

Other researchers suggest that females may face extreme risks of homicide at work because they are viewed as vulnerable and as easy targets. For example, Kraus *et al.*[94] suggest that criminals may perceive women as offering no resistance or being less likely to interfere during the course of a robbery. Thus, it appears that women may be the victims of workplace violence for different reasons than men.

Gender differences in the impacts of workplace violence

Researchers have consistently shown that experiencing an incident of workplace violence takes a negative toll on the victim.[95] When looking at the impacts of workplace violence on males and females, this toll appears to be greater for females. For example, Fisher and Gunnison[96] examined the economic costs of workplace violence incidents committed against male and female employees. They found that in incidents where a person was injured, females were slightly more likely to miss time from work than males. In addition, they found that in these incidents, female victims were absent from work for longer periods of time due to their injuries than male victims. On average, female victims who were injured lost 22 days from work, while male victims who were injured lost 8 days.

There are other financial impacts to be considered. Fisher and Gunnison also report that females were as equally likely as males to have lost pay due to injuries that were not covered by unemployment, insurance, sick leave or other sources. Finally, they found that female victims' household members were more likely to miss more than one day of work than were male victims' household members (49% compared to 35%). Thus, Fisher and Gunnison conclude that the economic consequences of workplace violence are far-reaching for females and that the victims' household members may be impacted as well.

Conclusion

Summary

Overall, our literature analysis suggests that gender differences more than gender similarities characterize workplace violence. First, the research suggests that while males are more likely than females to be killed in the workplace, homicide is the leading cause of death for females in the workplace. Secondly, the literature suggests that females have higher risks of being victimized in different occupations than do males. For instance, while males are at high risk of being victimized in justice/public order/safety occupations, females are at high risk of being victimized in retail and service industries, such as liquor stores, gasoline stations and grocery stores. Thirdly, certain sociodemographic factors (e.g. age) distinguish between the risks of work-related robbery and assault committed against males and females. Fourthly, females in the workplace are more likely than males to be victims of sexual assault, rape, and stalking by co-workers. Fifthly, although speculative at this time, cyberaggression and cyberstalking are two types of victimization that female employees may experience more often than male employees. Sixthly, the research indicates that female workers are more likely to be victimized by someone they know than are male workers. Seventhly, the motives behind the victimizations of females in the workplace may be different from males. Finally, it appears that while both males and females experience lost wages as a result of being victimized in the workplace, females may be more likely to miss more days of work.

Implications for security and violence prevention

We are cautious to draw broad, sweeping implications for security and violence prevention efforts for two reasons. First, the research that examines gender-related workplace violence issues is in its infancy stage. A clearer understanding of the extent and nature of the workplace violence committed against male and female employees would be a much needed contribution to the current gender and workplace violence research efforts. It may be somewhat premature to draw wide-sweeping security and crime prevention implications. Only by better assessing the gender and workplace violence relationship can our knowledge and understanding be put to good practice, not only for preventing violence but also for securing a safer workplace for males and females. It is clear that efforts have to be made to educate concerned parties – employers, employees, unions, professional organizations, government agencies – that gender differences in the extent, characteristics, victim–offender relationship, motives, and impacts of workplace violence exist. An education stage may be a first proactive step in the development of workplace violence prevention and security strategies and measures that address gender differences.

Secondly, overall, our results suggest that no one is immune from being violently victimized while at work or on duty. However, gender differences do exist with respect to the extent and nature of workplace violence – male and female employees experience different types of violence for different reasons and they experience different impacts from their victimizations. To date, it appears that few policies have been implemented in workplaces that specifically address the gender differences we have found in our analysis of the workplace violence data. Lessons from residential crime prevention evaluations have shown that generic 'one size fits all' crime prevention and security strategies may not be effective in preventing or reducing incidents.[97] Researchers have convincingly shown that such an approach does not necessarily result in reducing crime and, in fact, the opposite may happen and indeed has happened. This may happen in the workplace if a 'one size fits all' strategy is adopted. Instead, workplaces need to implement policies specifically aimed at the workplace violence issues that most pertain to women (e.g. stalking, sexual assault and rape).

The results we presented show there is variation among male and female workers in the frequency of the different types of workplace violence they experience and the characteristics of the incidents. This variation will pose challenges for those developing and implementing workplace violence prevention and security policies and programmes. These differences need to be addressed, as employers may be held liable for violence-related injuries suffered on the job.[98] Tailoring security and violence prevention strategies to fit the type of violence, the type of work, the victim–offender relationship and the motives of the perpetrator may be a valuable first step, since it is doubtful that a single strategy will be effective and appropriate in all workplaces for males and female alike.

Several efforts have been made to tailor prevention strategies to specific issues that females face in the workplace. For instance, one line of research details prevention strategies aimed specifically at preventing domestic violence in the workplace. Suggested prevention strategies include training managers and supervisors to recognize the signs of abuse and to help victimized employees.[99] It is recommended that this training include issues such as employee confidentiality, the dynamics and cycle of domestic violence, appropriate and inappropriate ways to approach a victim, and the availability of in-house and community-based resources for victims. In addition, employers should also develop domestic violence policies, perhaps including procedures enabling employees to confidentially report their abuse. Another suggestion is to allow victims of domestic violence in the workplace flexible working hours in order to attend medical and legal appointments. Suggestions for improved security include transferring victims to new work sites or changing their work shifts – this provides women with more security yet does not force them to leave their jobs. In addition, other security policies can be implemented, such as refusing to give out the phone numbers and addresses of employees, placing pictures of batterers near the front entrances of buildings in an effort to prevent access, escorting abused employees to their vehicles, designating parking spaces near the building for abused employees and offering silent alarms or mobile phones to females who are at risk of violence in the workplace.[100] Other suggestions for employers to prevent domestic violence in the workplace include assisting the victim in documenting the abuse, helping employees develop a safety plan, filing workplace orders of protection, providing general domestic violence education and prevention programmes, and providing resources and referrals for victims.[101]

It is important for employers to develop workplace violence prevention strategies not only for moral reasons (i.e. the social responsibility to prevent violence against their employees), but also for legal reasons.[102] Employers can be held liable for workplace violence that occurs due to an employer's failure to provide adequate security.[103] In addition, under the legal theory of 'respondent superior', an employer may be held liable for the violent actions of their employees. Finally, employers may also be held responsible for negligent hiring and employment retention for violent actions committed by co-workers.[104]

Future research

Future research should continue to explore the issue of gender differences in workplace violence. However, future research should also take into account some of the limitations of prior research. For instance, Castillo and Jenkins[105] note that in their study, and in other studies, rates of victimization were calculated using denominators that did not take into account hours of work. The distinction between full and part-time workers is important since data suggest that females are more likely than males to work part time.[106]

To accurately portray the risks of being a victim of crime in the workplace for each gender, studies should take into account the actual number of hours workers are exposed to these risks as well as the total number of workers by gender so that rates of violence can be estimated, especially rates by different occupational categories. For example, the job categories used in the NCVS are not suitable to calculating such rates because their categories do not correspond to the occupational categories used by the Bureau of the US Census and the Department of Labor.

In addition to correcting the problems of past research, future studies should look not only at the economic costs of workplace violence on victims but also at the psychological impacts, including an employee's quality of life, psychological well-being, and employment status after the victimization. New types of victimization that may be present in the workplace, namely stalking, cyberaggression and cyberstalking, need to be further examined. In addition, the workplace violence literature would be greatly advanced if researchers developed and tested theory-based hypotheses as to why gender differences and similarities exist in workplace violence.[107]

And, lastly, future researchers need to take stock of what is being done by employers and employees to address violence in the workplace. To date, little is actually known about either what types of general security and violence prevention strategies and measures have been implemented or what types of specific strategies and measures are directly targeted at male employees and female employees, respectively. A systematic inventory of these strategies and measures needs to be undertaken. Only then can evaluations be planned and executed to measure and test the 'effectiveness' of these strategies and measures in addressing workplace violence.

Notes

1. The violent crime rate included homicide, rape, robbery, and both simple and aggravated assault.
2. Bureau of Justice Statistics. Violent victimization rates by gender, 1973–99 (http://www.ojp.usdoj.gov/bjs/glance/vsx.txt).
3. Rennison, C.M. (2000) *Criminal Victimization 1999: Changes 1998–99 with Trends 1993–99.* Washington, DC: Bureau of Justice Statistics.
4. Rennison, C.M. and Welchans, S. (2000) *Intimate Partner Violence (Special Report).* Washington, DC: Bureau of Justice Statistics.
5. Tjaden, P. and Thoennes, N. (2000) *Extent, Nature, and Consequences of Intimate Partner Violence: Findings from the National Violence Against Women Survey (Research Report).* Washington, DC: US Department of Justice.
6. Tjaden, P. and Thoennes, N. (1998) *Stalking in America: Findings from the National Violence Against Women Survey (Research in Brief).* Washington, DC: US Department of Justice.
7. We are not suggesting that females have not been the focus of workplace violence studies. There are a few studies that have examined violence among female employees. For example, see Bell, C. (1991) Female homicides in the United States, 1980 to 1985. *American Journal of Public Health* 81(6), 729–32; Davis, H., Honchar, P.A. and Suarez, L. (1987) Fatal occupational injuries of women, Texas 1975–84. *American Journal of Public Health* 77(12), 1524–27.
8. However, see Santana, S.A. and Fisher, B.S. (2000) Workplace violence in the United States: are there gender differences? *Security Journal* 13(2), 39–52.
9. Crowell, N.A. and Burgess, A.W. (1996) *Understanding Violence against Women.* Washington, DC: National Academy Press.
10. Lord, V.B. (1998) Characteristics of violence in state government. *Journal of*

Interpersonal Violence 13(4), 489–503.

11. Bureau of Labor Statistics. Employment status of the civilian population by sex and age (http://stats.bls.gov/news.release/empsit.t01.htm).

12. Kraus, J.F., Blander, B. and McArthur, D.L. (1995) Incidence, risk factors and prevention strategies for work-related assault injuries: a review of what is known, what needs to be known, and countermeasures for intervention. *Annual Review of Public Health* 16, 355–79; Jenkins, L. (1996a) *Violence in the Workplace: Risk Factors and Prevention Strategies*. Washington, DC: National Institute for Occupational Safety and Health; Kinney, J.A. (1995) *Violence at Work: How to Make your Company Safer for Employees and Customers*. Englewood Cliffs, NJ: Prentice-Hall, 109–15; Toscano, G. and Windau, J. (1994) The changing character of fatal work injuries. *Monthly Labor Review* 117(10), 17–28.

13. Chappell, D. and Di Martino, V. (2000) *Violence at Work*. Geneva: International Labour Office.

14. See also Santana and Fisher op. cit.

15. For an excellent analysis of violence at work in England and Wales, see Budd, T. (1999) *Violence at Work: Findings from the British Crime Survey*. London: Health & Safety Executive and the Home Office, Information and Publications Group, Research Development and Statistics Directorate.

16. Sourcebook of criminal justice statistics (1999) (http://www.albany.edu/sourcebook/1995/pdf/t251.pdf).

17. This estimate reflects the sum of the categories 'very worried,' 'somewhat worried' and 'not too worried'.

18. Fisher, B.S. and Gunnison, E. (2001) Violence in the workplace: gender similarities and differences. *Journal of Criminal Justice* 29(2), 146–56; Mullen, E.A. (1997) Workplace violence: cause for concern or the construction of a new category of fear? *Journal of Industrial Relations* 39(1), 21–32.

19. Warchol, G. (1998) *Workplace Violence, 1992–96 (Special Report)*. Washington, DC: Bureau of Justice Statistics.

20. Davis *et al*. op. cit.; Fisher, B.S. (1996) *Analysis and Report of the National Crime Victimization Survey 1987–92: A Summary Report to DHHS, PHS, CDC, NIOSH, and ALOSH*. Cincinnati, OH: University of Cincinnati, Department of Political Science; Fisher, B.S. (1997) *Analysis and Report of the National Crime Victimization Survey 1992–96: A Summary Report to DHHS, PHS, CDC, NIOSH, and ALOSH*. Cincinnati, OH: University of Cincinnati, Department of Political Science; Goodman, R.A., Jenkins, E.L. and Mercy, J.A. (1994) Workplace-related homicide among health-care workers in the United States, 1980 through 1990. *Journal of the American Medical Association* 272(21), 1686–88; Peek-Asa, C., Erickson, R. and Kraus, J.F. (1999) Traumatic occupational fatalities in the retail industry, United States 1992–1996. *American Journal of Industrial Medicine* 35, 186–91; Warren, J., Brown, D., Hurt, S., Cook, S., Branson, W. and Jin, R. (1999) The organizational context of non-lethal workplace violence: its interpersonal, temporal, and spatial correlates. *Journal of Occupational and Environmental Medicine* 41(7), 567–81.

21. Warchol op. cit.

22. The Bureau of the Census administers the NCVS to all individuals aged 12 or

older living in a sample of approximately 50,000 housing units throughout the USA. The final sample contains more than 90,000 individuals. Each housing unit remains in the sample for three and one-half years, with each of the seven interviews taking place at six-month intervals. Each eligible member of the housing unit is questioned about his or her victimization experiences within the six-month bounding period.

23. Fisher (1996) op. cit.; Fisher (1997) op. cit.; Fisher and Gunnison op. cit.
24. Fisher (1997) op. cit.
25. Fisher and Gunnison op. cit.
26. Cohany, S.R. (1998) Workers in alternative employment arrangements: a second look. *Monthly Labor Review* 121(11), 3–21.
27. Fisher and Gunnison op. cit.
28. Warchol op. cit.
29. Jenkins (1996a) op. cit.
30. The National Institute for Occupational Safety and Health (NIOSH) maintains the NTOF system. The system is a death certificate-based census of occupational injury deaths to workers aged 16 years and older. Data are collected from all 50 states and the District of Columbia. This provides for complete coverage of all workers in the USA (see Jenkins, E.L. (1996b) Workplace homicide: industries and occupations at high risk. *Occupational Medicine: State of the Art Reviews* 11(2), 219–25).
31. Kraus *et al.* op. cit.
32. Castillo, D.N. and Jenkins, E.L. (1994) Industries and occupations at high risk for work-related homicide. *Journal of Medicine* 36(2), 125–32.
33. Sygnatur, E.F. and Toscano, G.A. (2000) Work-related homicides: the facts. *Compensation and Working Conditions* 5(1), 3–8.
34. Sygnatur and Toscano op. cit.; Toscano, G.A. and Windau, J.A. (1998) Profile of fatal work injuries in 1996. *Compensation and Working Conditions* 3(1), 37–43.
35. Jenkins (1996a) op. cit.; Jenkins (1996b) op. cit.; Kraus *et al.* op. cit.
36. US Department of Labor (1997) *BLS News: National Census of Fatal Occupational Injuries, 1996. US Department of Labor Report 97–266.* Washington, DC: US Department of Labor, 7 August. The fatality census uses multiple data sources, such as death certificates, workers' compensation reports and claims, Occupational Safety and Health Administration files and new articles to compile the most complete count of fatal work injuries possible.
37. Toscano, G. and Weber, W. (1995) Violence in the workplace. Office of Safety, Health, and Working Conditions (http://stats.bls.gov/osh/cfar0005.pdf).
38. Kraus, J.F. (1987) Homicide while at work. *American Journal of Public Health* 77(10), 1285–89.
39. Howe, H.L. (1995) Differences in workplace homicides by sex, 1993. Bureau of Justice Statistics (http://www.bls.gov/oshwc/cfar0001.pdf).
40. Warchol op. cit.
41. Ibid.
42. Fisher and Gunnison op. cit.
43. Fisher (1997) op. cit.
44. Alexander, B.H., Franklin, G.M. and Wolf, M.E. (1994) The sexual assault of

women at work in Washington State, 1980 to 1989. *American Journal of Public Health* 84(4), 640–42.

45. Warchol op. cit.
46. Fisher and Gunnison op. cit.
47. Tjaden and Thoennes (1998) op. cit.
48. Chenier, E. (1998) The workplace: a battleground for violence. *Public Personnel Management* 27(4), 557–68.
49. See also Mullen op. cit.
50. Tjaden, P. and Thoennes, N. (1999) *Violence by Co-Workers: Findings from the National Violence Against Women Survey.* Washington, DC: National Institute of Justice.
51. Miceli, S.L., Santana, S.A. and Fisher, B.S. (2001) Cyberaggression: safety and security issues for women worldwide. *Security Journal* 14(2), 11–27.
52. Tjaden, P. (2000) *A Proposal to Examine Cyberaggression.* Denver, CO: Center for Policy Research.
53. Betts, M. and Maglitta, J. (1995) IS policies target e-mail harassment. *Computerworld* 13 February, 12.
54. Warchol op. cit.
55. The SOII is an annual survey of approximately 250,000 business establishments in the private sector. Excluded from the sample are the self-employed, small farmers and government workers (e.g. police and other law enforcement officers).
56. Toscano and Weber op. cit.
57. Nonfatal assaults in the SOII include: hitting, kicking, beating, squeezing, pinching, scratching, twisting, biting, stabbing, shooting, all other specified acts (e.g. rape, threats) and unspecified acts. Assaults in the NCVS include an unlawful physical attack excluding rape or sexual assault. This can include attack with a weapon, attack without a weapon when serious injury occurred and attack without a weapon either resulting in no injury or minor injury (e.g. cuts, scratches).
58. Fisher and Gunnison op. cit.
59. Fisher (1996) op. cit.; Fisher, B.S., Jenkins, E.L. and Williams, N. (1998) The extent and nature of homicide and non-fatal workplace violence in the United States: implications for prevention and security. In Gill, M. (ed.) *Crime at Work.* Leicester: Perpetuity Press; Fisher and Gunnison op. cit.
60. Warren *et al.* op. cit.
61. Jenkins (1996b) op. cit.; Peek-Asa *et al.* op. cit.
62. Jenkins (1996b) op. cit.
63. Ibid.
64. Mustaine, E.E. and Tewksbury, R. (1997) The risk of victimization in the workplace for men and women: an analysis using routine activities/lifestyle theory. *Humanity and Society* 21(1), 17–38.
65. The authors do not distinguish type of crime. They only state the victimization happened while the victim was working or on the way to or from work.
66. Warren *et al.* op. cit.
67. Hurrell, J.J., Worthington, K.A. and Driscoll, R.J. (1996) Job stress, gender, and

workplace violence: analysis of assault experiences of state employees. In VandenBos, G.R. and Bulatao, E.Q. (eds.) *Violence on the Job: Identifying Risks and Developing Solutions*. Washington, DC: American Psychological Association.

68. Alexander *et al*. op. cit.
69. Ibid., 640.
70. Supportive of gender variation in workplace violence found in the USA, Mayhew (Chapter 2 of this volume) reported that when males and females did similar jobs, females tended to experience more verbal abuse than males. Males tended to experience more overt threats and physical assaults than females. Similarly, Hopkins (Chapter 4 of this volume) reported gender differences in his study of small businesses in the Belgrave and West End areas of Leicester, England. He found that males experienced higher rates of abuse and violence than females.
71. Castillo and Jenkins op. cit.
72. Fisher and Gunnison op. cit.
73. Wooldredge, J., Cullen, F. and Latessa, E. (1992) Victimization in the workplace: a test of routine activities theory. *Justice Quarterly* 9(2), 325–35.
74. Keim, J. (1999) Workplace violence and trauma: a 21st century rehabilitation issue. *Journal of Rehabilitation* 65(1), 16–20.
75. Hurrell *et al*. op. cit.
76. See Tjaden and Thoennes (1999) op. cit.
77. Jenkins (1996a) op. cit.; Peek-Asa *et al*. op. cit.
78. Jenkins (1996a) op. cit.; Lord op. cit.
79. Tjaden and Thoennes (1999) op. cit.
80. The NVAW employed a sample of 8,000 women drawn from a national, random-digit-dialling sample of households in the USA. It was administered from November 1995 to May 1996. The survey asked respondents about their experiences with non-fatal forms of violence that involved a co-worker.
81. Bachman, R. (1994) *Violence and Theft in the Workplace*. Washington, DC: US Department of Justice.
82. The National Crime Survey was redesigned during the early 1990s. The redesigned version is titled the National Crime Victimization Survey. Its administration was implemented in 1992.
83. Bachman op. cit.
84. Howe op. cit.
85. Warchol op. cit.
86. Toscano and Windau (1998) op. cit.
87. Lord op. cit.
88. Ibid.
89. Collins, P.A., Scarborough, K.E. and Southerland, M. (2001) *Workplace Violence: The Family Connection. Working Paper*. Richmond, KY: Loss Prevention and Safety Department, College of Justice and Safety, Eastern Kentucky University.
90. Ibid., 9.
91. Moracco, K.E., Runyan, C.W., Loomis, D.P., Wolf, S.H., Napp, D. and Butts, J.D. (2000) Killed on the clock: a population-based study of workplace homicide, 1977–1991. *American Journal of Industrial Medicine* 37(6), 629–36.

92. US Department of Justice (2001) Business, employers, and labor organizations (http://www.ojp.usdoj.gov/vawo/agendaforthenation/tab15.htm); US Department of Justice (2000) Workplace violence (http://www.ojp.usdoj.gov/ovc/assist/nvaa2000/academy/chap22-5.htm).
93. Mullen op. cit.
94. Kraus *et al.* op. cit.
95. See Warren *et al.* op. cit.
96. Fisher and Gunnison op. cit.
97. See Rosenbaum, D.P. (1988) Community crime prevention: a review and synthesis of the literature. *Justice Quarterly* 5(3), 323–95.
98. See Hughes, S.M. (1999) Violence in the workplace: identifying costs and preventive solutions. Undergraduate Gold Medal paper awarded from the First Annual Student Paper Writing Competition, American Society of Industrial Security, February 2000.
99. US Department of Justice (2000) op. cit.
100. US Department of Justice (2000) op. cit.; US Department of Justice (2001) op. cit.
101. US Department of Justice (2000) op. cit.
102. Ibid.
103. Ibid.
104. Ibid.
105. Castillo and Jenkins op. cit.
106. Castillo and Jenkins op. cit.; Fisher and Gunnison op. cit.
107. Fisher and Gunnison op. cit.

Chapter 7

Prevention of violence affecting workers: a systems perspective

Mark Braverman

The nature of the crisis in the modern workplace

Paul Shrivastava (p. 176), a professor of management, provides a powerful description of the current state of our world: 'We live in a crisis-prone and crisis-laden world. A world in which crises are omnipresent and proliferating. Every aspect of society faces damaging disruptions, upheaval and restructuring, which are the hallmarks of crises.'[1] In Shrivastava's analysis, crisis is global. It is reflected at every level of society, including the modern corporation. In Shrivastava's view, the corporations that will prosper are those that recognize crisis as opportunities for positive and important change rather than as unpleasant disruptions that threaten the status quo and should be avoided. 'Sustainable corporations', he writes, are companies that are open to constant change and restructuring. The extent to which corporations recognize and respond to these crises will determine how well a company is prepared for the crises it will face.

In a similar vein, Pauchant and Mitroff,[2] two writers who have also studied the way crises have affected modern corporations, offer a compelling model in which they contrast the 'crisis prone' with the 'crisis prepared' organization. Focusing on the proliferation of human and environmental crises that characterize modern society, they argue that corporations that deny the possibility of crisis inevitably expose themselves to the most severe and potentially disastrous situations:

> Managers in crisis-prepared organizations have learned this fundamental lesson; *crisis management concerns the totality of their*

organization . . . and is an expression of the organization's fundamental purpose or strategic vision. If an organization is not positioned well with regard to crisis management, then it is probably not well positioned to compete successfully in the new global economy.[3]

Like Shrivastava, these writers hold that the concept of *crisis* is crucial for an understanding of the challenges facing the modern corporation. They see the growing global crisis reflected in the novel, complex situations that are faced at a constantly increasing rate by managers in companies and work organizations of all kinds. Furthermore, they agree that the solutions are social, *not* technological:

> The sociotechnical systems that we call 'corporations' are so complex and interdependent that they have become extremely fragile . . . a minor event, even a single individual, can now have a drastic effect on an organization as a whole and on its community and environment. These events will not diminish in this century; they are, in fact, increasing rapidly.[4]

This quotation sums up a fundamental leadership and management issue of our time. Crises are no longer isolated, episodic events in the life of a company. Rather, they have to do with complex and 'non-technological' issues, such as stress, communication, trust, flexibility and caring. Furthermore, crisis management is not something that can be pigeonholed as the responsibility of a single function, such as Safety, Corporate Communications, Legal or Human Resources. Dealing with crises has become the daily occupation of managers at all levels and functions. Today, a key leadership capability is the capacity to understand the inevitability of crisis and to be prepared for it.

Leadership and crisis management: beyond public relations

The term 'crisis management' originated in the public relations industry to describe the manipulation of public and stockholder opinion in the midst of a corporate disaster or scandal such as product contamination, environmental, industrial or transportation disaster, or employer misconduct. Well-known examples include the Bhopal, India chemical spill, the *Exxon Valdez* oil spill, the *Tylenol* tamperings and the *Challenger* space shuttle explosion. These events all had the potential to threaten the very existence of the corporations and agencies that presided over them. The way they were handled (or mishandled) by the leadership at the time had profound consequences for the recovery of the organization.

But corporate crises are not limited to disasters that cause mass casualties, widespread environmental damage or two-inch headlines. Crises come to the attention of corporate executives, human resource managers, safety directors, corporate lawyers and risk managers on a weekly, if not daily, basis and have a profound effect on employees. These effects extend beyond the immediate circle of victims. They involve the health, productivity, loyalty, morale and even employment longevity of employees from the line level through middle and upper management. Having systems in place to handle the *internal* effects of crisis has become the responsibility of companies large and small, public and private, white and blue collar.[5] Unions, too, are staking out new territory in crisis management. Progressive forces in several labour organizations are realizing that protecting workers from the damaging and sometimes fatal effects of crises at work will have to be a central feature of labour's role in the new century.[6]

The learning organization: systems theory and workplace violence

Systems theory bears directly on the issue of violence and the crises that surround threat and violent behaviour in the workplace. Peter Senge's *The Fifth Discipline,* published in 1990, introduced a generation of managers to systems theory.[7] In his description of the 'learning organization', Senge explains that in order for any business to function successfully, its leaders must understand that every act has an effect on every other act, and that each organizational function is part of an interconnected system. In a learning organization, people strive to understand why something has gone wrong by looking at the entire interconnected system of events and decisions. In contrast, in a poorly functioning organization, every misfortune or setback is followed by a search for someone or something to blame. The assumption is that a single act or decision is responsible for the disaster. For example, after the *Exxon Valdez* oil spill, one dysfunctional response was to blame the captain of the ship; speculation abounded he was drunk at the time of the accident. The corporation could just as easily have targeted for blame the person or persons who made the decision to use a shipping channel that was too narrow, or the decision to use a single-hulled ship despite safety warnings. In fact, a systems thinking approach would suggest the disaster happened only because *all* these conditions were met. In a systems theory analysis, one would examine the faulty systems for communication, prevention and decision-making that allowed these conditions to prevail.

The classic example of unheeded warning signals is the Space Shuttle

Challenger disaster. After the tragedy, it became known that warnings from several sources about faulty design and the dangers of launching in cold weather were ignored or blocked.[8] Crisis-prone organizations face a 'double jeopardy': first, the lack of systems thinking allows for poor risk management because no one is looking at the whole picture. It is as if all the pieces of the puzzle are lying on the table but no one thinks to assemble them. Mounting evidence of unacceptable risk or explosive conditions can literally be rendered invisible in this way. Secondly, this same lack of co-ordination allows even the clearest, most alarming signals to be silenced, since there is little communication or accountability.

Crisis prepared or crisis prone?

Effective workplace violence prevention is best understood using a model of organizational crisis management. Pauchant and Mitroff use the term 'crisis prone' and 'crisis prepared' to differentiate between companies that have recognized the reality of crisis, and those which, at their peril, have not.[9] At the centre of their model is the importance of early detection of, and response to, warning signals. The ability to detect signals accurately and in time to take action is the difference between *reactive* and *proactive* crisis management, as illustrated in Figure 7.1.

Traditionally, crisis management practice has taken place on the *reactive* side of this model. The crisis occurs: a system malfunctions

Figure 7.1   The phases of crisis management

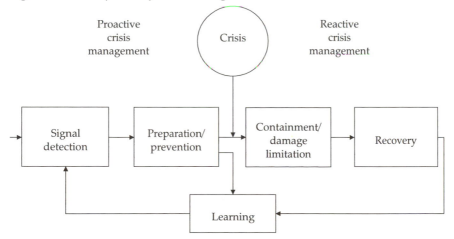

Interactive crisis management

Pauchant and Mitroff, 1992

causing death or injury; an employee 'blows the whistle' on a scandalous or illegal practice; a flawed or dangerous product is suddenly exposed; a disturbed, unhappy employee threatens or commits violence. The organization responds with the first reactive stage: *damage control*. This usually includes public relations activity to protect the image of the company and the punishment of an individual or number of individuals who are blamed for the crisis. The final stage of reactive crisis management is *recovery*. According to Pauchant and Mitroff, recovery in the reactive mode almost always means the covering up or denial of the real meaning of the crisis or disaster: 'It was the fault of one individual. He or she has gone, so we'll be fine from now on.' 'This was a fluke. Things like this don't really happen to us. It won't happen again.' The effect of this reactive mode of behaviour is to block any learning or change that might result from the crisis.

In contrast, some organizations develop the capacity for proactive crisis management by learning from experience. A look at Figure 7.1 shows that when a company moves past damage control and recovery into a willingness to learn from the crisis, it will discover there were warning signs and clear antecedents. These signals may point to problematic individual behaviour, flawed organizational systems, or an interaction between these factors. Becoming crisis prepared means developing the means to detect and respond to these signals. More important, it means the ability to *continue* to learn from subsequent crises so that crisis management capability continues to grow and, eventually, becomes a part of the organization's culture.

Violence as crisis

Every act of violence is the outcome of a series of events. Every situation involving a threat or act of violence is preceded by early signs of trouble. The warning signals for hostility and violence are as varied as the multiple systems and organizational levels that exist in every workplace. The signs may be on an organizational level, such as high levels of grievances, incidents of assaults or threats from clients or customers, or requests for increased security entering or leaving a facility. Alternatively, a warning signal may originate from a single employee who has submitted a claim for stress, complained of harassment or reported domestic abuse. In a crisis-prone organization, these early signs of possible violence or conflict will go undetected. To be sure, there will be actions taken in response, but the form of these actions will be dictated by standard disciplinary, labour relations, security or occupational health practice. Crisis response will occur only when the problem has reached a level where emergency response is required. By that time, it is often too late to prevent the damage to individuals or to the health, safety or general morale of the workplace.

Workplace violence as a policy issue

Surfacing first in the 1980s in the USA, significant concern about workplace violence as a hazard has now also emerged in Europe and Australia. Quite often, the anxiety about this issue relates to stress and insecurity about downsizings and organizational change. Job loss and violence are two events that seem to be inextricably linked in the minds of managers, and there is a wisdom in this connection. One can easily associate losing one's job with one's deepest fears: humiliation, isolation and loss of physical support. Indeed, these experiences can lead to severe breakdown and violence in some people, so it is important to be prepared to handle these events wisely and carefully. Responding simply out of fear, however, leads to hasty solutions based on simplistic analyses: 'If we improve our screening and our security, we will be safe. If we send some of our managers to a training on how to "profile" the violent employee, we will be safe. If we promulgate a policy of zero tolerance, we will be safe.'

This focus on screening and protection is misguided. The issue of workplace violence is not about the violence that is the occasional end result of this stress; it is about the stress itself. As we will see in the analysis that follows, workers under stress can exhibit breakdowns in performance and in behaviour that may lead in some cases to conflict, threat or violence itself. An organization under stress will exhibit breakdowns in communication, poor judgement by leadership and poorly co-ordinated or non-existent response to crisis situations. These organizational failures increase the risk that violence from individuals will occur. The very phrase 'workplace violence', therefore, misleads employers and practitioners to focus on only one single dimension of the problem, rather than on the cause to be found in a climate of stress, alienation, desperation, and isolation. Bowie, in proposing a type 4 'organizational violence' (set out in detail in Chapter 1 of this volume), describes the threat to health and safety when the employer abrogates responsibility for the health and safety of employees during times of organizational stress. To confront this issue effectively, therefore, employers must go beyond the search for protection from legal liability, knowledge of the relevant issues in employment law and issues in clinical prediction or forensics. The issue of workplace violence really asks us to look at what kind of human environments we are creating in our workplaces. It asks us to look at our definitions of disability, deviance and impairment, as well as to examine the systems we have in place to handle these phenomena.

Some crucial issues

In order effectively to confront the violence issue, business and labour leaders must confront a range of issues.

The limits of our present concepts about worker rights and employer responsibility

Dealing with threats of violence from both within and outside the workplace challenges what we know about best practice in handling issues of inter-employee conflict, impaired workers and actual threats and acts of violence. Repeatedly, human resource managers, sometimes in concert with internal security or legal departments, stumble in trying to deal with these complex and frightening situations. Time-honoured principles of employment law, such as workers' rights to privacy and protection from defamation or discrimination, have shaped employment policy and practice. Unfortunately, they have also created a dispute-centered, adversarial context that can be hazardous in its own right. In union as well as non-union environments, increased stresses on employees and organizations has created an urgent need for alternative methods of dispute resolution and conflict management.

The limits of current occupational health and disability policies and procedures

Violent or threatening employees almost always interact with the occupational health system, whether on their own or through the intervention of management. These systems are not equipped to address the suffering or desperation of these employees or to provide useful information or guidance for the concerned employer. Because of the increase in job stress due to structural and economic changes in the workplace, and fundamental changes in healthcare policy and delivery, it is crucial we examine the role of healthcare and disability policy in the handling of workplace violence.

The need for fresh approaches to safety and health

Safety and health in the workplace can no longer remain the province of mid-level managers responding to government regulations and compliance standards. It can no longer serve as a convenient arena for power struggles between labour and management. Furthermore, the hazards have expanded beyond issues of environmental or physical factors. Safety and health now has to do with the greatly increased stress brought on by fundamental changes in the structure of work and shifts in the employment contract. These changes have increased performance pressure, economic insecurity and potential for conflict and competition among workers. They have disrupted crucial structures of trust and communication. The implications for innovations in policy and practice are fundamental.

Industrial relations

Finally, workplace violence episodes bring to the surface crucial issues of industrial relations and have implications for the legal, labour relations, dispute mediation and health professions. The processes designed to handle labour disputes, while appropriate for resolving disputes about pay, job security, work rules or other issues that might be part of a labour agreement, are often not helpful as an approach to issues involving threat, intimidation, or dangerous behaviour. This is because an adversarial process designed to protect rights and ensure due process may often interfere with prompt and effective response to a violence or safety-related emergency. It is important, therefore, for management and union to join together to craft violence prevention policies that may depart in some ways from established labour relations procedures. The added benefits from this approach include more effective use of discipline, reduced grievances, improved morale and reduction of costs associated with labour disputes, stress claims and disability cases. While ensuring that employee rights are protected, joint labour–management approaches based on the need for specific violence and safety-related information ensure rapid and reliable crisis response.

In the current climate of sweeping change, unions face unprecedented challenges. Union members in traditionally 'protected' industries (such as government and utilities) now face repeated and unavoidable down-sizings. Collective bargaining is of limited – if any – use in protecting members' job security in the face of these developments. These challenges are not limited to particular industries. Employers and unions across the globe are recognizing the need for new approaches to new realities. As a current writer observes, '...employers around the world are seeking ways to effectively handle disputes arising over the changes in employment practices required to survive in an increasingly global economy'.[10] Never have unions been more motivated to find ways to work with the employer to defuse conflict and decrease the frequency of threatening and violent incidents.

The problem with our systems: the need for new tools

The standard tools and methods applied by employers and labour organizations to deal with issues of occupational health and safety and discipline are inadequate and inappropriate in responding to the problem of workplace violence. In fact, the methods and approaches commonly in use to handle more commonplace situations or disputes regarding performance or health and behaviour problems actually worsen the problem when applied to cases of violence or threat. Failures in multiple systems, including discipline, occupational health and disability, security and labour relations, are responsible for a wide range of violence phenomena affecting people at work. Indeed, impaired or innocent employees are hurt or victimized because of systems that cause employers to over-react or to respond with well-intentioned but fundamentally flawed actions. Even when employers, recognizing the hazard, take steps to implement systems for violence prevention, these solutions may have limited effectiveness. This is because employers do not consider the sources of stress leading to a climate of violence or hostility in their workplaces, or do not attempt to confront the system deficiencies that allow violence or threats to go undetected.

To understand the many forms of violence in the workplace, therefore, we must look at the individual as well as the system in which his or her behaviour is occurring. Workplace violence in the form of threat or actual violence against people or property is almost always the result of the *interaction* between a violence-prone individual, precipitating events, and a system that provokes the violence or allows it to happen. Once we understand that violence is the result of this interaction, we will be led directly to concrete methods for preventing its occurrence (see Figure 7.2).

The person: when violence is the outcome of stress

Studies of the human stress response indicate that unbearable stress will result in one or more of four outcomes: serious or chronic physical illness, emotional breakdown, suicide or violence. In the assessment of violence potential, we look most closely at the individual's *interpersonal*

Figure 7.2   The sources of violent behaviour

Workplace violence

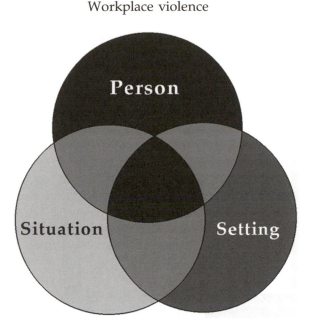

functioning – the way in which they see themselves in relationship to other people: what behaviours and styles do they use in their interactions with others? Do they try to understand the other's point of view or do they use manipulation or intimidation? Are they able to take responsibility for the consequences of their own actions, as opposed to blaming others or 'the system' for what goes wrong in their life? Can they feel shame and guilt, or is their sense of right and wrong determined by what they think they can 'get away with'? Can they control their impulses by anticipating consequences, or do they 'act first and think later'? In addition, we must pay attention to aspects of personal and cultural background that may have shaped attitudes about the uses and acceptability of violence. Has the person resorted to violent behaviour in the past? If so, under what circumstances?[11]

The situation: reaction to helplessness

Establishing that a person has a predisposition for violence does not yet allow a prediction about violence. The recipe for violence includes a situation that pushes the person towards violent or threatening behaviour. In the workplace context, we look for indications of loss, humiliation and a sense of interpersonal isolation. The most familiar examples include loss of employment at mid or late career, loss of job security, injury or illness leading to disruption of body image or limitation of function, and rejection or threat of abandonment at home.

The setting: where systems make the difference

The factors discussed above are not enough to produce the violent event itself. A crucial ingredient is the capacity of workplace-based systems to recognize the warning signs of stress-related breakdown and to initiate action that will interrupt the process. The employer has little control over the first circle: the person hired may possess characteristics that will be impossible to detect at the time of hiring. The employer may or may not have control over the second circle, which may involve a family issue, crime in the community or illness. Even if the situation is workplace generated – for example, a change in working conditions or a layoff – this may be relatively out of the control of the employer. Effective violence prevention depends on the ability of the social or organizational setting to eliminate or moderate the effect of those stressors on the individual. The *potential* for violence will be generated through the interaction of the first and second circles. But it is in the third circle that the employer exercises the most control, and it is here that both his or her responsibility and opportunity lie.

Early notification and effective reduction of acute stressors are the primary components of violence prevention. Figures 7.3(a)(b) illustrate the role of intervention in cases of threats of violence. Figure 7.3(a) shows how the response of a crisis-prone organization can lead to a violent or self-destructive outcome. At the left are listed some of the possible stressors that can lead to a violent or self-destructive outcome. Depending on individual factors, an employee subjected to any of these stresses may display one or more of the conditions or behaviours listed in the next box. These are the *warning signals* available to the employer. In the crisis-prone scenario, the signs of distress in the individual are met by the dysfunctional response of an unprepared organization. The most common among these are avoidance of the disruptive or inappropriate behaviour, punishment through standard disciplinary procedures and a narrow, beaurocratic approach to illness or apparent disability.

When the early signs of trouble are missed or mishandled, the at-risk individual moves through increasing distrust, fear and isolation until reaching the violent or self-destructive result. As this scenario develops, the organization, having missed the opportunity to change this outcome, moves towards a condition in which reactive crisis management will be the only option.

Figure 7.3a   The effect of organizational response on violence potential

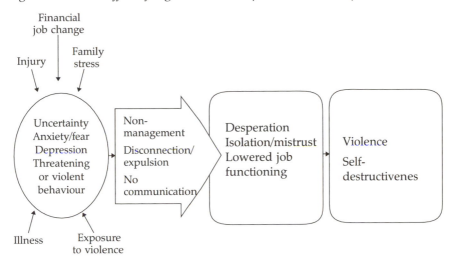

Figure 7.3b The effect of organizational response on violence potential

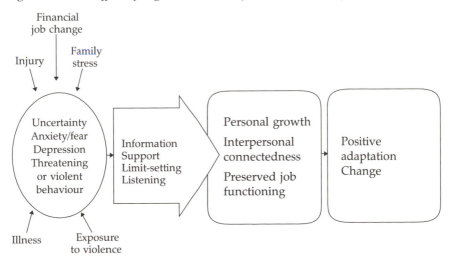

Figure 7.3(b) illustrates the alternative approach. Establishing clear standards of unacceptable behaviour opens up communication with the employee who is suspected of violating them. This allows almost all cases of potential violence to be identified before an actual emergency develops. 'Because of the statements you made, you are in violation of our workplace violence policy,' says the crisis-prepared employer. 'Now tell us what has been going on from your point of view.' For the employee who is at risk for violence or who is perceived as threatening, this kind of communication is vital because it *reduces* feelings of helplessness and isolation. In setting clear limits, the employer has actually cleared the way for effective *listening* to the employee's account of his or her experience. As discussed above, this is precisely what is needed to defuse the violence potential in an individual who is feeling isolated and helpless. In place of increasing isolation and helplessness, there is now a clearly defined set of alternative actions. First, the unacceptable behaviour is identified. Through information-gathering, assessment and analysis, the parties can propose solutions and reach agreement on consequences or necessary changes in the job situation.

Components of workplace violence prevention

The principles outlined above can be carried out through the following components of violence prevention practice.

Support from senior management

Violence prevention can be undertaken successfully only through the visible support and participation of the top level of company (and union) leadership. Most programmes to prevent workplace violence require some modifications in industrial relations, injury management and other occupational health and employee relations practices. This may translate into profound change in the organizational culture over time. In the absence of visible, tangible support from the highest levels, even the most well designed programme will fail to produce the necessary level of change. Leadership's first demonstration of this support is the appointment of a 'taskforce' or a 'team', composed of employees empowered to make decisions. A team like this can only be assembled with the direction and support of someone near the top of the organization. When a single, middle-level person from a function such as training, safety, legal or health is alone shouldered with the task of developing a policy or a training programme, the success of the entire effort is in doubt.

The team

The team is composed of stakeholders representing a range of functions. Depending on how these jobs are positioned in a particular workplace, the group should include health and safety, legal, human resources, labour relations/employee relations, employee assistance, union and operations. Keeping in mind the principle of involvement from the top, a high-ranking executive should be on the team, actively in the beginning, and then perhaps *ex-officio* once the programme is launched.[12] The team begins by designing the audit process (see below) and developing the policy. After the policy has been crafted and roles defined, the team designs and takes part in the training sessions. Once the programme is underway, designated members will receive and process requests for assistance and reports of tension or threat. The team will continue to oversee the programme and monitor its effectiveness.

Workplace violence risk audit

Policy development should be guided by an understanding of the actual constellation of violence-related risks in a particular workplace. Every workplace faces its own unique combination of threat from people outside the workplace or from within. Furthermore, factors such as physical security, organizational structure and culture, and existing policies will all effect the way in which violence-related situations are managed. A company-wide audit provides information about past experience, current exposures and the range of warning signs. An audit should provide the following information:

- *Employee opinions and concerns.* This information can be obtained through a combination of written surveys, interviews and focus groups. Focus groups tend to yield the fullest, most candid picture of employees' concerns and perceptions.

- *Past experience with violence and conflict.* Interviews with key people and a review of records will yield information about the frequency and nature of incidents, as well as the circumstances surrounding these occurrences. These data will guide the development of policy and procedures.

- *Current policies and systems.* It is crucial to analyze the existing systems that relate to violence prevention capability. This will suggest what new policies must be developed and what existing structures and procedures may need to be modified.

Policies and procedures

Once the audit is complete and the team has analyzed the results, the policy can be finalized. The components of a workplace violence policy include: 1) a definition of workplace violence (in concrete detail, set out as a simple list of behaviours and situations); 2) a statement of the 'zero tolerance' standard and the range of specific consequences; 3) reporting procedures; and 4) assurance of safety and non-retaliation for reporters.

It should be clear that the creation of an effective policy depends on the completion of the first three steps discussed above. Without support from the top, there will be no team to represent the important organizational functions and stakeholders. Without an audit, the policy will not reflect the specific violence risks the company is facing or the actual procedures that will work for the organization.

Training

The purpose of training is to ensure the implementation of the policy and the procedures that support it. Its purpose is not, as some assume, to impart the ability to 'predict' or 'spot' dangerousness. For a workplace violence prevention programme to be effective, employees at all organizational levels must be equipped to provide early and reliable notification of possible signals. The most troublesome cases typically begin with a manager failing to bring a situation to the attention of people at the proper levels early enough. Individual managers – at any level – should not be making judgement calls about these issues. Rather, they should be trained to identify criterion situations and behaviours and report them properly so that an appropriate process of fact finding and response can take place.

Easy, non-punitive access to medical and mental health expertise

A common error is to tie dangerousness assessments or threat investigations to disciplinary, occupational health or other administrative procedures developed for more routine circumstances. Standard procedures for assessing job-linked health conditions are not appropriate for handling threats or possible dangerousness. Indeed, the use of standard methods for assessing health issues or suitability for work can be dangerous and destructive to the process itself. A threat of violence assessment has different goals from these standard occupational health activities. Whereas the purpose of a standard 'Fitness for duty' assessment is to determine if someone is fit to do his or her job, the goal in the case of a possible threat of violence is to determine if someone is dangerous, and, if not, to identify the nature of the problem so that corrective steps can be taken.

The way the assessment is handled is perhaps the linchpin of the entire process of responding to a threat of violence. Failing to prepare for this step can bring disastrous consequences. If the employer has selected the proper professionals and has worked out procedures carefully, he or she will be able to proceed assured of two critical elements: 1) the employee will feel comfortable and open about entering into the assessment process, and 2) there will be *immediate and legal* access to critical information about dangerousness.

Terminations and layoffs: using common sense and planning

The return of the fired employee to exact murderous revenge has become the symbol of the overall fear of workplace violence, despite what statistics may tell us about the actual probability that this will occur in one's own work setting. This fear accurately represents the rage and insecurity that pervade a workplace in the throes of change or a community struggling with economic contraction. Job loss, even for the most vulnerable of individuals, however, need not spell danger. *No one ever took revenge simply for being fired.* Employees who become threatening always talk about *the way they were made to feel* in the process of losing their jobs.[13]

One factor in particular increases the risk of violence or threat connected with a termination: the length of time that elapses between the actions that led to the termination and the termination itself.[14] This period is often *years,* and it is a major risk factor. This is because a delay between the time the behaviour is first noticed and the employer finally acts causes a worsening of the problem. In the typical case in which a termination is contemplated because an employee has reportedly threatened others or is perceived as dangerous, the intimidating, harassing or even threatening behaviour has been going on for months and often years. However, there is usually little, if any, documentation of administrative actions taken in response to this long-standing pattern. This is because most threatening behaviour is used to control and intimidate others, and it usually works. In the absence of company policies regarding violence and threats, this sort of behaviour is often ignored: the offender is given 'wide berth'. When the situation has become intolerable, management is in a weak position because the behaviour has been tolerated for so long. Giving the person 'another chance', without taking action or exploring the causes for the behaviour, or ignoring the behaviour out of fear, is clearly unwise. Doing so out of compassion is similarly misguided. If a union is present, and union and management collude by passively allowing adversarial, rule-bound procedures to drive the process, they are jointly abdicating their responsibility to preserve the safety of the workplace and, not least of all, the safety of the employee him or herself.[15]

Conclusion: beyond profiling

Preventing violence requires much more than simply publishing a policy, groping for a 'profile', or responding to emergencies. It is about self-awareness and learning. If your organization has not experienced change or growth as a result of an act of violence, a frightening threat or a 'close call', then you have reinforced your reactive crisis orientation. Where there has been no self-examination, you have fostered powerful, dangerous illusions: 'This was an isolated event.' 'He was a bad apple, but he is gone now.' And the conditions which led to the crisis will persist.

The way a corporation, a federal or private agency, a small business or a town deals with the reality of violence and threats has implications for its very survival. When a threat or act of violence occurs, it is a signal thrown up from the myriad of crises that confront the workplace continually: the stress of families living on increasingly thin ice; the unrelenting pressure of wrenching organizational change and competition on a global scale; a crisis in healthcare that threatens the availability of mental health care for a growing sector of the population; people at risk every day from the societal and political violence that continues to plague our species. If the threat of violence within their walls and intruding into its boundaries moves managers and union leaders to attend to these fundamental issues, then this very real crisis will have provided an opportunity of considerable value.

Notes

1. Shrivastava, P. (1993) Crisis theory/practice: towards a sustainable future. *Industrial and Environmental Crisis Quarterly* 7(1), 23–42.
2. Pauchant, T.C. and Mitroff, I.I. (1992) *Transforming the Crisis-Prone Organization: Preventing Individual, Organizational, and Environmental Tragedies.* San Francisco, CA: Jossey-Bass.
3. Ibid., 126 (emphasis added).
4. Ibid.

5. Braverman, M. (1992) Posttrauma crisis intervention in the workplace. In Quick, J.C. *et al.* (eds.) *Stress and Well Being in the Workplace*. Washington, DC: American Psychological Association.
6. Barab, J. (1996) When arbitration is not the answer: the union perspective. In Narita, J. (ed.) *Proceedings of the Forty-Ninth Annual Meeting of the National Academy of Arbitrators*. Washington, DC: Bureau of National Affairs.
7. Senge, P.M. (1990) *The Fifth Discipline*. New York: Doubleday.
8. Pauchant and Mitroff op. cit.
9. Pauchant and Mitroff (ibid.) offer a comprehensive and excellent discussion of the forms of institutional denial and self-delusion in the face of crisis.
10. Gleason, S.E. (ed.) (1997) *Workplace Dispute Resolution: Directions for the 21st Century*. East Lansing, MI: Michigan State University Press, 6.
11. The thinking of acknowledged authorities on violence prediction goes against the conventional wisdom that 'a history of violent behaviour is the best and only reliable predictor of violence'. Monahan (in Monahan, J. (1981) *The Clinical Prediction of Violent Behavior*. Washington, DC: US Department of Health and Human Services, National Institutes of Health) looks at how the sociocultural background of the individual might render violence acceptable, and under what circumstances. Monahan emphasizes the importance of the context of the threat situation, the availability of weapons, vulnerability of the victim and the social approval of violence. Robert Fein (in Fein, R.A., Vossekuil, B. and Holden, G.A. (1995) *Threat Assessment: An Approach to Prevent Targeted Violence*. Washington, DC: US Department of Justice, National Institute of Justice) reinforces this contextual perspective in his work. His recent research on threats on public figures further casts doubt on the 'violent history' hypothesis.
12. The importance of stakeholder input in the design phase has also been recognized by workers in the field of alternative dispute resolution. One writer points out the importance of CEO involvement in the successful design and implementation of alternative dispute resolution systems. See Rowe, M. (1997) Dispute resolution in the non-union environment. In Gleason, S.E. (ed.) *Workplace Dispute Resolution*. East Lansing, MI: Michigan State University Press.
13. Work applying philosophical and social psychological constructs sheds more light on this observation. See Skarlicki, D.P., Ellard, J.H. and Kellin, B.R.C. (1998) Third-party perceptions of a layoff: procedural, derogation, and retributive aspects of justice. *Journal of Applied Psychology* 83, 119–27.
14. Gavin de Becker (*The Gift of Fear*. Boston, MA: Little, Brown & Co., 1997) offers an excellent discussion of the dangers of protracted or delayed terminations and a list of practical suggestions.
15. The issue of labour relations and workplace violence is discussed in more detail by the author in Braverman, M. (1999) *Preventing Workplace Violence: A Guide for Employers and Practitioners*. Thousand Oaks, CA: Sage.

Chapter 8

Standards for violence management training

Brodie Paterson and David Leadbetter

Introduction

Violence at work in many respects continues to represent a largely unexplored area with a knowledge base which is often incomplete, imprecise or contradictory.[1] Work-related violence can result in serious physical injury or death, and working in an atmosphere of continuing threat may be profoundly damaging to the confidence, morale and ultimately psychological health of staff exposed or affected.[2] Continuing lack of recognition of the problem, inconsistencies in definition and endemic under-reporting in some settings have combined to hinder attempts to understand and thus to prevent, reduce or minimize the harm resulting from violence in the workplace.[3] The reality of practice for many workers in this new millennium can involve being sworn at, spat upon, insulted on racial grounds or being physically attacked in the course of their work.

Homicide is overwhelmingly the most dramatic aspect of workplace violence and the loss of life at work is properly the source of concern.[4] In some nations, for some occupations, homicide may be the most frequent cause of work-related injury death. The need for action to reduce the risk of such incidents cannot therefore be overemphasized.[5] Fortunately it appears that the overwhelming majority of workplace violence experienced is not fatal. However, while 'non-fatal' violence may attract less media interest than high-profile workplace homicides,[6] it also represents a serious potential risk to the welfare of employees and it may be under-reported, particularly in such settings as health and social care where the incidence of verbal abuse, threatening behaviour and assault can be high.[7]

Many employers in these sectors are now, however, increasingly recognizing the issue of violence in the workplace. Faced with the demand to do something quickly, it appears that many managers have interpreted the problem as an issue for training, but this viewpoint is simplistic.[8] The management of aggressive and violent behaviour must be seen within a context in which both the individual and the organization working in partnership have an active role in taking steps to reduce the likelihood of violence and in forming and maintaining social norms against violence.[9] Viewing the management of violence primarily as the responsibility of the individual practitioner and as an issue of individual competency to be addressed via training is, therefore, inappropriate. The practice of teams and individuals forms only one part of the co-ordinated effort that is a necessary pre requisite of effective action at the organizational level. The underlying idea is of a total organizational response.[10] encompassing issues such as building design, service culture and values,[11] operational policies, procedures and working practices,[12] core staff skills and training – all complementing the actions of individual practitioners. This perspective argues that organizations have a responsibility to be proactive in identifying and reducing the risks staff are exposed to from aggression and violence.[13]

This process of risk assessment and the active steps to reduce incidence by changing the environment of care and working practices must be seen as an essential element in any strategic approach.[14] This can be illustrated with reference to an example of this 'ecological perspective' in action. In a UK hospital Accident and Emergency department, violent incidents were often reported to be associated with patients who were under the influence of alcohol. The perception of nursing staff, however, was that while alcohol was undoubtedly a significant contributory factor, another problem was the time patients spent waiting before being seen by a doctor, which, at times of peak demand, could be several hours. The organization concerned could not realistically refuse to see patients under the influence of alcohol, many of whom were also in need of acute care, but it decided it could do something about waiting times. It therefore decided to reorganize and streamline admission procedures to decrease waiting times and, as part of this strategy, it increased the autonomy of nursing staff to deal on their own with less serious injuries – obviating the need for all patients to be screened by a doctor. The consequent reduction in waiting times appeared to contribute to an overall reduction in recorded violent incidents. Failure to adequately appreciate the role of the organization[15] may thus lead workers and trainers to be blamed for what is perceived by administrators as ineffective learning or a failure to apply taught aggression management skills when in fact the organizational structures and processes continue to contribute to the violence workers are exposed to.[16]

Training in aggression and violence management skills should therefore form only one component of a multi-modal violence reduction strategy that needs to be owned by the organization at the highest level. This must be adequately funded with a dedicated budget and a training plan which is subject to periodic monitoring and annual review. There is a substantial role for training, but standardized training packages must be considered with caution. Leadbetter and Paterson[17] suggest that training must be individually tailored to each particular workplace. Training needs will always vary widely, depending on the role and situation of the staff involved. Training should always be based on a training need analysis that identifies and closely matches the provision of training to identified need. It must incorporate research findings, be designed around identified competencies and be carefully evaluated and monitored. The constant review and development of approaches on the basis of the evaluation of operational experience are the vital factors.[18]

Training content

There is some agreement on the potential core constituents of training, including the necessity to address the following:

- *Core values* Training should promote the core values of the service (e.g. least restrictive environment, anti-oppressive practice).

- *Risk assessment* Attempting to identify who is at what form of risk from what.

- *Definitions of aggression and violence* Necessary for reporting purposes for staff to understand how their organization defines violence and thus what they should report.

- *Safe systems of work* Office design and layout, the use of alarms, developing and testing security procedures, incident-reporting procedures, etc.

- *Information in relation to particular user groups* People who are elderly, people experiencing mental illness, learning disabilities, acquired brain injury, etc. in order that staff can focus on primary prevention rather than reactive strategies.

- *Theoretical models of aggression and violence* Such that staff have an informed understanding of why aggression may occur both in their clients and in themselves.

- *Setting conditions and triggers* Prediction of aggression and violence (such that staff can anticipate and thus defuse potential situations before they occur).

- *De-escalation, theoretical models and practice strategies* Core skills in responding to potentially aggressive situations.

- *Legal and ethical issues* Relevant to particular practice area such that staff are aware of their rights and responsibilities.

- *Physical contact skills* So that staff (where physical violence is anticipated) can block an attack and escape by breaking away and/or initiating restraint procedures. Depending on identified need, 'weapons awareness' may also need to be addressed.

- *Immediate management of hostage situations* Hostage situations do occur in health and social care settings and staff may be involved either as a hostage or during 'first-on-scene' negotiations.

- *How to support staff who may be exposed to violence both pre- and post-incident* Staff exposed to aggression and violence may need both practical support and specialist psychological intervention.

Training needs to focus on the discreet needs of at least three major staff groups:[19]

1. *Management* Managers requirements tend to differ from direct service workers, and the more senior they are, the less likely they may be to experience violence. Their primary needs, therefore, are to understand their legal obligations for worker safety and to develop an awareness of effective organizational approaches to the management of violence. This however does not mean they may not require basic personal safety training.

2. *Support and administration staff* Support and administrative staff roles may vary in terms of the degree of contact these staff have with clients. They may have no contact, limited direct client contact (e.g. by telephone) or substantial contact (e.g. a cleaner in a psychiatric hospital ward). Their need for training will therefore vary (see Table 8.1).

Table 8.1 *Organizational training matrix.*[20]

	Responsibility of organization for worker safety	Effective organizational approaches to managing violence	Basic personal safety training	Dealing with verbally abusive clients	Verbal de-escalation	Blocking and escape techniques	Restraint	Teaching and presentation skills	Duration (hours)
Senior and middle management	✓	✓	✓	✗	✗	✗	✗	✗	7–15
Office staff (non-patient contact)	✗	✗	✓	✗	✗	✗	✗	✗	3.5–7
Receptionist	✗	✗	✓	✓	✗	✗/✓	✗	✗	7
Emergency room nurse	✗	✗	✓	✓	✓	✓	✗/✓	✗	14–21
Psychiatric	✗	✗	✓	✓	✓	✓	✓	✗	21–35
Acute in-patient unit trainers	✓	✓	✓	✓	✓	✓	✓	✓	35–70

3. *Direct service staff* Direct service staff are likely to have substantial direct client contact and may thus require skills in dealing with a continuum of aggressive incidents ranging from verbal aggression to attempted assault. These skills (where appropriate) must complement existing skills in working therapeutically with the client group concerned.

Each of these groups has different but inter-related and overlapping training needs. However, failure to address the need for aggression management training for any of these groups could seriously limit the effectiveness of aggression management across the organization.[21] Within each workplace training needs will vary in accordance with individual roles but the example of a typical training matrix developed for a UK national health service trust is shown in Table 8.1 could be used as a guideline. The suggested content guidelines should be read in conjunction with the content guidance in the text. The guidance on duration represents the minimum acceptable time considered necessary by a majority of experienced aggression trainers internationally. Any reduction in training duration beyond these suggested minimums will inevitably compromise the quality of the training programme.

Train-the-trainer-workshop programmes

Of particular concern (and an important area in which minimum standards need to be set) are train-the-trainers programmes in aggression management.[22] Much training in this area operates on the 'cascade principle', where an individual (once trained as a trainer) goes on to train other workers. This approach can operate successfully but must involve continuing objective and independent competency-based evaluation of both trainer and student performance. The preparation of trainers should comprise an absolute minimum of 35 hours of face-to-face contact. Ideally, an instructor programme would follow some time after attendance at an initial introductory programme so that the potential trainer could consolidate and apply his or her own skills in practice before adopting a training role.

Content

The content of a 'train-the-trainers' programme should include the following:[23]

1. A basic introduction to the course and revision of previous training.
2. Explanations of how and why people learn.
3. The characteristics of a good trainer and communicator.
4. Methods of instruction and the use of educational media.
5. Lesson planning and delivery.
6. The teaching of physical intervention skills.
7. Presentation skills.
8. Dealing with difficult situations in training.
9. Theoretical models of violence and contemporary research into violent behaviour.
10. Presenting a workshop on coping with violence.
11. Methods of evaluating and modifying teaching and learning.

Does training work?

This is a more complex question than it first appears and depends how one defines 'works'. There are relatively few published studies describing or evaluating programmes intended to equip human services workers with the necessary skills to practise in this area. A variety of measures have been used in these studies both pre- and post-training, including attitudinal scales, total numbers of violent incidents, numbers of injuries to staff and/or clients, staff stress levels, role conflict and measures of acquisition of new skills.[24] In general, staff participating in such courses appear to evaluate them positively,[25] and there is some evidence that certain programmes appear to contribute to a reduction in recorded incidents of violence,[26] levels of stress[27] and burnout amongst staff.[28, 29]

However, the quality of the research methodology and/or analysis in many of the contributions is weak. Many studies give relatively limited or inadequate details of the content[30] or duration of training[31] and, in practice, there appears to be wide variation in programme content and duration, both nationally[32] and internationally.[33] This makes it frankly foolhardy to offer generalizations about the effectiveness or otherwise of training. As Bowie[34] observes: 'An increase in people's confidence in their ability to handle violent situations...does not demonstrate any actual long term increase in their violence management skills.' The increased emphasis on developing evidence-based practice has led to a number of reviews of the available research literature on training in the management of violence and particularly about restraint.[35] A review by the Royal College of Psychiatrists[36] based on the Cochrane protocols concluded that 'There was weak quantitative evidence that training and experience in coping with aggression reduced injuries to staff. It is not clear whether incidents of violence are reduced.' A meta analysis conducted by David Allen[37] on behalf of the British Institute of Learning Disabilities concluded that:

> The existing research literature suggests that training carers in behaviour management skills can produce a variety of positive direct and indirect benefits. Staff that receive training appear to be more knowledgeable about appropriate behaviour management practices. They are also likely to feel more confident (although this effect may be less significant for female staff), and can be effectively taught physical intervention skills. In the workplace staff training can decrease rates of *challenging* behaviour and the use of reactive strategies. Injuries to both carers and service users may also be reduced. Unfortunately, the research indicates that none of the above outcomes can be guaranteed from training, and negative results have also been observed in each of the above areas.

The observation that some programmes appear ineffective and may even be dangerous[38] (carrying an excess risk of injury to participants[39] during training or resulting in an increased rather than decreased risk of injury to staff post-training) is a serious concern.[40]

As noted in the UK, a frequently observed effect of the aforementioned increased recognition of the issue of occupational violence, and the tendency to frame the problem as a training issue, has been the widespread adoption by many agencies of 'packaged' training programmes. In some instances, regrettably, these appear to have been purchased because of availability and/or on the basis of assurances from training or academic organizations that are often unsupported by valid evaluative studies. Some of these packages contain physical intervention techniques that generate substantial concerns on the grounds of ethics, safety and effectiveness.

Industry standards for aggression management training

There is thus a strong case for establishing industry standards that can ultimately be subject to rigorous evaluation. The purpose of standards is to provide a set of objective guidelines that may be used by training managers and their organizations to compare the length, the content and the potential impact of their aggression and violence management training with a set of standards developed by a network of experienced providers and consumers for such training.[41] Such standards would enable organizations to:

- assess their level of need for such training;

- compare available internal and external training programmes; and

- make an informed selection of such programmes based on the same level of background information that similar decisions currently require.

In the UK, central government has appeared reluctant to issue definitive guidance on acceptable forms of restraint for any service sector. The revelation of poor practice in learning disability services by the BBC has acted as a spur for a range of policy and standards initiatives.[42] The Department for Education and Employment[43] and the Department of Health have issued draft guidance, which includes criteria for acceptable physical restraint.[44] These reflect existing advice[45] and conclusions from the limited available research on fatalities and injuries during restraint. Collectively, these initiatives highlight the potential dangers of a range of commonly used approaches, including prone restraints, basket holds, locks across joints, going to the ground and mechanical restraints. The necessity for investigative journalists rather than government agencies to play the lead role in the analysis of dangerous practice in both the UK and USA is, however, significant.[46]

The British Institute of Learning Disability has taken a lead role in the UK in the development of standards. Building on its work on policy development[47] with Department of Health funding, it has developed a *Code of Practice on Physical Intervention Training*[48] and is developing a scheme of academic accreditation in conjunction with the Open College network. Its code of practice addresses eight key areas effective training should address:

1. policies
2. best interest criteria
3. techniques for physical intervention
4. health and safety during training
5. course organization
6. monitoring performance
7. evaluation and record-keeping
8. professional conduct.

It is to be hoped these initiatives will, in due course, raise standards, drive unscrupulous trainers from the marketplace and promote a much needed evidence-based debate on acceptable practice and standards. The effectiveness of training must be judged in terms of whether it is effective in preventing incidents and minimizing the impact of violence that cannot be prevented, as well as providing a reasonable cost-effective protection against foreseen risks. The content of training for any staff group must be designed to ensure they are adequately equipped with the appropriate values, knowledge and skills base to practise within their clinical area. The role of staff and thus their requirements for training will vary significantly. Where the remit of any staff member involves the clinical treatment of individuals with a problem of aggression and violence, it is absolutely vital he or she is adequately prepared to undertake therapeutic work with the individual concerned to reduce the likelihood of aggression and violence, as well as in the interim to safely manage the presenting behaviour.[49]

A number of key questions need to be asked when assessing the suitability of training in areas of physical intervention, and such questions are also broadly applicable to aggression management training generally.[50]

What is the values base of training?

Training involves more than the acquisition of skills and knowledge; it involves either explicitly or implicitly the transmission of a culture and and a values base. Training programmes should, therefore, have an overt focus on values and the legal and ethical principles that will apply to their practice setting.

Does the training adopt a hierarchical approach based on the principle of least restrictive intervention?

The concept of least restrictive intervention requires that any intervention should represent the minimum restriction of liberty possible applied for the minimum period of time.[51] Where there is a physical skills element to any programme, it must be part of a range of graduated interventions that start with non-physical procedures. The level of intervention must be adjusted in proportion to the risk involved in individual situations.[52] This will involve the teaching of such procedures as distraction and de-escalation techniques before physical intervention procedures.[53] Physical intervention procedures themselves should reflect a hierarchy and may contain blocking and breakaway procedures as well as combinations of one-person, two-person and three-person procedures for standing, seated and prone restraint situations. Such training must be regularly updated and reinforced. The inoculation view of training (which assumes that attendance on a violence management training course inevitably confers instant and permanent competence) has been discredited, and periodic updating is necessary. In addition, supervision in practice is of the utmost importance to ensure that overly restrictive procedures are not used inappropriately or excessively by staff.[54]

Physical contact skills (where applicable) cannot and should not be taught in isolation but only as a part of an integrated curriculum ensuring that staff have a values base and competencies that actively limit such physical contact to the last resort in a violent situation.[55] The overarching principle is always that no alternative to the use of force/restriction of liberty exists.[56]

Is equipment going to be used?

Training programmes that have a physical skills component may advocate or demonstrate the use of equipment to restrict the client's movements 'mechanically' by some form of device that may involve specialist chairs, wrist and/or hand cuffs, restraint vests and body wraps.[57] A wide range of such devices is available, but there have been concerns about their misuse and the potential risks involved. Appropriate specialist training in the use of any equipment should therefore be sought and its use in practice subject to careful recording and monitoring.[58]

Will the standards work in our environment?

The physical environment
Training may presume certain conditions apply; these might involve access to alarms, the availability of quiet areas for interview or the ability to exclude other clients temporarily. Where there is a physical component in the training, its effectiveness might be influenced by aspects of the physical environment, including furnishings or even the width of corridors, doorways or staircases. If such presumptions are inaccurate, skills transfer from the training environment to the workplace will be adversely affected and the trainers should, therefore, always be invited to visit and review the environment where it is anticipated the skills are going to be used.

Staffing profile
The relevant height, weight, fitness and strength of those attempting to

restrain in comparison to the person being restrained will obviously affect the likelihood of success. In most care settings in the UK, women form the overwhelming majority of the workforce and may be involved in attempts to restrain men or large adolescent males. Physical intervention procedures should therefore emphasize technique, as a strength or weight advantage cannot be guaranteed in any context.

Staffing ratio
Techniques may presume access to three or four members of staff when common working practices may involve lone workers. The techniques should be practicable in the working environment in which they are going to be applied.

Moving someone
In certain contexts there may be an urgent need for someone to be moved under restraint. There should, therefore, be procedures that allow a reasonable prospect of safely moving an individual under restraint.

Are the techniques relevant?

Any programme must be as relevant as possible to the work situation in which it will be applied. This means the nature of violence in the individual workplace concerned should be understood such that the content of the training closely matches staff needs. An example from my own experience as a trainer dealing with the issue of physical violence will be used to illustrate this point. For a number of years we had taught student nurses how to escape from a situation where an aggressive client had grabbed their hair. We had always taught this particular procedure with both parties standing. An audit of the experience of a group of students whom we had trained revealed they were indeed (albeit rarely) having their hair pulled, but it transpired this did not occur when they were standing but more usually when they were kneeling to provide immediate care for someone (e.g. on the toilet or leaning over a bed). The standing procedure could not be readily applied when the student nurse was bending over or kneeling and thus had to be modified.

The audit also revealed that we needed to increase the content of our curriculum on communicating with patients experiencing dementia as a significant number of incidents involved patients experiencing this condition. Techniques taught should, therefore, be based on an audit and examination of violence, and only these procedures either of proven relevance to the workplace or that could reasonably be anticipated should be taught. Extraneous or irrelevant procedures should be ruthlessly culled and the time saved used instead for 'over learning'. The frequent repetition of as small a number of techniques as possible is necessary both for acquisition and retention of the procedures taught. All techniques taught should be as simple to use as possible, involving gross rather than fine motor movements to promote retention and recall, particularly under conditions of stress.

What risks are involved?

No physical procedure is free from risk but the potential risks should have been subject to prospective assessment (i.e. an examination in a simulated situation by a neutral expert before been used in the workplace).[59] A written evaluation of every technique and the situation in which it was assessed should be available for inspection. Further, the safety of every procedure with regard to the welfare of the users and of the approach of the staff and the clients should be monitored and the content of training and practice reviewed at least annually. Good practice would suggest videotaping every procedure so as to produce a permanent record and to allow an external review by a panel of neutral experts drawn from physical therapy, medicine and occupational health. Any safety review must however, consider the implications when a technique is used in accordance with the guidance, as well as the potential misapplications – whether accidental or deliberate – that could result in heightened risk.

Is the training effective?

The effectiveness of the training will be affected by a range of variables in any given situation. These include the issues already discussed in this chapter, such as the dynamics of workplace violence in a particular situation, the culture of the workplace and the degree to which supervision promotes the application of new skills. If there is a physical element to the training, factors that will obviously influence effectiveness include the physical environment and the height, weight and strength of the parties concerned. However, the effectiveness of all procedures should be routinely evaluated as a guide to their usefulness: 'Any approach must offer a realistic chance of success, that is, it must actually work in the real world with a highly resistant and aggressive client as well as in controlled simulations.'[60]

Are the techniques ethical?

There are those who would argue that physical restraint is usually avoidable and, thus, almost inevitably unethical. However, in the absence of effective alternatives to protect staff and services users, its continued use in highly controlled circumstances seems inevitable. In such circumstances it seems, therefore, desirable that staff are trained in how to attempt restraint in a way that minimizes risk to all parties rather than allow them to rely on experience or guesswork as a guide to how to restrain safely. Further, failure to train in physical intervention (where such an event is a foreseeable part of the worker's role) may represent a failure by the employer to discharge their duty of care towards their workforce, with consequent legal ramifications.

Where practicable, formal consideration of the risk to all parties is desirable before action. When restraint is used in care settings, it should always represent the maximal intervention within a graduated hierarchical response. However, if physical intervention is being considered, the process of risk assessment should identify, record and evaluate alternatives to restraint and the physical and psychological consequences of each response.[61] These interventions should be discussed with the client, carers and relatives so that, where practicable, restraint is based on a consensus of opinion that has involved rigorous scrutiny and, ideally, the testing of alternative interventions. If restraint is ultimately seen as necessary, consideration should be given to maximizing the physical safety and psychological welfare of all parties concerned and to minimizing the duration of restraint. The use of 'pain compliance' in the restraint should be avoided completely in the case of certain populations including young children and people with severe learning disabilities (mental retardation) or dementia.[62]

The 'culture of quick fixes'

Training programmes of short duration cannot in themselves provide a solution to the complex and multifaceted problem of difficult and violent behaviour in health or social care. It is unrealistic to expect them so to do. The effectiveness of training in this area must be evaluated, not only in terms of whether it is effective in preventing incidents, but also in terms of the extent to which it promotes positive change in the service users' behaviour. Reducing the probability of violent incidents resulting in injury to service users and staff is clearly a legitimate aim. However, a common failing of many 'systems' based approaches is that they focus excessively on the management of 'critical incidents' and do not adequately address the complexities of longer-term intervention. There are genuine concerns that training in crisis management where physical restraint is emphasized over the primary prevention of violence may actually increase incidents when greater attention to the underlying causes of individual violence (including, perhaps, deficits in the staff knowledge and skills base, in service design, and in culture and care planning) might have averted violence.

Enhancing the ability of staff to deal with critical incidents is obviously desirable, but such training may do little to change the underlying culture or values base of services. The overall pattern of preparation for any staff group must be designed to ensure they are adequately equipped with the appropriate values, knowledge and skills base to practise within their area. Where such practice requires they engage in therapeutic work with individuals with a problem of aggression and violence, it is essential they have the appropriate knowledge, value and skills base and are continually focused on the need for interventions that will reduce the likelihood of aggression and violence and promote positive change. This, however, requires action by the organization in terms of policy development and implementation complemented by a substantial investment in the development and retention of highly skilled staff. These staff must have regular access to expert support and supervision such that they can develop and implement 'evidence-based' practice. Training programmes of relatively short duration are highly unlikely to be able to promote the necessary level of expertise.

Conclusion

As Bowie[63] notes, aggression and violence management training is still more of an art than a science, but the industry continues to grow and a plethora of training programmes has sprung up in Australia, the UK, the USA and elsewhere.[64] This review of training has concentrated on one of the most contentious areas of training practice: that of the physical management of violent behaviour where there is probably least agreement. There are obvious dangers arising from unregulated practice in this area, with continuing controversy about the safety of particular procedures and suggestions that some approaches may increase rather than decrease the risk of injury or even death. Training can form part of the solution to the complex problem of workplace violence but, on the basis of the available research, success cannot be assumed.[65]

Purchasers of training should investigate potential providers extremely carefully before selecting, preferably looking at several providers and talking to similar organizations about their experiences.[66] As noted in this chapter, a number of initiatives are, however, ongoing in this area in the UK, the USA and elsewhere that seek to promote agreement on standards and to regulate for good practice in an area that has, effectively, been unregulated to date.[67] Questions remain, however, about the effectiveness of aggression and violence management training. This should serve as a continuing spur to further research into determining what works best and where.

Notes

1. Chappell, D. and Di Martino, V. (1998) *Violence at Work*. Geneva: International Labour Office.
2. Barling, J. (1996) The prediction, experience and consequences of workplace violence. In VandenBos, G.R. and Bulatao, E.Q. (eds.) *Violence in the Workplace*. Washington, DC: American Psychological Association.
3. Mershaw, L.J. and Messite, J.M. (1996) Workplace violence: preventive and interventive strategies. *Journal of Emergency Medicine* 38(10), 993–1006.
4. Bulatao, E.Q. and VandenBos, G.R. (1996) Workplace violence: its scope and the issues. In VandenBos, G.R. and Bulatao, E.Q. (eds.) *Violence in the Workplace*. Washington, DC: American Psychological Association.
5. National Institute for Occupational Health and Safety (1993) *NIOHS Alert: Request for Assistance in Preventing Homicide in the Workplace*. Washington, DC: US Department of Health and Human Services.
6. Lanza, M. (1996) Violence against nurses in hospitals. In VandenBos, G.R. and Bulatao, E.Q (eds.) *Violence in the Workplace*. Washington, DC: American Psychological Association.
7. Leadbetter, D. and Paterson, B. (1995) De-escalating aggressive behaviour. In Stark, C. and Kidd, B. (eds.) *Management of Aggression and Violence in Health Care*. London: Gaskell and The Royal College of Psychiatrists.
8. Cox, T. and Cox, S. (1993) *Psychosocial and Organisational Hazards: Control and Monitoring. Occupational Health Series* 5. Copenhagen: World Health Organization.
9. Fein, A.F., Garreri, E. and Hansen, P. (1981) Teaching staff to cope with patient violence. *Journal of Continuing Education in Nursing* 12(2), 21–26.
10. Rice, M.E., Harris, G.T., Varney, G.W. and Quinsay, V.L. (1989) *Violence in Institutions: Understanding, Prevention and Control*. Toronto: Hoefgre & Huber.
11. Ibid.
12. Cox and Cox op. cit.
13. Greaves, A. (1994) Organisational approaches to the prevention and management of violence. In Wykes, T. (ed.) *Violence and Health Care Professionals*. London: Chapman & Hall.
14. Royal College of Nursing and the NHS Executive (1998) *Safer Working in the Community: A Guide for NHS Managers on Reducing the Risks from Violence and Aggression*. London: Royal College of Nursing.

15. Paterson, B. and Leadbetter, D. (1999) Managing physical violence. In Turnbull, J. and Paterson, B. (eds.) *Aggression and Violence: Approaches to Effective Management*. Basingstoke: Macmillan.

16. Leadbetter and Paterson op. cit.

17. Ibid.

18. Bowie, V. (1996) *Coping with Violence: A Guide for the Human Services*. London: Whiting & Birch.

19. Ibid.

20. Adapted from Stark, C. and Kidd, B. (eds.) (1995) *Management of Aggression and Violence in Health Care*. London: Gaskell and The Royal College of Psychiatrists, 3.

21. Bowie (1996) op. cit.

22. Bowie, V. (1998) Managing violence at work: an international perspective on proposed standards for aggression management training. Keynote address, 'Good Practice in Managing Violence at Work' conference, Stirling, October.

23. Ibid.

24. Sailas, E. and Fenton, M. (1999) Seclusion and restraint as a method of treatment for people with serious mental illnesses (Cochrane Review). In *The Cochrane Library. Issue 3*. Oxford: Update Software (Cochrane Library no.: CD001163).

25. Ibid.

26. Wright, S. (1999) Physical restraint in the management of violence and aggression in in-patient settings: a review of the issues. *Journal of Mental Health* 8(5), 459–72.

27. Infantino, J. and Musingo, S.Y. (1985) Assaults and injuries among staff with and without training in aggression control techniques. *Journal of Hospital and Community Psychiatry* 36(12), 1312–14.

28. Fein *et al.* op. cit.

29. Rosenthal, T.L., Edwards, N.B., Rosenthal, R.H. and Ackerman, B.J. (1992) Hospital violence: site, severity and nurses' preventative training. *Issues in Mental Health Nursing* 13(4), 349–56.

30. Wong, E.W. (1992) Violence prevention and the literature. *Journal of Hospital and Community Psychiatry* 44(11), 1158–200.

31. Bowers, L., Whittington, R., Almvik, R., Bergman, B., Oud, N. and Savio, M. (1999) A European perspective on psychiatric nursing and violent incidents: management, education and service organisation. *International Journal of Nursing Studies* 36(3), 217–22.

32. Phillips, D. and Rudestam, K.E. (1995) Effect of non-violent self-defense training on male psychiatric staff members' aggression and fear. *Psychiatric Services* 46(2), 164–68.

33. Robinson, S. and Barnes, J. (1986) Continuing education in relation to the prevention and management of violence. In Wilson-Barnett, J. and Robinson, S. (eds.) *Directions in Nursing Research*. London: Scutari Press.

34. Bowie, A Risky Management Approach: A Presentation for Safety Week 2000, at Sutherland Hospital NSW Australia, by Vaughan Bowie, University of Western Sydney (9).

35. Sailas and Fenton op. cit.

36. Royal College of Psychiatrists (1998) *Managing Imminent Violence*. London:

Gaskell, 22.

37. Allan, D. (2000) *Training Carers in Physical Interventions: Towards Evidence-Based Practice*. Kidderminster: British Institute of Learning Disabilities. (55)

38. Tarbuck, P. (1992) Use and abuse of control and restraint. *Nursing Standard* 6(52), 30–32.

39. Leadbetter, D. (1994) Need for care over methods of restraint. *Community Care* 18–24 August, 13.

40. Parkes, R. (1996) Control and restraint training: a study of its effectiveness in a medium secure psychiatric unit. *Journal of Forensic Psychiatry* 17(3), 525–34.

41. Bowie (1998) op. cit.

42. *McIntyre under Cover*. BBC Television October 2000.

43. Department of Education and Employment (2000) *Promoting Positive Handling Strategies for Pupils with Severe Behavioural Difficulties (Draft)*. London: Department of Education and Employment.

44. Department of Health (2001) *Draft Guidance on the Use of Physical Interventions for Staff Working with Children and Adults with Learning Disability and/or Autism*. London: Department of Health.

45. Centre for Residential Child Care (1997) *Clear Expectations, Consistent Limits Good Practice in the Care and Control of Children and Young People in Residential Care*. Glasgow: Centre for Residential Child Care, University of Strathclyde.

46. *Hartford Courant* (1999) Deadly restraint. A *Hartford Courant* investigative report (http://www.courant.com/news/special/restraint/index/stm).

47. Harris, J., Allen, D., Cornick, M., Jefferson, A. and Mills, R. (1996) *Physical Interventions: A Policy Framework*. Kidderminster: British Institute of Learning Disability Publications.

48. British Institute of Learning Disability (2001) *Draft Code of Practice for Trainers in the Use of Physical Interventions: Learning Disability: Autism and Pupils with Special Educational Needs*. Kidderminster: British Institute of learning Disability Publications.

49. Bowie (1996) op. cit.

50. Bowie (1998) op. cit.

51. Klein, J.I. (1992) The least restrictive alternative: more about less. In Grinsoon, L. (ed.) Psychiatry 1982, *The American Psychiatric Association Annual Review*, American Psychiatric Association, Washington DC. Washington, DC: American Psychiatric Press.

52. Paterson, B., Leadbetter, D. and Tringham, C. (1999) Critical incident management, aggression and violence case study. In Mercer, D. *et al.* (eds.) *Forensic Mental Health Care Planning: Directions and Dilemmas*. Edinburgh: Churchill Livingstone.

53. Paterson, B., Leadbetter, D. and McComish, A. (1997) De-escalation in the short-term management of violence a process based approach. *Nursing Times* 93(7), 58–61.

54. Moss, M., Sharpe, S. and Fay, C. (1990) *Abuse in the Care System: A Pilot Study by the National Association of Young People in Care*. London: National Association of Young People in Care.

55. Paterson, B., Tringham, C., McComish, A. and Waters, S. (1997) Managing

aggression and violence a legal perspective on the use of force. *Psychiatric Care* 4(3), 128–31.

56. Ibid.

57. Frank, C., Hodgetts, G. and Puxty, J. (1996) Safety and efficacy of physical restraints for the elderly review of the evidence. *Canadian Family Physician* 42, 2402–409.

58. Miles, S.H. and Irvine, P. (1992) Deaths caused by physical restraints. *The Gerontologist* 32(6), 762–66.

59. Paterson and Leadbetter op. cit.

60. Ibid., 132.

61. Lyon, C. (1994) *Legal Issues Arising from the Care, Control and Safety of Children with Learning Disabilities who also Present Severe Challenging Behaviour*. London: Mental Health Foundation.

62. Smith, P.A. (1999) Standards of practice for human service professionals who are responsible for the care and supervision of individuals with assaultive behaviour. In Smith, P.A. *et al.* (eds.) *Professional Assault Response Training: Instructor's Manual*. Citrus Heights, CA: Professional Assault Response Training, 11.

63. Bowie (1998) op. cit.

64. Bowie (1996) op. cit.

65. Allan op. cit.

66. Paterson and Leadbetter op. cit.

67. General Accounting Office of the United States (1999) *Report to Congressional Requesters: Mental Health: Improper Restraint or Seclusion Places People at Risk*. Washington, DC: US General Accounting Office.

Chapter 9

Why workplace bullying and violence are different: protecting employees from both

Oonagh Barron

Introduction

This chapter has been written in order to provide an examination of the issues relevant to employee safety when dealing with workplace violence or workplace bullying. It also provides a brief overview of the key issues in relation to the prevention of both workplace bullying and workplace violence, focusing in particular on potential risk factors revealed by international research.

The chapter works from the premise that workplace bullying and workplace violence are different, but in some respects should be dealt with together especially through the occupational health and safety (OHS) paradigm. In particular, strategies used for dealing with workplace bullying may provide some insight into how to address workplace violence that originates from a source internal to the workplace.

When undertaking an exploration of a complex area it is important to clarify definitions of concepts and to agree on understandings of relevant terms. The next section of this chapter examines some definitions and issues relevant to assist in the differentiation between workplace bullying and workplace violence.

The difference between workplace bullying and workplace violence

There has been a tendency in Australia for a mixing or misuse of the terms workplace bullying and workplace violence. This is evidenced by the use of 'workplace bullying' for situations which should be described as workplace violence.[1] Both concepts are concerned with abuse of power in the work setting, and workplace violence, like workplace bullying, is located within the work setting. Yet workplace violence concentrates on behaviour that usually has criminal aspects to it (or would be considered criminal behaviour if it occurred outside the work setting) – i.e. assaults, threats, damage to property, verbal obscenities, sexual harassment, etc. Behaviour that falls within the concept of workplace bullying is less likely to have criminal elements.

The author has written about the tendency in Australia to confuse the concept of workplace bullying with that of workplace violence.[2] They are essentially different workplace phenomena, in relation to the types of behaviour each concept covers or describes, the legal options for individuals to seek redress and the strategies that can be used for intervention or prevention. An element contributing to this confusion is caused by a form of workplace violence that has aspects in common with workplace bullying. This form of workplace violence is perpetrated against someone within the workplace by someone employed within the same workplace, just as employees who are bullied at work are most often bullied by someone else employed within their organization. Forms of workplace violence that originate from a source external to the workplace are not so readily confused with workplace bullying. However, psychological forms of aggression – like bullying at work – that may result in injury to an employee are causing increasing concern in various countries:

> Attention has traditionally been focused on physical violence, and the typical profile of violence at work which has emerged has been largely one of isolated, major incidents...in more recent years, however, new evidence has been emerging of the impact and harm caused by non-physical violence, often referred to as psychological violence.[3]

In 1998 an International Labour Office (ILO) report into violence at work discussed the problems of establishing a clear definition of workplace violence.[4] Currently, there is still no internationally agreed definition of workplace violence and the examination of psychological forms of violence or aggression is contributing to confusion.

The differentiation between various forms of workplace violence and workplace bullying is essential to assist in developing strategies to intervene and prevent these behaviours occurring. And while there is no agreed international definition of either workplace violence or workplace bullying there is agreement in relation to the behaviours that form the basis of categorizing workplace violence or workplace bullying. The next section of this chapter looks more closely at definitions of workplace bullying and then workplace violence and also examines differences between the two workplace phenomena.

Workplace bullying

Workplace bullying has been characterized in a number of ways. In an Australian context, the Queensland government Division of Workplace Health and Safety has developed guides for both employers and workers on the issue of workplace bullying. In these guides bullying was defined as: ...'the repeated less favourable treatment of a person by another or others in the workplace, which may be considered unreasonable and inappropriate workplace practice'.[5] This definition relies on the concept of *repeated* behaviour; the necessity for the behaviour to be repeated is a key factor that differentiates workplace bullying from workplace violence.

At an international level, a definition developed in the previously referred to ILO report into violence at work described workplace bullying in the following manner: 'Workplace bullying constitutes offensive behaviour through vindictive, malicious or humiliating attempts to undermine an individual or groups of employees. These specifically negative attacks on their personal and professional performance are typically unpredictable, irrational and unfair.'[6] This definition is an indication of the diversity of definitions of workplace bullying that can be encountered. Reference to irrationality within this definition does not fit as well as the aspects of unpredictability or unfairness. Some forms of workplace bullying are rational, because they have arisen out of a previous workplace dispute. A Norwegian researcher, Stale Einarsen, categorized workplace bullying into two differing types, based on the motivation behind the bullying behaviours. Einarsen's two forms of bullying in the workplace are bullying that is dispute related (arising out of workplace conflict), and bullying that is predatory (where the target is opportunistic, and no previous conflict has taken place).[7]

At this point in the discussion it may be helpful to describe some of the workplace behaviours that will fall into the category of workplace bullying. These behaviours can include persistent criticism; freezing people out of the workplace (or sending someone to Coventry); withholding information that is vital for effective work performance; undervaluing effort; spreading malicious rumours; and taking credit for other people's ideas.[8] In some cases, workplace bullying can turn into workplace violence, where the escalation of oppressive behaviours continues unchecked for such time that it culminates in an assault, threat to harm or other violent act.

Most definitions of workplace bullying do not encompass threats of, or actual violence; they refer instead to the escalation of aggressive behaviours that culminate in the eventual victimization of the subject of the bullying. The majority of definitions focus on the impact or effect of the bullying on a target. Researchers in this area agree on the following aspects of workplace bullying:

- It is characterized by a pattern of behaviour (single incidents fall outside the accepted definition of workplace bullying).

- It escalates in severity over time.

- The perpetrator is always known to the target of the bullying.

- The victim/target is unable to defend him or herself.

- The bullying is always situated within the organization.[9]

Workplace violence

The term workplace violence covers a range of behaviours and circumstances where violence arises out of a work situation, and where the subject of the violence or aggression is usually an employee. A quite comprehensive definition of workplace violence is one used by Stanton: 'physical assault, threatening behaviour or verbal abuse, and racial and sexual harassment occurring in a work setting.'[10]

As with other forms of violence, workplace violence may manifest and be perpetrated in a wide variety of ways. In an Australian context some work has been done to attempt to define closely what is meant by the term workplace violence. Both Mullen[11] and Bowie's[12] work divides workplace violence into subsets or categories of how, when and where it happens, as well as who perpetrates it. This categorization is very important because workplace violence is clearly not a singular phenomenon – it comes in a variety of forms and occurs in differing contexts and situations.[13] Mullen developed three distinct categories that reveal the main forms of workplace violence. The categories Mullen developed are as follows:

- Intra-organizational conflict (this is located within the workplace and covers conflict between workers).

- Occupational violence (this is located where the job is performed and is perpetrated by outside parties, such as customers and clients).

- Violence from the general public (which is often random or opportunistic, such as robbery).

Mullen's categories are useful in understanding the permutations and dynamics of workplace violence that must be addressed in the development of preventive and intervention strategies. Protecting employees from each type of workplace violence logically involves differing approaches, especially when it comes to dealing with aggressors or perpetrators from sources that can be external or internal to the workplace. The behaviours that exemplify the various forms of workplace violence include: threats to cause physical harm; assaults; damaging property; pushing; punching; stalking; and sexual harassment. Bowie includes a further concept of 'organizational violence', where an organization's lack of appropriate intervention in a workplace violence situation contributes to the impact of the violence on a victim.[14]

Workplace violence and workplace bullying are different, but one form of workplace violence, intra-organizational violence, has some elements in common with workplace bullying. The location of both is the workplace and perpetrators are employees of the organization. Forms of workplace violence perpetrated by members of the public, service users or clients do not usually have elements in common with workplace bullying. However, some employees experience forms of bullying from members of the public or service users/clients (e.g. being threatened with an unfounded complaint to a superior).

It is where workplace bullying and intra-organizational violence have similarities that confusion most often arises. Also confusion may arise in describing intra-organizational violence as workplace bullying when the original behaviour started as bullying and escalated into violence. Failing to describe such incidents accurately as workplace violence has implications in relation to how employers, authorities and other relevant parties respond to reports. Describing violence as bullying also has implications on how people subjected to workplace violence would view reporting what happened to them to the proper authorities; potentially they might be concerned they would not be taken seriously. Job Watch as a practitioner in this area has had direct experience of employers, police and OHS authorities failing to view physical assault against an employee in a workplace as a serious matter.

A further difference between workplace bullying and workplace violence, in particular intra-organizational violence, becomes evident when legal options available to employees who experience either behaviour in their workplace are examined. Employees who are subjected to violence in the workplace perpetrated by a co-worker or superior have a broader range of options, particularly in an Australian context, to seek legal redress. Such options include criminal charges, actions through occupational health and safety laws, claims of workers compensation for injury or income support for time off work, actions for unfair/unlawful or constructive dismissal, claims of unlawful discrimination where appropriate and claims for crimes compensation.[15] Legal actions available in relation to redressing workplace bullying are less straightforward but can include claims for workers' compensation as well and, where significant injury (such as severe psychological distress or the development or exacerbation of psychiatric disorders) has occurred, civil action for personal injury caused by an employer's negligence may be available. However, in the main, employees subjected to workplace bullying have far less legal options than those who have been subjected to workplace violence.

Research and available data

Much of the information available at an international level on workplace violence is through crime report statistics.[16] This source of data relates particularly to occupational violence and violence from the general public, but is a problematic source for data on crimes arising out of intra-organizational violence. In Job Watch's anecdotal experience, the police are reluctant to see assault or other forms of violence perpetrated within the workplace by an employee of that workplace as criminal acts. Job Watch clients have been told by the police that what has happened to them is a civil matter because it occurred in the workplace and therefore cannot be addressed through criminal investigation or charges. Currently there is no consistent source for data on intra-organizational violence.

The data available on subjects of bullying and perpetrators of bullying are often collected from the victim's perspective. Information about intra-organizational violence can also come from the same source as that of workplace bullying: the target of the violence. For example, a 1998 Morgan Poll found that 46% of Australians reported being verbally or physically abused by someone they worked with;[17] and a report published by Job Watch is based on interviews with employees who reported experiencing intra-organizational violence at work. Job Watch's report reveals that in the majority of cases victims do report what happened to them and they report it to more than one place. It also reveals that employers are often aware that intra-organizational violence is happening in their workplaces and that perpetrators of workplace violence have usually been violent to other workers.[18]

The other two forms of workplace violence have differing data sources which include (as mentioned earlier) crime report data, crime compensation data and workers' compensation data. From July 2000, Australia's National Occupational Health and Safety Commission implemented a national reporting system for incidents of workplace violence where workers' compensation claims have been made. The first of these comparative data should be available in 2002. In the 1998 ILO report,[19] the problems of accessing data to quantify levels of the incidence of workplace violence on an international basis were discussed and, as revealed in the discussion above, the available data are not necessarily consistent, particularly as intra-organizational violence may be under-reported or under-represented in crime statistics.

While there may be problems with the available data, they form a starting point to examine factors present in the industry, workplace or work environment that may have contributed to violence or bullying incidents occurring. The next section examines information on risk factors gathered from such data that may provide information on why these workplace behaviours occur.

Risk factors

Much of the research that has been undertaken in the areas of workplace bullying and workplace violence assesses and explores risk factors that may contribute to the occurrence of either. Establishing the main risk factors for workplace bullying and the varying forms of workplace violence is an essential step in the prevention process.

In examining risk factors it is important to differentiate between workplace bullying and workplace violence, as well as to differentiate between the three forms of workplace violence. The risk factors for all these are logically different and unlikely to cover every case scenario. Workplace bullying is a workplace phenomenon that occurs exclusively within an organization, and one form of workplace violence, intra-organizational violence, also occurs exclusively within an organization and the victim is likely to know the perpetrator.

Workplace violence risk factors

In the ILO report, Chappell and Di Martino[20] discussed established risk factors for the forms of workplace violence that originate from sources outside the workplace, occupational violence and violence from the general public. These were forms of workplace violence where data were gathered from crime report statistics. The main risk categories for these two forms of workplace violence were:

- handling cash
- providing care, advice or training
- carrying out inspection or enforcement duties
- working with disturbed, drunk or violent people
- working alone.

The aspects described above indicate there are certain industries and occupations that are more likely to be subject to occupational violence and violence from the general public. Transport workers, health and community service workers, police and retail workers all perform duties that fall within the mentioned risk factors. Except where the violence is perpetrated by the clients or service user, the perpetrators of these forms of workplace violence are not likely to be known to the victim.

Establishing risk factors in relation to intra-organizational violence is not as clear cut, partly because not much data are available on the subject and where data are available (such as from the USA in relation to occupational homicide), information has been gathered after critical incidents and this focuses on the characteristics of the perpetrator of a crime (usually an ex-employee). Risk factors that may have contributed to the occurrence of serious incidents and that have been put forward after the examination of the post-incident scene and other relevant information (such as perpetrator profiles) include:

- disgruntled and vengeful workers
- job insecurity
- workers with a strong sense of entitlement who feel cheated.[21]

Other types of intra-organizational violence, the non-critical type of incident (which includes sexual harassment), are a less examined area. But research has revealed the following aspects as risk factors for the non-critical forms of intra-organizational violence:

- Labour-force participation levels (this relates in particular to sexual harassment, where low numbers of female employees in an industry, compared to high numbers of male employees, have seen more reports of sexual harassment than in areas where women have a higher proportional representation in the workplace).

- Non-traditional areas of employment (this is similar to the above risk factor, where female workers employed in non-traditional areas of employment have reported higher levels of sexual harassment).
- Loss of self-esteem and stability among workers.[22]

The report referred to earlier (*Working in Fear*), examining the experiences of victims of intra-organizational violence looked at differing factors present in the workplaces of the research subjects. The following factors were present in nearly two-thirds of workplaces where non-critical intra-organizational violence occurred:

- lack of recognition of workers
- high demands on work performance
- an authoritarian management style.[23]

The elements described above have aspects in common with findings in relation to research conducted into workplace factors evident in work-places where bullying has occurred.

Workplace bullying risk factors

In 1990, Leymann reported there were four factors that could be present in the work situations of targets of bullying or mobbing. These four things were: 1) deficiencies in work design; 2) deficiencies in leadership behaviour; 3) a socially exposed position of the victim; and 4) low morale.[24] Leymann's four factors provide an interesting framework from which to examine workplace bullying situations. These four factors may also be useful when examining the issue of risk factors for intra-organizational violence, as a result of the elements bullying and intra-organizational violence have in common (especially where the perpetrator of the violence is known to the victim).

Risk factors in relation to workplace bullying can be very broad: who is a potential victim? Who is a potential bully? Which workplaces might become the site of bullying? And so on. Leymann's factors assist in breaking this down: where there are deficiencies in leadership behaviour, managers and supervisors are at risk of becoming bullies. Where employees are isolated or in any other way socially exposed, they may be at risk of being bullied. Where workplaces have low morale and poor work design, bullying may be happening.

One of the largest studies of workplace bullying in the UK involved members of the UNISON union. Charlotte Rayner[25] examined the data gained from the study and found that managers were most likely to be the perpetrator of bullying; that bullies have usually bullied before; and that bullies often target more than one person. Rayner also made reference to work done by Einarsen and colleagues,[26] which found the following elements in victims of bullying workplaces:

- lack of constructive leadership
- lack of possibilities to monitor and control own work
- conflicting goals and priorities.

In April 2000 the Manchester School of Management (UMIST) published a study based on a survey population of over 5,200. The study found that 75% of the people who had been bullied had been bullied by a manager and that job insecurity was a risk factor, as were large workloads and increased working hours, usually caused by downsizing.[27]

Protecting employees from both bullying and violence in the workplace

Protecting employees' safety is a fundamental duty or obligation for employers. This obligation may originate from statute or common law and is the principal basis of OHS. OHS duties include protecting employees from 'foreseeable' risk of injury. Governments, industry organizations, unions and the police have roles to play in the protection of employees; however, an employer's obligation to the employee is paramount.

Intervention often relies on the legislative or statute power obligations on an employer. In the OHS arena, the duty to provide a safe workplace extends to the prevention of foreseeable risks. Employers who implement strategies to prevent workplace bullying and workplace violence are protecting themselves from legal liability as well as protecting employees from risk of injury. The 'foreseeable risk of injury' is unfortunately more straightforward in cases of workplace violence (especially those forms perpetrated by someone not employed in the workplace) than in situations of workplace bullying.

Prevention

Preventive strategies for dealing with both workplace violence and workplace bullying have been developing in line with the body of research mentioned earlier. The most common forms of workplace violence dealt with via preventive strategies are, as with research fields, focused on the external forms of workplace violence: occupational violence and violence from the general public. Due to the similarities between one form of workplace violence and workplace bullying, preventive strategies used for dealing with bullying may be useful for the intervention and prevention of intra-organizational violence.[28]

Addressing intra-organizational violence through OHS or other preventive strategies is a relatively new, though emerging, area. In the Australian context, Worksafe Western Australia has developed a code of practice for preventing and dealing with workplace violence, the National Children's and Youth Law Centre have run prevention training sessions for employers in New South Wales and in Victoria, a code of practice for the prevention of workplace bullying and violence is currently being developed.

Preventing workplace bullying and intra-organizational violence can be achieved in various ways, such as by adopting anti-bullying/violence policies and by regularly surveying employees about the presence of various risk factors in their workplace (e.g. low morale, job insecurity, conflicting goals and priorities, and negative leadership behaviour in managers). Other preventive strategies may involve checking for authoritarian managerial styles; the development of 'soft' (people) management skills, as recommended by Sheehan;[29] ensuring staffing levels are optimum; and ensuring employees are not working unnecessary or regularly long hours. Addressing such workplace issues is a likely to prevent workplace bullying and may also prevent intra-organizational violence.

Non-governmental organizations and prevention

In response to both bullying and intra-organizational violence, Australian non-governmental organizations (NGOs) and unions have been very active in publicizing the problems experienced by workers and in developing proactive strategies for prevention. In relation to the prevention of workplace bullying, the working women's centres have been very active, especially in relation to providing advice and support to workers. In particular, the South Australian Working Women's Centre has recently commenced the second part[30] of its workplace bullying project, which involves the piloting of a range of prevention strategies within organisations.

Another NGO that has been working for a number of years on the subject of bullying in general (but also bullying at work) is the Queensland-based Beyond Bullying Association.[31] In October 2000, the Australian union peak body, the Australian Council of Trade Unions (ACTU), ran its annual OHS campaign on workplace bullying around the theme of 'being bossed around is bad for your health'.

The Australian NGO, Job Watch (mentioned in the research section of this chapter) has been very active in the area of intra-organizational violence since 1995. This organization has approached prevention with a range of strategies, including: community education;[32] the provision of legal advice to targets; research;[33] conferences;[34] development of education materials for secondary school students;[35] media campaigns; lobbying government for law reform; and conducting legal cases for the most disadvantaged targets. In recognition of the broad contribution Job Watch has made to the prevention of violence at work in Victorian workplaces, the organization has received two Australian heads of government awards for violence prevention. Much of the work this organization has done has involved young workers, who appear to be vulnerable to the most extreme expressions of intra-organizational violence.

Additionally, NGOs and unions in the UK have been at the forefront of strategies to deal with workplace bullying. These include the Andrea Adams Trust, Success Unlimited, the Manufacturing, Science and Finance Union (MSF) and UNISON (the public service union).

The involvement of such organizations in publicizing emerging OHS problems, conducting research and developing prevention strategies has been vital to bringing bullying and violence at work to public attention. In fact, many of these organizations' approaches can inform later government responses to such problems. For example, at the time of the ACTU OHS campaign on bullying, the Victorian minister responsible for OHS in that state announced that a code of practice to prevent bullying at work would be developed.

Conclusion

What has been learnt from workplace bullying may assist in under-standing the dynamics of internal/intra-organizational violence. Clearly, further research that focuses on examining work process and work structure issues as indicators of intra-organizational violence will assist in understanding better this workplace phenomenon. Additionally, the contribution of NGOs and unions in enhancing preventive strategies and the knowledge base in this area should not be overlooked.

Ultimately the protection of employees from various forms of oppressive conduct occurring in their workplaces will involve a range of strategies that are relevant or specific to the workplace, industry or prevailing risk factors. Protecting employees as far as possible from internally based bullying and intra-organizational violence may involve examining work process, workload and work autonomy issues, as well as management training or competency in dealing with employees, making sure employees are not working long hours and that staffing levels are at an optimum. Regularly auditing organizations via risk management strategies may also be useful, as would assessing the success of existing strategies. In short, this means adopting the same OHS risk management approach as used for preventing occupational violence and violence from the general public. Such an approach will assist in removing the problems of intra-organizational violence and bullying from workplaces.

The views expressed in this Chapter are those of the author and do not necessarily reflect those of the Victorian WorkCover Authority.

Notes

1. Barron, O. (1998) The distinction between workplace bullying and workplace violence and the ramifications for OHS. *Journal of Occupational Health and Safety – Australia and New Zealand* 14(6), 575–80.
2. Ibid., 576.
3. Chappell, D. and Di Martino, V. (1998) *Violence at Work.* Geneva: International Labour Office, 11.
4. Ibid., 21.
5. Department of Employment, Training and Industrial Relations (1998) *Workplace Bullying: A Worker's Guide.* And *Workplace Bullying: an Employer's Guide.* Division of Workplace Health and Safety. Brisbane: Queensland.
6. Chappell and Di Martino op. cit., 11.
7. Einarsen, S. (1998) Dealing with bullying at work: the Norwegian lesson. Paper presented at the 'Bullying at Work 1998 Research Update' conference, Staffordshire University Business School, 1 July.
8. Source: Suzy Lamplaugh Trust (www.suzylamplaugh.org).
9. Barron (1998) op. cit., 577.
10. Stanton, J. (1993) Workplace violence. *Risk Management* June, 76.
11. Mullen, E.A. (1997) Workplace violence: cause for concern or the construction of

a new category of fear? *Journal of Industrial Relations* 39(1), 21–32.

12. Bowie, V. (1996) *Coping with Violence: A Guide for the Human Services*. London: Whiting & Birch.

13. Barron (1998) op. cit.

14. Bowie, V. (2000) Current trends and emerging issues in workplace violence. *Security Journal* 13(3), 13.

15. For further information on forms of action available to employees in situations of workplace violence, see Barron, O. (1999) Violence in the workplace: protecting the rights of the employee. Paper presented at University of Sydney Law School seminar 'Violence in the Workplace', 26 August.

16. See Chappell and Di Martino op. cit., 23–50.

17. Morgan Poll (1998) Finding no. 13091, 9 June.

18. Barron (2000) *Working in Fear: Experiences of Workplace Violence* (working title). Melbourne: Job Watch Inc.

19. Chappell and Di Martino op. cit.

20. Ibid., 46.

21. Mayhew, C. and Leigh, J. (1999) Occupational violence in Australian workplaces: defining and explaining the problem. Paper presented at the 'Occupational Violence' seminar, Faculty of Law, University of Sydney.

22. Ibid., 2–3.

23. Barron (forthcoming) op. cit.

24. Leymann, H. (1990) Mobbing and psychological terror and workplaces. *Violence and Victims* 5, 119–26.

25. Rayner, C. (1998) From research to implementation: finding leverage for intervention and prevention. Paper presented at the 'Bullying at Work 1998 Research Update' conference, Staffordshire University Business School, 1 July.

26. Ibid., 18.

27. Hoel, H. and Cooper, C. (2000) *Destructive Conflict and Bullying at Work*, Manchester School of Management, UMIST.

28. Barron (1998) op. cit., 578.

29. Sheehan, M. (1998) Bullying: signs and solutions. Paper presented at the 'Bullying at Work 1998 Research Update' conference, Staffordshire University Business School, 1 July.

30. Thomson, C. (1997) *Workplace Bullying Project*. South Australian Working Women.

31. The Beyond Bullying Association has published two books: *Bullying from Backyard to Boardroom* and *Bullying: Costs, Causes and Cures* (for more information, see their web site: http://cwpp.slq.qld.gov.au/bba/).

32. For example, in July 2000 Job Watch and the Victorian WorkCover Authority jointly published *Workplace Violence: Your Rights, What to Do, and Where to Go for Help*.

33. Barron (forthcoming) op. cit.

34. In November 2000, Job Watch and URCOT jointly conducted a conference: 'Sorry's not OK: Young Women and Violence at Work.'

35. In conjunction with VECCI, Job Watch produced the video and booklet: *No Bull: Say No to Bullying* and *Violence at Work*.

Chapter 10

Dealing with violence in the workplace: the experience of Canadian unions

Anthony Pizzino

Introduction

As an occupational health and safety hazard, violence in Canadian workplaces has been propelled from relative obscurity in the 1980s to one of the leading issues being addressed today. During the past ten years, unions have greatly contributed to efforts aimed at increasing the awareness of violence in the workplace among workers, employers and legislators. Despite the efforts, workplace violence continues to make prominent headlines, as anyone knows who watches the television news, listens to the radio and reads the newspapers or health and safety publications. This media exposure has led many to believe that workplace violence is a random, unpredictable act where the perpetrators are usually workers. They think that the 'disgruntled employee' perpetrator is the most serious threat facing workers. Paradoxically, by focusing on the rarest forms of violence in the workplace, the very headlines that have helped to raise awareness of the problem are also helping to obscure the true meaning and magnitude of this devastating occupational hazard.

The public's assumptions run contrary to the experiences of Canadian unions. During the past decade, the union's work has found that most fatal and non-fatal violent assaults are perpetrated by someone outside the workplace – a client, patient or student – and not by co-workers or former co-workers. They have found that changes in government policies are aggravating the problem and making public workplaces even more prone to violence,[1] and that assailants may be unhappy, dissatisfied or angry about the service being provided or about lengthy waiting periods.[2]

In Canada, unions in both public and private sectors are playing active roles in assisting their members with efforts to prevent violence at work. Much of the unions' activity has been geared to pressuring employers and governments for the recognition of violence as an occupational hazard and for the enactment of legislative, policy and collective bargaining provisions.

Due to the high rate of aggression and assaults committed against public sector workers, these unions have been at the forefront of the action. Among the most active in seeking legislative and collective agreement solutions to violence in the workplace is the Canadian Union of Public Employees (CUPE).[3]

The gap in statistics

Canadian workers are not likely to be killed in a violent incident at work. But they are very likely to suffer injuries as the result of violent acts in their workplaces. A gap in statistics becomes evident, however, when trying to determine the prevalence of the problem in Canada. It remains one occupational hazard that has not been studied thoroughly on a national scale. While incidents of such violence appear to be increasing, the extent and magnitude of the problem are still unclear.

Part of the difficulty in obtaining meaningful statistics arises from the fact that no central agency in Canada collects and provides thorough data on the nature, prevalence and severity of violence in the workplace. While most employers report workers' compensation data centrally to the provinces, which in turn report federally, government statistics on workplace acts of violence are difficult to access.

Unions have been encouraging Workers' Compensation Boards in each Canadian province to begin categorizing incidents of violence in a more consistent manner. Although most compensation boards have coding systems that capture injuries and deaths from workplace violence, these data do not reflect the actual numbers of incidents. In addition, there is the fact that all violent incidents may not result in injuries severe enough to require a workers' compensation claim. In other cases, workers are discouraged from filing claims and are encouraged to use sick days or vacations instead. In the majority of cases, under-reporting of workplace violent incidents to supervisors and joint union–management occupational health and safety committees remain a problem.

Unions have been attempting to identify reasons why statistics do not bear out the true nature and extent of the problem. In its search, CUPE has identified that workers:

- may not recognize that an incident was violent and should therefore be reported;

- recognize that an incident was violent, but do not report it because employers tell them that violence 'is part of the job';

- report the incident, but organizations do not record, classify and follow up; and

- report the incident to supervisors and managers, but not to the joint union–management occupational health and safety committees.

What is known about the prevalence of violence in Canadian workplaces? The International Labour Organization (ILO) has ranked Canada among the top five nations in terms of workplace assaults.[4] Work assaults are higher in Canada, and women have a 19% higher rate of physical or psychological[5] assault compared to the USA.

According to the Occupational Safety and Health Branch of Human Resources and Development Canada, since the early 1980s, violence against workers has increased 'in both perception and incidence'. It is reported that

> 'Employees as well as managers and supervisors have become all too frequent victims of assaults or other violent acts in the workplace which entail a substantial risk of physical or emotional harm.' (p. iii)[6]

A somewhat national perspective on the prevalence of violence in the workplace can to some extent be derived from the Association of Workers' Compensation Boards of Canada (AWCBC) *Work Injuries and Diseases* reports. In 1998, the AWCBC revealed that the number of fatalities and accepted time-loss injuries resulting from acts of violence in Canada went up sharply between 1995 and 1997 – increasing in that three-year period by 88%.[7]

In addition to the AWCBC, limited provincial data contribute an understanding of the extent and severity of the problem. In British Columbia, the provincial Workers' Compensation Board reports that wage loss claims by hospital workers due to acts of violence or force had increased by 88% since 1985. More than half the acts of violence in the province took place within the healthcare system.[8]

In Ontario, a 1992 request from the Ontario Nurses' Association (ONA) to the Ontario Ministry of Labour for an analysis of time-loss claims revealed that 59% of respondents had been physically assaulted at one time in their careers. The study found that 35% had been assaulted in the previous 12 months and 10% in the previous month. Almost all the assaults were at the hands of patients.[9]

In the Province of Manitoba, the Manitoba Teachers' Society (MTS) surveyed all school administrators and a random sample of teachers in 1990 and 1993. Of the teachers participating in the 1993 survey, 47% had experienced either physical or emotional abuse during the previous 17 months.[10] By contrast, only 37% had reported being assaulted during a similar time period in the 1990 survey.[11]

The paucity of, and variability in, available statistics have prompted at least two of the largest Canadian public sector unions, the Canadian Union of Public Employees, and the Public Service Alliance of Canada (PSAC),[12] to determine the extent to which their members are subjected to violence and abuse. The unions have shown that workers are being seriously injured – physically and/or psychologically – in increasing numbers.

In 1993, CUPE conducted one of the most comprehensive Canadian trade union studies of violence at work. The national survey, which also laid the foundation for policy and legislative campaigns, found that 61.2% of respondents had been subjected to an aggressive act in the previous two years. Of those, 55% had been subjected to three or more aggressive acts during the same time period. When asked to describe the details of their last assault, survey participants revealed that 38% were struck with an object; 30% were hit; and 30% were grabbed, scratched or kicked. Verbal aggression was reported by 69%.[13]

The PSAC survey found that 35% of members had been subjected to violence in the previous year. Verbal abuse accounted for 72% of the violence, with 70% of assaults occurring in offices. A total of 39% indicated they were struck, pushed, hit, grabbed or sexually assaulted. Interestingly, while clients accounted for 38% of the violence, supervisors were responsible for 22%.[14]

Risk factors

Looking at some of these numbers, it seems clear that violence is not a random, unforeseeable event. Violence is a risk for people working in specific jobs. Working with the public is one risk factor, but there are others.

CUPE has identified jobs and workplaces where the risk is highest:

- Workers who handle money, in the retail and non-retail sector.
- Workers who are seen by the public to be in positions of power (for example enforcing laws or inspecting premises).
- Anyone who must work alone in a building or in the community.
- Healthcare workers providing care to ill or aged persons.

The categories and the circumstances in which violence happens are important factors when unions suggest preventive programmes, and also assist unions in pushing to secure more progressive and protective provisions. Where employers are often satisfied with 'managing violence', unions go a step further in looking at workplace design and organization, in order to recommend preventive measures.[15]

Violence is preventable

A useful framework for investigating and solving workplace violence problems has been available in British government-sponsored materials since the 1980s. The Health & Safety Executive's (HSE) five-element analytical framework, developed in bipartite committees established by the HSE, is based on a sound public health principle: to attempt to find solutions for problems whether the root cause is known or not.[16]

Curiously, the majority of Canadian provinces and American states have largely ignored the practical method outlined by the HSE. However, these methods have heavily influenced CUPE's approach and response to violence at work. Although the model is simple, and each workplace is different, it is the basic principles that are important.[17] The five elements – 'assailant', 'employee', 'interaction', 'work environment' and 'outcome' – provide a basis for developing an exposure profile to investigate the hazard.

The first step is to determine if a problem exists. If there is a potential for violence, based on the previously identified risk factors, or where violence has been reported, a comprehensive violence prevention programme must be established. The principles involved are basically the same ones used to deal with other occupational health and safety hazards: to identify the problem; to solve it using a preventive focus; to involve the workers affected; and then to monitor the effectiveness of the preventive intervention.

Barriers to prevention

Beyond the statistics and sporadic efforts to understand and address violence in the workplace lies a remarkable lack of organizational reaction. While some employers have taken steps to address the hazard, a much greater number have failed to provide the minimum occupational health and safety legislative requirements for worker protection.

Besides organizational inaction, there exists a belief that solutions are not possible and that violence cannot be prevented. However, the literature and the unions' experiences say different. Violence at work can be controlled and the risks can be reduced. Enough is known about work processes to achieve this. It is essential that organizations look beyond the horror stories and sensationalistic media reports when investigating violence. It is also important not to focus on 'exposure' profiles or 'high-risk' occupations but, rather, to look at the entire workplace, its activities and work processes and organization.[18] Indeed, the logic of following a participative and programmed approach is, in fact, consistent with Canadian occupational health and safety laws in general and workplace violence regulations in particular.

Canadian unions are finding that programmes that focus a disproportionate amount of attention to worker-on-worker violence are succumbing to the sensational media coverage that accompanies these rare events. The 'disgruntled worker' assailant, although newsworthy, is a very small part of the workplace violence problem.[19] Unfortunately, in this regard Canada is being influenced by a proliferation of American-style consultants who are focusing employers' attentions on 'worker profiling' and 'zero-tolerance policies'. Worker profiling efforts claim to be able to screen out workers who are considered to be a risk for violent behaviour. Proponents of 'zero tolerance' policies argue they promote safer workplaces since they will be free from violence. Canadian unions are strongly opposed to these misguided approaches. Workplace violence interventions that target individual worker behaviour are mostly reactive and hardly preventive. Profiling workers based on personal characteristics is not an effective predictor of potential violent behaviour and may, in fact, be counterproductive when applied to workplace violence.[20] Unions believe that, in addition to being difficult and unevenly enforced, 'zero tolerance' policies focus organizational attention on individuals and may lead to violations of workers' rights if management discharges workers without carefully weighing facts and circumstances. Either way, these interventions and policies quite simply fail to address the root causes of violence in the workplace.

Part of the reason for the lack of organizational action may be simple denial. Another is that workers in certain occupations are forced by employers to accept the violence as 'part of the job'. In organizations that acknowledge the potential for violence, the lack of action is driven by two factors. One is that violence in the workplace is not preventable; the other is that workers are led to believe that workplace assaults are their fault and are the result of workers' actions or behaviour.

The unions' programme

The trade unions' suggestions for preventing violence in the workplace include designing and implementing a comprehensive violence prevention programme that:

- defines violence;
- recognizes violence as an occupational hazard;
- has a mechanism to report violence;
- involves the joint union–management occupational health and safety committee;
- provides information to workers about the potential for violence;
- provides training in appropriate responses to violence;
- recognizes the importance of workplace design and work organization; and
- provides support for affected workers.

The definition of violence in the workplace is a key part of a violence prevention programme. The most comprehensive definitions recognize that non-physical violence (including verbal abuse as well as sexual and racial harassment) is also part of the continuum. CUPE's definition of violence at work places violence in the context of a process that includes actions, causes and effects:

> 'Violence is any incident in which an employee is abused, threatened or assaulted during the course of her/his employment. This includes the application of force, threats with or without weapons, verbal abuse, sexual, racial and psychological harassment.'[21]

In order to encourage workers to report acts of workplace violence to their employers and to the joint occupational health and safety committee, CUPE has developed a 'Violent incident reporting form'. This form includes information on the assailant's characteristics, on the incident and on any injury sustained, and is provided to members at no cost. The forms are printed on carbon-less paper with the worker retaining a copy and the rest being distributed to the employer, the joint union–management occupational health and safety committee and the local union executive. Following the recording of incidents, the information collected can be classified based on the assailant, the nature of the incident and the work environment. The approach encourages methodical analysis of each component of a violent episode to determine the scope for intervention.

Legislated joint occupational health and safety committees offer one avenue for prevention, but unions and employers can work together in other ways to prevent violence in the workplace. Some employers and unions are recognizing the value of negotiating collective agreements, which include violence prevention provisions. The Canadian Labour Congress (CLC) has developed model collective agreement language on violence and harassment.[22] The provisions on violence would empower the joint health and safety committee to deal with workplace violence issues. The CLC model also suggests clauses requiring consultation with the committee on the development and implementation of physical and procedural measures to protect workers from physical violence and verbal abuse. It suggests training for workers in the recognition and management of abusive incidents. The CLC's detailed provisions on harassment commits the parties to recognize 'an employee's right to a working environment which is free of harassment on the grounds of race, sex and sexual orientation'.[23]

A key issue for Canadian unions has been that of control over work organization and workers' health, safety and well-being. Public sector workers, in particular, are often the people on the front lines. They are in positions to tell clients, patients or students they cannot do something for them. In some cases, they have authority to deny important client requests or to take legal action against clients. For example, they are in positions to refuse a municipal permit, to write a parking ticket or to take children into protective custody.

By the very nature of their jobs, they seem to have the power to determine what people can do, as well as when and how they do it. At the same time, with increases in workload and understaffing this is in fact far from reality – these workers have little or no control over their work situation, and rarely, if ever, make the rules they administer. They have not been involved in designing their work environment nor have they chosen their pace of work. They have little or no say in setting budgets or priorities. This lack of control over the organizational aspects of work and safety is not conducive either to problem-solving or, most importantly, to prevention.

Legislative solutions to the problem

At the present time, violence in the workplace is covered in occupational health and safety regulations in only 2 of 11 Canadian jurisdictions:[24] the provinces of British Columbia and Saskatchewan. In the rest of the country, violence in the workplace is covered in a very broad statement, or 'general duty clause', obligating employers to ensure the health and safety of workers.

Comprehensive regulations to cover violence have been developed in Nova Scotia, but even though they were submitted to the provincial legislators in 1996 as a bipartite consensus of unions and employers, the government has yet to enact them. In 1999, the Canadian federal government set up a tripartite working group consisting of workers, employers and government to develop regulations on violence under the federal Canada Labour Code (Part II) Occupational Health and Safety. A federal sector violence-at-work regulation is expected to become law following the consultative process. In the mean time, and in anticipation of new federal violence regulations, recent amendments to the Canada Labour Code (Part II)[25] for the first time specifically mention violence in the workplace. Employers are required to take prescribed steps to prevent and protect against violence in the workplace.[26]

British Columbia's regulation is performance based, outlining the employer's responsibility to develop and implement a violence prevention programme that will eliminate or minimize the risk to staff. The regulation provides a definition to help workers and employers recognize what the law covers. Workplace violence is defined as:

> 'The attempted or actual exercise by a person, other than a worker, of any physical force so as to cause injury to a worker, and includes any threatening statement or behaviour which gives a worker reasonable cause to believe that the worker is at risk of injury.'[27]

The regulation contains a requirement for the employer to perform a risk assessment of hazards that may lead to violence. If a risk of violence is found, procedures for communicating the risk to workers and then eliminating the risk must be developed. Finally, the regulation requires employers to implement incident-reporting procedures. All these activities require the active participation of the joint union–management occupational health and safety committees.

As part of wide-ranging revisions to workplace safety legislation in 1996, Saskatchewan's Occupational Health and Safety Regulations also contain provisions regarding violence in the workplace. The regulations define violence and outline the type of workplaces that are covered under the legislation. The 13 categories include: healthcare facilities; pharmaceutical-dispensing services; education; police, corrections, security and other law enforcement services; crisis counselling and intervention services; retail sales open between 11.00 pm and 6.00 am; financial services; premises where alcohol is sold or consumed; taxi and transit services.[28] The regulation defines the contents of an anti-violence policy statement, which employers are obliged to develop under the province's Occupational Health and Safety Act.

In addition to these anti-violence provisions, Saskatchewan is the only Canadian province that explicitly requires employers, as part of its occupational health and safety legislative scheme, to prevent harassment. The province's broad definition of harassment expands the human rights legislation and prohibits harassment where it 'constitutes a threat to the health and safety of the worker'.[29] In coupling the province's violence and harassment provisions and including psychological and social aspects in the definition of 'health and safety', Saskatchewan's Occupational Health and Safety Act the interpretation of violent incidents is broadened to a degree not seen in other Canadian jurisdictions.

Nova Scotia's proposed regulation[30] is similar in principle to the performance-based British Columbia and Saskatchewan regulations in that hazards from workplace violence must be identified and controlled. The regulation differs in one key area – employers are explicitly required to acknowledge that workplace violence is an occupational health and safety hazard they are committed to eliminating or minimizing. The hazard-identification process must take into account previous incidents, the occupational experience with violence in similar workplaces, the location and circumstances in which future work is performed and the presence of interactions or situations that may predict future violence.

Current union activities

A number of unions and central labour bodies continue to be at the forefront of efforts to ensure protection from violence at work. The Canadian Labour Congress (CLC), which represents two and one-half million workers, is co-ordinating federal efforts to ensure that legislative protection from violence for federal sector workers becomes law. The CLC's 19th Constitutional Convention stated that occupational health and safety legislation should be used to allow workers to leave a work site when they are threatened with harassment or front-line violence. The convention went on to say that, while jurisprudence in this area is contradictory, it is evolving slowly to recognize that workplace hazards to safety and health extend further than 'toxic chemicals or the outbreak of fire'.

The CLC convention also recommended that mandatory training for health and safety representatives and committee members be provided and should cover:

- violence against women;
- causes of violence and aggression;
- how to recognize potential violence;
- dealing with specific situations; and
- debriefing, support and follow-up after incidents of violence.

The CUPE's national convention policy on violence in the workplace calls for legislation in all jurisdictions to require:

- employers to develop and maintain work plans, policies, measures and procedures to eliminate the risk of violence;

- employers to assess patients or residents with respect to their aggressive or violent behaviour, to communicate the assessment to workers and to take steps to prevent the causes of violent or aggressive acts;

- training in procedures to be used in dealing with and handling violent or aggressive individuals;

- the maintenance of adequate staffing levels where workers must deal with violent persons;

- restrictions or prohibitions on working alone with violent or aggressive persons, and the provision of personal alarms and security measures; and

- the right to refuse dangerous work where adequate policies, measures and procedures are not maintained by employers.

The Public Service Alliance of Canada (PSAC) has identified cutbacks in employment and services, deregulation, privatization and hard economic times as the causes of violence in the federal public sector. The PSAC has adopted a policy stating that an employer must eliminate all hazards from the workplace, or isolate them when they cannot be eliminated. The policy also states that violence in the workplace must be addressed in the legislation of all territorial, provincial and federal jurisdictions. The PSAC recommends, among other things:

- developing or revamping of employer policies and guidelines regarding violence in the workplace;

- affirming that employees are not expected to put themselves at risk while performing their job;

- providing a systematic approach for the management of aggressive clients, patients, inmates or members of the general public; and

- requiring all assaults resulting in physical or mental injuries to be reported to provincial Workers' Compensation Boards.

The Canadian Automobile, Aerospace, Transportation and General Workers Union (CAW-Canada) has proposed that the federal government ensure the following protections in legislation:

- Enactment of a regulation making three-person crews mandatory in the armoured car industry.

- Mandatory precautions for all workplaces where workers are exposed to the risk of violence.

There is no doubt that Canadian unions will continue to study workplace violence issues and recommend useful solutions to the problem. Every major union in Canada is engaging its members in deliberations aimed at securing protections from this ever-growing hazard. As consultation with employers and government advances, so will union programmes aimed at eliminating the threat of violence.

Conclusion

Violence in Canadian workplaces is a serious occupational hazard. Like many such hazards, it is predictable and preventable, with effective, practicable solutions, but like some other health and safety hazards, it defies quick fixes and easy solutions. Nevertheless, there are many basic steps organizations can take towards effective and responsible prevention. Well defined prevention programmes that incorporate policies and practices can begin the process of prevention.

Canadian unions see the problem of violence, worker abuse, harassment and the psychological effects of being a victim or witnessing workplace violence as a challenge that, if practically addressed, will benefit workers and society at large. They will therefore continue to place workplace violence at the top of their health and safety agendas. They will also continue to pressure employers and governments to assume their legal responsibilities for reducing worker injury due to violence.

While some workplace resolutions to the problem lie in joint union–management processes, there is an obvious need for other, far-reaching solutions. Some of these include applying collective bargaining strategies as an effective tool for problem-solving. Others reside in the development of legislative schemes under safety legislation. The Canadian occupational health and safety legislative regime places the onus of responsibility on the employer to provide safe working conditions. It also gives workers the rights to participate in making recommendations to eliminate or reduce the likelihood of worker injury due to violence. The government, in turn, is responsible for enforcing employer responsibility and workers' rights. The violence prevention provisions currently contained in Saskatchewan and British Columbia legislation are reasonable models for other jurisdictions. The future federal regulation and the draft Nova Scotia violence regulation continue the established management pattern of joint union–employer occupational health and safety co-operation. The Canadian experience is showing that both the collective bargaining and the legislative approach are most effective when there is meaningful worker participation in violence prevention strategies together with strong employer commitment to the process. They provide evidence that prevention of this increasing hazard is not only possible but that it is also necessary.

Notes

1. Canadian Union of Public Employees (1999) *Overloaded and Underfire: Report of the Ontario Social Services Work Environment Survey.* Ottawa: CUPE.
2. Canadian Union of Public Employees (1991a) *Violence in Nova Scotia's Homes for Special Care: Report of the Hearings on Violence for the Nova Scotia Homes for Special Care Task Force.* Ottawa: CUPE.
3. The Canadian Union of Public Employees is Canada's largest union, representing 475,000 workers in over 3,500 locales. CUPE workers are employed in all ten provinces, in municipalities, school boards, hospitals and nursing homes, libraries, universities, social services agencies, public utilities, airlines and other institutions.
4. Chappell, D. and Di Martino, V. (1998) *Violence at Work.* Geneva: International Labour Office.
5. The ILO refers to psychological assaults as 'non-physical violence'.
6. Frappier, F. (1995) *Violence Prevention in the Workplace in the Federal Jurisdiction.* Ottawa: Legislative and Liaison Division, Occupational Health and Safety, Human Resources Development Canada.

7. Association of Workers/Compensation Boards of Canada (1998) *Work Injuries and Diseases, Canada 1995–97*. Ottawa: AWCBC.

8. Boyd, N. (1995) Violence in the workplace in British Columbia: a preliminary investigation. *Canadian Journal of Criminology* 37(4), 491–519.

9. Liss, G. (1993) *Examination of Workers' Compensation Claims among Nurses in Ontario for Injuries Due to Violence*. Toronto: Ontario Ministry of Labour.

10. Manitoba Teachers' Society (1993) *Report of Abuse of Teachers in Manitoba Schools*. Winnipeg: MTS.

11. Manitoba Teachers' Society (1990) *Report of the Task Force on the Physical and Emotional Abuse of Teachers*. Winnipeg: MTS.

12. The Public Service Alliance of Canada represents 150,000 members in all Canadian provinces and territories. The range of occupations includes office workers, customs officers, prison guards, inspectors and airport workers.

13. Pizzino, A. (1993) *Report on CUPE's National Health and Safety Survey of Aggression against Staff*. Ottawa: CUPE.

14. Public Service Alliance of Canada (1994) *Stop Workplace Violence: Report of the PSAC Survey on Workplace Violence*. Ottawa: PSAC.

15. Canadian Union of Public Employees (1991b) *Stopping Violence at Work*. Ottawa: Health and Safety Guideline.

16. Poyner, B. and Warne, C. (1986) *Violence to Staff*. London: Health & Safety Executive.

17. Poyner, B. and Warne, C. (1988) *Preventing Violence to Staff*. London: Health & Safety Executive.

18. Harrison, R. (ed.) (1995) Violence in the workplace. *Occupational Medicine: State of the Art Reviews* 11(2), iii.

19. Cabral, R. (1995) Workplace violence: viable solutions under collective bargaining. *New Solutions* 5(3), 15–22.

20. Braverman, M. (2000) Prevention of violence affecting workers: a systems perspective. *Security Journal* 13(3), 25–38.

21. Canadian Union of Public Employees (2001) *8th National Health and Safety Conference. Violence in the Workplace Workshop Proceedings*. Montreal, February.

22. The CLC's Health and Safety and Environment Department has developed a 'Toolbox for Collective Bargaining', which includes anti-violence contract clauses.

23. This is one of the contract clauses in the CLC's toolbox.

24. Canadian occupational health and safety laws are administered provincially and federally. The 10 provinces and the federal sector each have separate and distinct statutes covering health and safety. There are, therefore, essentially 11 jurisdictions for occupational laws in Canada.

25. The Canada Labour Code covers workers in federally regulated workplaces, including the federal public service, railway and highway transport, telephone and telecommunications systems, airports, banks and Crown corporations. The Labour Code was amended following tripartite consultations in September 2000.

26. Canada Labour Code, Part II, R.S., c. L-1, s. 1 (s. 125 (1) (z. 16) Duties of Employers).

27. Violence in the Workplace Regulation, BC Regulation 296/97, as amended by BC

Regulation 185/99. Workers' Compensation Board of British Columbia.

28. Occupational Health and Safety Regulations. Chapter O-1.1 of the Statutes of Saskatchewan.

29. Ibid.

30. Regulations Respecting Violence in the Workplace made pursuant to ss. 82(1) of Chapter 7 of the Statutes of Nova Scotia, 1996 (the Occupational Health and Safety Act).

Chapter 11

The Assaulted Staff Action Program (ASAP): ten year analysis of empirical findings

Raymond B. Flannery Jr

Introduction

Violence in healthcare worksites is a serious and continuing threat. Although healthcare providers may be victims of homicides, rapes and robberies, the most common form of workplace violence is that of patient assault on staff.[1] These assaults may result in death, permanent disability, medical injury, increased industrial accident claims and utilization of sick leave, lost productivity, weakened morale, medical and legal expense and intense human suffering in the form of psychological trauma.[2] In the USA the seriousness of this issue has led the federal government to issue guidelines for preventing violence in healthcare and social service settings.[3]

The characteristics of assaultive psychiatric patients have been the subject of three decades of empirical research (see the reviews[4]). The traditional assaultive patient has been identified as an older male with schizophrenia (or other neurological impairment), and past histories of violence towards others and substance-use disorder. More recent research (see review[5]) has noted the presence of a second high-risk group of assaultive patients: younger, equally male or female, personality-disordered individuals with past histories of violence towards others, personal victimization, and substance-use disorder. In both inpatient and community-based settings, the staff most at risk are the younger, less formally educated, less experienced mental health workers or community residential counsellors.[6]

Although medical injury services receive prompt attention, the psychological sequelae of these incidents often remain unaddressed and staff victims continue to suffer unnecessarily.[7] One approach to these needs is to provide crisis intervention services in critical incident stress management (CISM) approaches.[8] CISM represents a comprehensive, multifactorial model of crisis intervention procedures that spans a continuum from pre-incident training through acute crisis intervention to post-incident response.

Pre-incident training includes setting appropriate expectations for potential critical incident experiences as well as providing the cognitive and behavioural skills and resources to cope with these events. The acute-care phase refers to the delivery of differing types of individual, group, and family service interventions as the critical incident dictates. Post-incident response refers to any additional medical, psychiatric, financial, legal, or family services. Recent narrative[9] and empirical reviews[10] appear to demonstrate the efficacy of CISM interventions.

In 1990, I was asked by the director of nursing of a traditional state psychiatric hospital to design a psychological intervention programme for the facility's staff victims of patient assault. This programme, known as the Assaulted Staff Action Program (ASAP), is a voluntary, system-wide, peer-help, crisis intervention programme for staff victims of patient assault (physical and sexual assaults, non verbal intimidation and verbal threats).[11] ASAP is a CISM approach[12] in that it provides pre-incident training, an array of acute crisis interventions, and a range of post-incident responses.

This chapter will focus on the structure and functions of an ASAP and on the empirical findings of ASAP's ten years of service to its victim colleagues.

ASAP: its general nature

Philosophy

The basic domains that contribute to good physical and mental health include: reasonable mastery, the ability to shape the environment to meet one's needs; caring attachments to others, a network of social supports that provide companionship, information and instrumental support; and a meaningful purpose in life, a goal that motivates an individual to invest energy in the world each day to accomplish a task.[13] When violence occurs, each of these domains may be disrupted. Staff victims may additionally experience the symptoms associated with psychological trauma, especially hypervigilance, exaggerated startle response, sleep disturbance, intrusive recollections of the event, and a tendency to avoid the setting where the violence took place.[14] The purpose of all ASAP interventions is to restore reasonable mastery, to put in place a network of caring attachments, to help the victims make sense of why the violence has occurred, and to resolve any traumatic symptoms that may be present.

In addition, ASAP[15] is guided by five basic assumptions. First, ASAP believes that patient assaults can precipitate a crisis in staff victims. Secondly, ASAP believes that employees are worthy of the same compassionate care that is being provided to the patients. Thirdly, while staff may make errors in performing their duties, ASAP believes it is not the fault of staff when violence erupts. (Deliberate criminal behaviour by staff is dealt with by legal means.) Fourthly, ASAP believes it is easier for staff victims to talk to their peers about these critical incidents than to managers; and, fifthly, that talking helps to mitigate the immediate crisis and prevents or mitigates the subsequent development of post traumatic stress disorder (PTSD).[16]

All ASAP team members volunteer their services to their colleagues. No one is paid for his or her time, although compensatory time off is given if the team member is required to travel back to the facility during offshift hours to provide ASAP services. Participation in ASAP by staff victims is entirely voluntary. Since victims may blame themselves as a method of restoring the illusion of control and, thus, may not come forward for assistance, ASAP is a systems-wide programme in which each staff victim is contacted and offered assistance.

Its structure

The basic structure of ASAP includes first responders, ASAP team supervisors, and ASAP team leaders.[17] The first responders provide individual crisis interventions to staff victims. They are each part of an oncall beeper rotation for 24-hour periods during which they respond to each individual assault. They attend a weekly ASAP team meeting to review all cases and a monthly inservice educational programme to rehearse intervention skills and develop an extended knowledge base about psychological trauma, critical incidents and crisis intervention procedures.

The ASAP team supervisors are also on call by beeper on a weekly rotation. Supervisors provide second opinions to first responders in complicated situations, are available to do individual crisis interventions in cases of multiple assaults, and co-lead ASAP group interventions. They attend both the weekly team meetings and the monthly inservice education programmes. The ASAP team leader is the chief administrator and is responsible for monitoring the quality of all ASAP services that are rendered, for co-leading some of the group interventions, for providing inservice education for the team, and for providing crisis intervention services to ASAP team members, should circumstances warrant. ASAP maintains data anonymously and in the aggregate to monitor and improve the quality of ASAP services. ASAP team leaders record the data for each assault that occurs in their programmes. The team leaders themselves have a monthly team leaders' meeting with the director of the ASAP programme to address the needs of individual teams as they arise and to plan programmatic efforts as needs emerge.

Its services

As a CISM approach,[18] ASAP offers a range of crisis intervention services to meet specific facility needs as they are required at differing times.

Individual crisis counselling

When an assault occurs, the charge nurse on the unit is mandated to call ASAP. The first responder on call is activated by beeper and goes to the patient care site where the incident has taken place. The team member checks for safety on the unit and ascertains that all necessary medical attention has been completed. The staff victim is then offered the ASAP.

If the victim accepts, the ASAP representative reviews the facts of what has happened, assesses for disruptions in mastery, attachment and meaning and any PTSD symptoms, and provides the victim the opportunity to share his or her concerns and feelings. As the interview concludes, the team member seeks to restore in the victim some beginning sense of renewed mastery, a support network to talk with and a sense of why the event has occurred. The same ASAP team member contacts the staff victim three days later and, then again, ten days later to see if the victim is coping adequately or is in need of further ASAP services.

If the victim declines ASAP, the staff victim is given a set of handouts about the symptoms associated with psychological trauma and individual and family strategies for coping with the crisis. The victim is also given a card with the team member's facility phone extension, in case the victim decides at a later point that ASAP service might prove of assistance. Many victims do read these materials and later call for ASAP assistance.

Group crisis intervention

Some patient assaults are extensive and involve entire patient care sites. In these circumstances, ASAP provides group crisis interventions utilizing the critical incident stress debriefing model.[19] This approach reviews the facts, thoughts, and feelings experienced by victims in a series of seven steps. This intervention is done in group format and is co-led by the ASAP team leader and supervisors. This intervention is provided within 72 hours, if staffing and scheduling permit.

Staff victims' support group

For some staff victims, the individual ASAP crisis interventions need to be supplemented with additional services. One of these services is the staff victims' support group. Co-led by the ASAP team leader and supervisors, this group intervention provides an additional forum for staff victims to receive ongoing support and to review the impact of its critical incidents. The group is scheduled to overlap the first and second shifts so that all employees in need can attend.

Staff victim family outreach

Another additional ASAP service for some staff victims includes family crisis intervention. This issue is sometimes encountered by staff who are single parents. The staff victim may go home with a visible injury. The victim's children fear becoming orphans and do not want the parent to return to work. However, the parent needs to return to work to support the children. The staff victim parent is thus placed in a double-bind predicament. In these cases, ASAP team members who are also specialists in family therapy interventions will meet with the family to provide family crisis intervention.

Professional referrals

On occasion, an episode of assault at work precipitates intrusive recollections of past episodes of violence in the victim's life that are not work related. For example, a nurse is assaulted by a patient but suddenly is flooded with painful memories of physical abuse at the hands of a step-parent. In these cases, ASAP team members stabilize their colleague and referral is made to private therapists who specialize in trauma counselling.

All ASAP interventions focus on restoring mastery, attachment and meaning as well as resolving any symptoms associated with psychological trauma.[20] All ASAP services have been approved by unions and managers and are offered as free employee benefits. Only in the case of private referrals for personal issues does the employee's health insurance pay for services rendered.

All ASAP interventions are held in complete confidence. They do not become a part of the employee's medical or personnel record or employee performance review. Any administrative review of the incident is held after the ASAP intervention to avoid re-traumatizing the staff victim and is conducted with the information contained in the facility's incident report. ASAP information on the incident is not necessary and is not available for this administrative review. ASAP team leaders keep all original ASAP reports under separate lock and key. When this information is forwarded for quality management purposes, it is sent in anonymous aggregate format to the director of the ASAP, where the information is added to the database in a software program on a dedicated line that can only be accessed by the director.

The ASAP is modular and, therefore, flexible in meeting the differing needs of facilities. The size of any given team is a function of the number of assaults per week, the number of patient care sites to be served, the distance between these sites, and the total number of employees to be served. Teams can be housed within one facility (e.g. large state hospital) or be mobile across sites (e.g. a community-based residential housing programme with 29 sites in three towns). Although this chapter focuses on healthcare settings, ASAP could easily be fielded in school settings, correction facilities, and industrial environments where repeated acts of violence may be reasonably expected.

ASAP: empirical findings

From April 1990 to April 2000, there were 16 ASAP teams in three states. These teams have had over 500 members, and volunteered 420,000 hours of service to 3,500 employees. Four of these teams were deactivated due to downsizing and facility closure. Currently, 12 teams remain online in these states. During this period, the 13 Massachusetts teams that were fielded responded to 1,033 incidents of assault. ASAP was accepted in 929 cases (90%) and declined in 104 incidents (10%). There were 572 male (55%) and 457 female (45%) staff victims in both inpatient (77%) and community settings (23%).

The studies reported here in summary format are based on data gathered from the 13 Massachusetts teams during this 10-year period. All data were gathered within the context of the ASAP[21] and all studies have been peer reviewed. Full references are provided for readers who may wish to read any particular study in its entirety. The studies are grouped according to the CISM phases of pre-incident training, acute care services and post-incident response.

Pre-incident training phase

ASAP pre-incident training in Massachusetts routinely includes setting appropriate expectations for assault incidents as well as the provision of cognitive and behavioural resources to cope more effectively. These include the training of all employees in non violent self-defence procedures, restraint and seclusion interventions, alternatives to restraint and seclusion, and effective communication with patients. Employees are additionally instructed in the profiles of the patients most statistically likely to be assaultive.

Since ASAP routinely gathers information about the characteristics of patient assailants at the time of each incident, three ASAP studies[22] have been able to provide additional information on patients that present high risk for assault. The first study[23] was an examination of the characteristics of assaultive patients in both inpatient and community-based settings during this 10-year period. In addition to documenting the continued presence of the traditionally assaultive patient (older male with schizophrenia or other neurologic abnormality and past violence towards others and substance-use disorder),[24] this paper was among the first to document the newer category of assailant who is younger, equally likely to be male or female, personality disordered and to have histories of violence towards others and substance-use disorder. (A study of the repetitively violent patients during this 10-year period is currently being conducted.)

The second study[22] examined in greater detail the possible inter-relationships between past violence towards others, personal victimization, and substance-use disorder and later subsequent violence. All three variables were examined individually and jointly and all three were associated with subsequent violence. Violence towards others and personal victimization together had a statistically significant association with subsequent violence than either singly. Substance-use disorder in combination with violence towards others and personal victimization had an increased statistically significant association with subsequent violence than with either violence towards others or personal victimization alone.

The third study related to pre-incident issues[25] and was an inquiry into the time when assault incidents took place. Staff did not appear at equal risk during all work hours. This study confirmed that in inpatient settings assaults tended to occur more frequently during meal times during the first shift, when general ward activity was heightened. In community-based residential settings, the greatest risk occurred during the second shift in the later evening, when patients were preparing for bed.

Acute care phase

Four ASAP studies have examined the provision of acute care-crisis intervention services.[26]

A 10-year analysis of the characteristics of staff victims served by ASAP[27] confirmed earlier findings[28] that younger, less experienced, less formally trained employees in both inpatient and community settings were at highest risk for victimization. The findings also revealed substantial reductions in disruptions in the domains of mastery, attachment and meaning, as well as the symptoms associated with psychological trauma,[29] after ASAP interventions were completed.

Two ASAP studies examined the role of gender in both victims and assailants.[30] One study[31] examined this issue during ASAP's first 2 years; the second,[32] its last 6 years. In the first study,[33] female inpatient staff were found to be at increased risk from same-gender assaults (female staff victim–female patient assailant) and female residential counsellors to be at increased risk of different-gender assault (female staff victim–male patient assailant). The second study[34] documented a significant shift in risk for female residential counsellors. While female inpatient staff confronted the same-gender risk, female community staff were at equal risk from both male and female patients. Male staff were at risk from male patients in all settings in both studies.

The final acute care study considered the cost-effectiveness of the ASAP approach,[35] and used staff turnover as the outcome measure. In the first ASAP, 15 staff turnovers were associated with patient assaults during the 2 years prior to ASAP. During the 2 years after ASAP was fielded, US$40,000 in volunteered time and a replacement cost per employee of US$12,000, the first ASAP team saved its hospital US$268,000 on this one outcome measure alone during its first 2 years of operation.

Post-incident response phase

In all facilities with ASAP, post-incident assistance included private referrals, when indicated, and an administrative/clinical review of each assault incident to ensure safety and to review the patient's treatment plan so that the risk of additional assaults was reduced.

ASAP has often been associated with an additional post-incident response of sharp reductions in assault rates in facilities where ASAP has been fielded properly. An unanticipated finding of a sharp reduction in the assault rate after ASAP was fielded in its original setting[36] has been replicated in each of three state hospitals[37] and in two community mental health settings[38] and suggests that ASAP may be a risk management strategy in its own right. It may be that, as staff feel supported, they become less anxious. As they become less anxious, the patients may become less anxious and assaults decline.

To be sure this decline was due to ASAP and not some other variable such as staff enthusiasm for ASAP, a meta-analysis was conducted which indicated that the declines in assault appeared, in fact, to be a function of ASAP.[39]

Research issues

Taken collectively, these findings provide initial support for the effectiveness of ASAP in enhancing workplace safety and in providing high-quality care to staff victims of workplace violence when it does occur. However, these are preliminary findings and there remains the need for ongoing research.

Although extensive anecdotal evidence from staff victims suggests the helpfulness of ASAP interventions, there remains the need for a true randomized controlled study to assess whether ASAP is effective in mitigating acute stress disorder and in mitigating or preventing PTSD.[40] Research of this nature needs to be cognizant of the ethical issue of withholding ASAP interventions from a facility or individual staff victim, since ASAP is associated with sharp declines in levels of assault. For this reason, ASAP research to date has utilized multiple baseline designs. However, if some institution decided not to field ASAP, it might then be compared to a similar matched institution where ASAP was fielded and a true randomized study might then be possible.

All employees in the second institution would need to be evaluated for PTSD prior to fielding ASAP and critical incidents befalling staff that were unrelated to patient assault at work would need to be monitored during the course of the study. ASAP would then be fielded in the first constitution. Those employees who were staff victims of patient assault but who were not victims of other potentially traumatizing events could then be compared pre- and post-ASAP interventions for possible remaining signs of acute stress disorder or PTSD.[41] Staff victims in the control facility could similarly be tested. This same methodology could also be used to evaluate any decline in assaults after ASAP was fielded by comparing the assault rates in both facilities during the course of the study.

Additional future studies need to address the severity of assaults and the severity of the impact on staff victims. Studies of the different types of assaults by gender of both staff victim and patient assailant may yield important information on the differing impact of different types of assault.

The need to assist staff victims of patient assault is widespread. The ASAP[42] at the moment is the most widely researched crisis intervention programme in the world. It appears to offer one reasonable approach to alleviate the human suffering of staff victims of patient assault.

Notes

1. Blair, D.T. (1991) Assaultive behaviour: does provocation begin in the front office? *Journal of Psychosocial Nursing* 27, 21–26; American Psychiatric Association (1992) *Clinician Safety. Task Force Report* 33. Washington, DC: American Psychiatric Association; Davis, S. (1991) Violence in psychiatric inpatients: a review. *Hospital and Community Psychiatry* 42, 585–90; Flannery, R.B. Jr, Hanson, M.A. and Penk, W.E. (1994a) Risk factors for psychiatric inpatient assaults on staff. *Journal of Mental Health Administration* 21, 24–31.
2. Caldwell, M.E. (1992) The incidence of PTSD among staff victims of patient violence. *Hospital and Community Psychiatry* 43, 586–88; Hunter, M. and Carmel, H. (1992) The cost of staff injuries from inpatient violence. *Hospital and Community Psychiatry* 43, 586–88; American Psychiatric Association (1992) op. cit.; Blair op. cit.; Davis op. cit.; Flannery *et al*. (1994a) op. cit.
3. Occupational Safety and Health Administration (1996) *Guidelines for Preventing Workplace Violence for Health Care and Social Service Workers*. Washington, DC: United States Department of Labor.
4. Blair op. cit.; Davis op. cit.; Flannery *et al*. (1994a) op. cit.
5. Flannery, R.B. Jr (2001) Characteristics of assaultive inpatients: updated review of findings 1995–2000. *American Journal of Alzheimer's Disease and other Dementias* 16, 153–156.
6. Blair op. cit.; Flannery *et al*. (1994a) op. cit.; Flannery (2001) op. cit.
7. Caldwell op. cit.
8. Everly, G.S. Jr and Mitchell, J.T. (1999) *Critical Incident Stress Management (CISM): A New Era and Standard of Care in Crisis Intervention* (2nd edn). New York: Plenum.
9. Everly, G.S. Jr, Flannery, R.B. Jr and Mitchell, J.T. (2000) Critical incident stress management (CISM): a review of the literature. *Aggression and Violent Behavior: A Review Journal* 5, 23–40.
10. Everly, G.S. Jr, Flannery, R.B. Jr and Eyler, V. (2001) Critical incident stress

management (CISM): a statistical review of the literature. *Psychiatric Quarterly* in press.

11. Flannery, R.B. Jr (1998) *The Assaulted Staff Action Program (ASAP): Coping with the Psychological Aftermath of Violence*. Ellicott City, MD: Chevron Publishing.

12. Everly and Mitchell, op. cit.

13. Flannery, R.B. Jr (1994) *Post-Traumatic Stress Disorder: The Victim's Guide to Healing and Recovery*. New York: Crossroad Publishing.

14. American Psychiatric Association (1994) *The Diagnostic and Statistical Manual of Mental Disorders* (4th edn). Washington, DC: American Psychiatric Association.

15. Flannery (1998) op. cit.

16. Flannery (1994) op. cit.; American Psychiatric Association (1994) op. cit.

17. Flannery (1998) op. cit.

18. Everly and Mitchell op. cit.

19. Mitchell, J.T. and Everly, G.S. Jr (1996) *Critical Incident Stress Debriefing (CISD): An Operations Manual for the Prevention of Traumatic Stress among Emergency Services and Disaster Workers* (2nd edn). Ellicott City, MD: Chevron Publishing.

20. American Psychiatric Association (1994) op. cit.

21. Flannery (1994) op. cit.

22. Flannery, R.B. Jr, Schuler, A.P., Farley, E.M. and Walker, A.P. (2001) Characteristics of assaultive psychiatric patients: ten year analysis of the Assaulted Staff Action Program (ASAP). *Psychiatric Quarterly* 72, 237–248; Flannery, R.B. Jr, Stevens, V., Juliano, J. and Walker, A.P. (2000) Past violence and substance use disorder and subsequent violence toward others: six year analysis of the Assaulted Staff Action Program (ASAP). *International Journal of Emergency Mental Health* 2, 241–247; Flannery, R.B. Jr, Corrigan, M., Tierney, T. and Walker, A.P. (2001) Time and risk of psychiatric patient assault: ten year analysis of the Assaulted Staff Action Program (ASAP). *Journal of Health Care Safety, Compliance, and Infection Control*, 5, 31–35.

23. Flannery, Schuler *et al.* (2001) op. cit.

24. Blair op. cit.; Davis op. cit.; Flannery *et al.* (1994a) op. cit.

25. Flannery, Corrigan *et al.* (2001) op. cit.

26. Flannery, R.B. Jr, Stone, P., Rego, S. and Walker, A.P. (2001) Characteristics of staff victims: ten year analysis of the Assaulted Staff Action Program (ASAP). *Psychiatric Quarterly* 72, 239–250; Flannery, R.B. Jr, Hanson, M.A., Penk, W.E. and Flannery, G.J. (1994b) Violence against women: psychiatric patient assaults on female staff. *Professional Psychology: Research and Practice* 25, 182–84; Flannery, R.B. Jr, Lizotte, D., Laudani, L., Staffieri, A. and Walker, A.P. (2001) Violence against women and the Assaulted Staff Action Program (ASAP): psychiatric patient assaults on female staff. Administration and Policy in Mental Health, in press; Flannery *et al.* (1994a) op. cit.

27. Flannery, Sculer *et al.* (2001) op. cit.

28. Blair op. cit.; Davis op. cit.; Flannery *et al.* (1994a) op. cit.

29. Flannery (1994) op. cit.; American Psychiatric Association (1994) op. cit.

30. Flannery *et al.* (1994b) op. cit., Flannery, Lizotte *et al.* (2001) op. cit.

31. Flannery *et al.* (1994b) op. cit.

32. Flannery, Lizotte *et al.* (2001) op. cit.

33. Flannery *et al.* (1994b) op. cit.
34. Flannery, Lizotte *et al.* (2001) op. cit.
35. Flannery *et al.* (1994a) op. cit.
36. Flannery, R.B. Jr, Hanson, M.A., Penk, W.E., Flannery, G.J. and Gallagher, C. (1995) The Assaulted Staff Action Program: an approach to coping with the aftermath of violence in the workplace. In Murphy, L. *et al.* (eds.) *Job Stress Intervention*. Washington, DC: American Psychological Association.
37. Flannery, R.B. Jr, Hanson, M.A., Penk, W.E., Goldfinger, S., Pastva, G. and Navon, M. (1998) Replicated declines in assault rates after the implementation of the Assaulted Staff Action Program. *Psychiatric Services* 49, 242–43.
38. Flannery, R.B. Jr, Penk, W.E. and Corrigan, M. (1999) The Assaulted Staff Action Program (ASAP) and declines in the prevalence of assaults: community-based replication. *International Journal of Emergency Mental Health* 1, 19–22; Flannery, R.B. Jr, Anderson, E., Marks, L. and Uzoma, L. (2000) The Assaulted Staff Action Program (ASAP) and declines in rates of assault: mixed replicated findings. *Psychiatric Quarterly* 71, 165–75.
39. Flannery, R.B. Jr, Everly, G.S. Jr and Everly, V. (2000) The Assaulted Staff Action Program (ASAP) and declines in assaults: a meta-analysis. *International Journal of Emergency Mental Health* 2, 143–49.
40. Flannery (1994) op. cit.; American Psychiatric Association (1994) op. cit.
41. Flannery (1994) op. cit.; American Psychiatric Association (1994) op. cit.
42. Flannery (1998) op. cit.

Chapter 12

Violence at work: supporting the employee

Noreen Tehrani

Introduction

When asked to describe traumatic incidents in the workplace many people will describe major incidents such as the *Piper Alpha* Disaster, the Omagh bomb or the Australian Bush fires. Less well acknowledged are the horror and distress caused by less dramatic incidents, including workplace violence, bullying[1] and victimization.[2] Unlike major disasters that affect a relatively small number of employees, interpersonal conflicts and other traumatic experiences have a profound effect on the physical and psychological well-being of a large number of employees.[3] Unfortunately, many of these traumatic incidents go unreported and therefore the size of their impact on employee health is largely unrecognized. The under-reporting, although unfortunate, is less surprising when one considers the attitudes held by many workers exposed to high levels of violence, victimization and abuse who have come to regard personal attacks and violent abuse as 'part of the job'. This macho culture has been found to be particularly prevalent in hospitals and GP practices,[4] the police force,[5] public houses[6] and the construction industry.[7] Whilst individual incidences of violence, abuse or victimization may not immediately result in psychological trauma to the exposed employee, the prolonged exposure and gradual build up of traumatic experiences can lead to a cumulative form of traumatic stress.[8]

There is a wide range of incidents that can lead to employees suffering from traumatic stress. Table 12.1 details organizational incidents that can result in employees experiencing traumatic stress symptoms. It is not surprising that interpersonal conflict and violence are some of the most common causes of traumatic stress.

Table 12.1 Four types of traumatic events found in organizations

Operational	Interpersonal
• Exposure to biological hazard (AIDS) • Exposure to a carcinogen (asbestos) • Exposure to noxious fumes • Destruction of workplace • Institutionalized victimization • Community opposition and violence	• Death of a colleague • Witnessing a colleague being injured • Exposed to a violent strike/picketing • Suicide of colleague at work • Bullying • Victimization and verbal abuse
Criminal	Physical injuries caused by
• Bomb threat • Mugging • Blackmail • Violent attack/threats • Sabotage/vandalism	• Vehicle crash • Equipment failure/misuse • Small-scale fires • Lifting and handling • Pranks/'jokes'

The development of trauma care systems

The development of trauma care systems and interventions within organizations has been strongly influenced by the experience of organizations whose employees regularly deal with life-threatening and distressing events. Warfare is one of the most traumatic events with armed conflict leaving psychological scars on almost everyone involved.[9] The psychological impact of war on armed forces has been documented over the centuries, yet little has been done to relieve this suffering of traumatized soldiers until the latter stages of First World War.[10] During that war one of the main findings was the importance of providing immediate trauma treatments close to the scene of the action. The principles (immediacy, proximity and expectancy) involve the provision of immediate support, in the proximity of the action, with the expectancy that the soldier would be returning to the scene of conflict as soon as possible. These basic principles continue to influence present-day trauma care programmes. The actual interventions used in the early years were not particularly systematic, being based on individual symptomatology. However, research by the Israeli Army during the war with Lebanon has produced a more systematic approach, which includes psychological first aid and the use of group support.[11]

Emergency services, in particular the fire services, have also had a strong influence on the development of organizational approaches to trauma care. A major disaster, the Coconut Grove fire, which occurred in Boston, Massachusetts in 1943, was particularly important. The magnitude of the fire (which killed over 400 people) required those involved in supporting the victims to develop a more standardized and systematic approach than had been previously the case. Lindermann, a psychiatrist involved in dealing with the disaster, designed a system of crisis management that has been influential in the development of present-day trauma care.[12] In recent years other workers have built upon the principles of crisis management and developed a systematic approach to the provision of psychological first aid, social support, assessment, debriefing and treatment following violent incidents and disasters.[13, 14] These approaches established the principles on which current-day trauma care programmes within organizations have been established.

Organizational trauma care programmes

Organizations that regularly expose their employees to violent or traumatic incidents cannot avoid the psychological consequences of this exposure on their employees. The organizational cost of traumatic stress is high and is paid for in terms of sickness absence, medical retirements and costly litigation. The need to deal with the psychological impact of exposure to violent incidents and disasters has prompted the introduction of organizational trauma care programmes. In a comprehensive review of UK trauma management programmes[15] it was found that most programmes followed a similar pattern that involves three main stages, namely: immediate crisis management, trauma debriefing and trauma counselling. Some organizations have taken a more proactive view in the development of their programmes. These organizations have undertaken risk assessments, developed employee selection criteria, provided awareness training for new recruits, increased employee coping skills and trained managers and peers to help traumatized colleagues.[16–20]

The key stages of a trauma care programme

A systematic approach to dealing with violent and traumatic incidents in the workplace is essential. Table 12.2 illustrates the core trauma care programme adopted in the UK Post Office. The Post Office employees were involved in a wide range of traumatic incidents ranging from armed raids, physical attacks, threats of violence and verbal abuse. This programme has six main stages. The first stage begins before the traumatic event and the final stage is involved in the audit and evaluation of the total programme. The successful execution of each stage of the programme is important to the success of subsequent stages of the programme.

Table 12.2   The core trauma care programme developed in the Post Office

Stages of response for a trauma case programme		
Stage –1	Selection, pre-incident information and induction	Pre-trauma training to help employees develop the appropriate level of knowledge and skills to deal with a traumatic incident
Stage 1	Crisis management and diffusing	Immediate personal and organizational needs are met. This may include first aid, personal support, dealing with the police and media. During stage 1 employees are also given an opportunity to talk about the traumatic incident to a peer or manager, and information on debriefing and traumatic stress responses will be given to the employee
Stage 2	First-line debriefing	Recognizes the operational and organizational aspects of the trauma and provides an early opportunity for the traumatized employee to make sense of his or her experience. An opportunity to provide education and information on the nature of traumatic stress and traumatic stress reactions
Stage 3	Psychological debriefing	A more in-depth debrief where the thinking and emotional aspects of the trauma can be explored fully and an

		assessment of the ongoing needs undertaken. Training in how to deal with the major trauma responses, including arousal, re-experience and avoidance, is provided.
Stage 4	Trauma counselling /psychiatric care	Where the employee requires further support, a referral for trauma counselling and/or psychiatric care is offered
Stage 5	Auditing and evaluation	Individual cases are followed up to ensure that progress is maintained and delayed reactions identified. Performance is measured against agreed criteria (e.g. employee satisfaction data, reductions in sickness absence and medical retirements)

Stage -1: selection, induction training and education

In stage −1, the organization assess all potential employees for their suitability for the work, which is likely to involve dealing with traumatic incidents. Following selection a recruit is provided with training and education on how to avoid situations that are psychologically damaging and on the coping skills that will help him or her deal with his or her responses to traumatic stress. The implementation of stage −1 helps the overall programme by reducing the number of employees who are particularly susceptible to becoming traumatized following a distressing incident, and it also helps employees to recognize when they need additional post-trauma support.

Stage I: crisis management and diffusing

This stage is important. The way employees are treated immediately following a traumatic incident can have a significant impact on their recovery and on the way the organization is perceived. Handling a crisis involves a number of skills, including evaluating the situation and anticipating needs, maintaining communications, delegating authority to act and dealing with the stress of the situation.[21] In the Post Office checklists were provided, which helped managers to work through what needed to be done in a systematic way. Following a traumatic experience, many employees need an opportunity to talk about what has happened to them. The process of diffusing is very important to the programme as it provides an opportunity for the traumatized employee to talk about his or her experience. Although diffusing is frequently disregarded in the formal trauma care programme, in most organizations it is a naturally occurring phenomenon. Employees who have shared an experience will take time to discuss their experience in an attempt to understand what has happened.

Stage 2: first-line debriefing

In the trauma care model designed in the Post Office, first-line debriefing was carried out by peers or managers trained in these skills. Unlike other models of debriefing, this model does not explore thoughts or feelings but rather works systematically through the actual traumatic incident gathering information on what actually happened (i.e. what was seen, heard, touched, tasted and smelt). The debriefing starts before the event and ends at the present. There are two first-line debriefing models; the first deals with groups of employees and the second with individuals.

Stage 3: psychological debriefing

This debrief[22] is suitable for individuals and is undertaken by a trained psychologist, counsellor or other health professional. In the psychological debrief the story is gone through three times: in the first telling of the story, the facts are elicited; in the second telling, the thoughts connected to those facts are established and then finally the feelings evoked by the facts and thoughts are described. This gradual unfolding of the trauma story has the effect of reducing the emotional responses to the traumatic event.

Stage 4: trauma counselling and psychiatric care

The Post Office did not undertake any trauma counselling or psychiatric care internally. Referrals were made to an external counselling organization or to the employee's general practitioner. Following counselling or psychiatric interventions, the employee would be followed up and, where necessary, rehabilitation programmes would be established.

Stage 5: auditing and evaluation

Occupational health physicians and the occupational health psychologist monitored the trauma care programme in the Post Office. This process involved looking at the levels of sickness absence and monitoring the progress of individual employees.

The programme developed within the Post Office was successful in addressing the needs of the employees and the organization, with 90% of users being satisfied or very satisfied with the service and the organization achieving a 50% reduction in sickness absence and medical retirements.[23] The success of the Post Office trauma care programme in providing a service that was valued by both employees and organizations was dependent upon a number of issues. However, one important factor was the tailoring of the programmes to suit the needs and culture of the business. Experience in the introduction of trauma care programme has shown that, unless the programme is integrated with existing policies and procedures, the likelihood of an effective implementation will be low.[24]

Organizational culture

It has been recognized that introduction of counselling and trauma care programmes requires the provider to have a clear understanding of the organisational culture.[25] Hofstede[26] describes a number of organizational cultural types. Two of the cultural dimensions are of particular importance to the introduction of trauma care. These dimensions are 'power versus autonomy' and 'tender-heartedness versus tough-mindedness' (Figure 12.1). The interactions between these two dimensions create four organizational culture types (paternalistic, macho idol, supportive and survival of the fittest). Power cultures, which are dominated by a central power source, encourage an environment where

Figure 12.1   Organizational cultures and their impact on trauma care

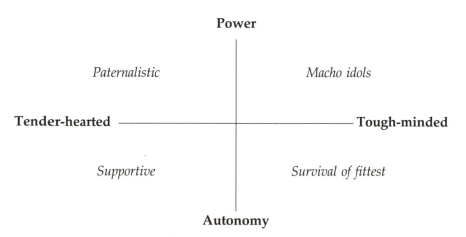

employees expect to be told what to do. Where the power culture is accompanied by tender-heartedness, the organization will have a paternalistic approach to its employees. 'Paternalistic' organizations will be anxious that anyone affected by a traumatic event is provided with trauma care, whether or not he or she wants that care. Where the power culture is associated with tough-mindedness, the organization is likely to have developed a mythology relating to the 'macho idols' from past traumatic incidents. These organizations will tend to emphasize the need to train their employees on how to cope with traumatic situations and may even glory in recounting the achievements of horrifying events from the past where the 'macho idols' were able to deal with the horrors of a disaster without problems. In this culture it is unlikely that an employee would feel able to discuss his or her feelings and will be inhibited in asking for help. 'Macho idol' organizations are likely to be resistant to the introduction of trauma care programmes, as they do not believe they are required.

Autonomous cultures give power to the individual and where the autonomous culture is tender-hearted, there will be a strong emphasis on people and relationships. In these 'supportive' organizations management and employees will wish to support each other in the aftermath of a traumatic event. When developing trauma care programmes in these supportive organizations it is important to recognize and respect the need of management and peers to be involved with the provision of care. This often results in the immediate support being provided by the employees, who would be trained and supported by trauma experts. In organizations where the culture is tough-minded and autonomous, the environment is one in which only the fittest can survive. The 'survival of the fittest' organization attracts employees who want to be seen as individuals where everyone is expected to look after themselves. In these organizations, senior managers reward the strong and get rid of the weak. In the 'survival of the fittest' organizations, the main focus is on how to identify the employee who will cope well with traumatic events. Trauma care programmes in this type of organization are often tasked with looking for a test or technique the organization can use to make sure it only recruits employees who are 'psychologically robust' and to eliminate those who are likely to be vulnerable to traumatic stress.

When introducing a trauma care programme, the organizational culture will also determine the way in which the programme will be judged. A criterion that is regarded as vital to the academic researcher, such as establishing and comparing a randomized treatment group with a control group,[27] is likely to be viewed as unworkable and unnecessary by most organizations. Experience gained in the development of a number of trauma care programmes has shown that the success criteria most frequently chosen relate directly to the organizations need to manage an effective business operation. The measures organizations value are those that provide tangible evidence of success and that, ideally, are related to an estimate of financial benefit. An over-complex programme that requires a large investment of management time and resources is unlikely to be acceptable. An analysis of the success criteria chosen by six organizations identified five areas of importance (Table 12.3). The success of the programmes was monitored by feedback from the users obtained from questionnaires and focus groups.

Table 12.3   Trauma care programmes: organizational success criteria

Area	Criteria for success
Organizational appropriateness of the programme	Does the programme match the needs of the organization?
Level of satisfaction or benefit recorded by the users of the programme	How do the users rate the programme? Would they use the service again? Would they recommend it to a colleague?
Reduction of sickness absence and medical treatments	Did the programme reduce the levels of sickness absence and medical retirements? What was the financial benefit?
Quality of the training educational materials	How useful was the training? How informative was the educational material?
Quality of professional support to employees and managers	What was the quality of professional support? Did it meet agreed service standards?

Organizations tend to be less interested in the clinical evaluation of interventions, instead concentrating their interest on the practical benefits that can be achieved by introducing trauma care. Where traumatic stress questionnaires are offered as part of a programme, their acceptance is more likely to be due to their value as a means of identifying employees who may require additional counselling or support rather than as a means of evaluating the effectiveness of the programme. Organizations are more likely to choose a business-related outcome, such as a reduction in sickness absence, as their preferred evaluation tool.

Evaluation studies

One of the important main elements of trauma care programmes is that of debriefing. Although debriefing is widely used and there is evidence it is valued by both debriefers and employees,[28] there is little evidence from clinical research to support it as an effective treatment. In a major review of debriefing[29] it was found that the experimental design and control of much of the published research on debriefing were inadequate. The review identified only six studies that met the minimum levels of design and control and found that of the six studies two showed that debriefing had a positive outcome, two demonstrated no effect and two identified some negative effects. It is clear that there is a need for further evaluation studies. However, it is important to look at some of the existing studies as a means of understanding some of the issues involved.

Work-based studies

Deahl et al.[30]
This study looked at the impact of debriefing on soldiers who had taken part in the Gulf war. The findings were that debriefing did not reduce trauma symptoms and that debriefing had no effect on the development of psychiatric disorders. There were a number of serious methodological problems with this study, the most serious being that the groups were formed on the basis of self-selection rather than by random assignment, and the fact that no baseline measures were taken. The authors of this research were aware of this methodological problem but reported that they were still committed to the principles of debriefing.

Kenardy et al.[31]
This study looked at rescue personnel who had been involved in an earthquake. No differences were found between employees who had been debriefed and those who had not been debriefed. However, once again the groups that were self-selected were asked whether they wished to be debriefed or not. Despite the lack of hard evidence on the

effectiveness of debriefing, the researchers reported that 80% of those debriefed found the debriefing helpful.

Tehrani [32]

This study looked at the effect of the introduction of a trauma care programme where debriefing formed a major element. The employees in these organizations had been exposed to armed raid, physical attacks, verbal abuse and threats of violence. The study showed that, in one organization, there was a 50% reduction in sickness absence and medical retirements compared with the pre-introduction levels. In the second organization there was a 32% reduction in stress-related sickness absence and medical retirements compared with pre-introduction.

These studies do not evaluate debriefing as the debriefing was only undertaken as part of the larger trauma care programme.

Non-work-based studies

Lee et al. [33]

In this study women who had suffered an early miscarriage were offered debriefing. These women were randomly put into one of two groups, one of which was debriefed. The women were screened at intervals and no differences were found between the two groups on the Impact of Events Scale (IES) and Hospital Anxiety Depression Scale (HADS). This study has been criticized on the grounds that this was not a suitable group for debriefing and that a single hour of consultation was a totally inadequate response to a bereavement of this nature.[34]

Hobbs et al. [35]

This study looked at road-traffic crash victims. There were two randomized groups. The debriefing was undertaken in hospital between 24 and 48 hours following the crash. No differences were found between the debriefed group and the control group on most of the measures. This study has been criticized on the grounds it is inappropriate to undertake debriefing while an individual is suffering physical pain and injury. Dyregrov[36] describes this study (at best) as bad clinical practice and (at worst) as highly unethical.

Bisson et al. [37]

The subjects in this study were burns victims. There were two groups, with the debriefing taking between 30 minutes and 120 minutes. The results showed the debriefed group had higher levels of traumatic stress at 13 months. This study has been criticized on two major grounds. First, that the people in the debriefed group had suffered more trauma in the past than the control group and, secondly, that the timing of the debriefing was inappropriate.[38]

These findings are used to challenge the continuing use of debriefing[39] and have left organizations confused about what to do to make sure their trauma care programmes are actually assisting in the recovery of their traumatized employees.

The criticisms of debriefing have led to a heated debate among trauma experts from Australia, the USA and Europe and have led some organizations to discontinue their use of debriefing[40] Other organizations (convinced that debriefing is an important element of their trauma care programme) have continued its use but with an increasing awareness of the need to undertake some form of evaluation.[41]

A case study

On 5 October 1999, at one of the busiest times of the day on the rail network, two commuter trains, packed with passengers, crashed a few minutes outside the mainline Paddington railway station in London. A number of carriages were severely damaged by the impact and the resultant fire destroyed sections of the train. The crash occurred at Ladbroke Grove on a section of track that was overlooked by blocks of flats, a supermarket and a railway bridge. Some of the first people on the scene were employees of the supermarket who not only found ladders to help passengers climb up from the rail track to the safety of the supermarket's car park but also provided immediate first aid, emotional support and comfort. The supermarket's employees handled this major disaster with efficiency and a level of human kindness that have been acknowledged by passengers, bereaved families and the wider community. This story has touched the hearts of the British public. However, there is also another story that is perhaps not so widely known. The supermarket's management has learnt over the years that, when employees are faced with incidents that expose them to situations that involve actual or potential death or serious injury, there is a need to provide immediate and ongoing support. The supermarket's violence at work policy that had previously been used to deal with work-related incidents (such as armed raids and threats of violence) was activated immediately by the occupational health service. A small team of occupational health advisers was present in the store on the day of the incident and remained throughout the following week. Informal diffusing and the identification of all those involved in the rescue were undertaken. The atmosphere during this early stage was highly emotional: the problems of recovering bodies and clearing the track took over two weeks, during which time the employees were faced with a constant reminder of what had happened. One week after the crash, all the employees were invited to a group debriefing session. A psychologist specializing in traumatic stress led this debriefing session, supported by two occupational health advisers. The session began with each of the employees completing a trauma questionnaire[42] and with a short presentation on post-trauma stress, which was designed to allow the employees to ask questions and gain clarification on why they were having particular symptoms or reactions to the incident. The employees were then offered an opportunity to take part in a group debrief. All the employees opted to take part in the group debrief, which went through their experience of the incident in great detail, focusing on their behaviours together with the things that were seen, heard, smelt, touched and tasted. The debrief allowed gaps in the story to be filled, and participants were given an opportunity to check their understanding and share their knowledge. Perhaps even more significant were the changes in attitude that had occurred. At the beginning of the debrief, the participants talked about those things they would have liked to have done, but did not do. At the end of the debrief colleagues were telling each other what they had done allowing for the group recognition they had done a good job, despite the difficulties.

Employees who had high scores on the trauma questionnaire were offered an opportunity to have individual trauma counselling. This was undertaken during the following month.

Four months after the crash, the employees completed the trauma questionnaire a second time. The results showed that the symptoms for all the employees had reduced dramatically and the employees reported that the support that had been provided by the store manager, the personnel manager, the occupational health service and by the psychologist was very helpful in the recovery process.[43]

Discussion

There are few organizations where there is a total absence of violent attacks, be they physical or psychological. There is a clear need for organizations to respond appropriately to all forms of violence in order to protect the psychological well-being of employees. With the increasingly complex and technological world, the likelihood of organizations having to deal with large-scale disasters is growing. Unless organizations consider this possibility and put plans in place for handling the full range of incidents from bullying, physical attacks, threats, serious injury and death, they may find they are unable to respond appropriately to the needs of business and their workforce. Although many organizations have introduced trauma care programmes, few have undertaken evaluations of these programmes that meet the rigour required by academic researchers, yet organizations and employees appear to have a high level of satisfaction with the effectiveness of this support in helping the recovery process.

The current debate raises a number of important questions:

- To be successful, is it enough to show that a trauma care programme meets organizational expectations (e.g. highly valued by the users and reduces levels of sickness absence)?

- In order to evaluate trauma care programmes, is it ethically and morally acceptable to withhold interventions from some employees in order to 'prove' that debriefing or some other aspects of the trauma care programme are effective?

- Can we trust the validity and reliability of clinical assessment tools designed for use in hospitals or laboratory settings with the normal employees found in the workplace?

Despite the current debate trauma care programmes adopted by organizations meet a number of needs. First, they enable the organization to deal with the traumatic event in a systematic way, ensuring the needs of the employees and of the business are met. Secondly, they demonstrate an organizational commitment to employees and their well-being. Thirdly, they provide an opportunity for employees to share their experiences with their peers in order to increase awareness and to build a shared understanding of the meaning of the incident to the working team. Finally, they help the organization to identify those employees who need additional help. It is difficult to know exactly where trauma care is going in the future. It seems strange that so much effort should go into evaluating debriefing, which forms a very small part of the overall organizational approach. Perhaps what is required is for organizations to be more involved in telling the academic world what they regard as success criteria so that a balance can be achieved between the clinical and the organizational benefits of a trauma care programme. Despite some limitations, there are some clear indications that organizational debriefing is an effective and valued part of the trauma care programme. Demands for the withdrawal of this approach without considering the positive evidence gathered in organizational settings are premature and may lead to countless employees suffering psychological symptoms unnecessarily.

Notes

1. Lipsedge, M. (2000) Bullying, post-traumatic stress disorder and violence at work. In Baxter, P.J. *et al.* (eds.) *J.M. Hunter's Diseases of Occupations.* London: Arnold; Leymann, H. and Gustafsson, A. (1996) Mobbing at work and the development of post traumatic stress disorders. *European Journal of Work and Organisational Psychology* 5(2), 251–75.
2. Joseph, S., Williams, R. and Yule, W. (1997) *Understanding Post-Traumatic Stress: A Psychosocial Perspective on PTSD and Treatment.* Chichester: Wiley.
3. Wynne, R. and Clarkin, N. (1995) Workplace violence in Europe – it is time to act. *Work and Stress* 9(4), 377–79.
4. Brady, C. and Dickson, R. (1999) Violence in health care settings. In Leather, P. *et al.* (eds.) *Work-Related Violence: Assessment and Intervention.* London: Routledge.
5. Paton, D. and Smith, L. (1999) Assessment, conceptual and methodological issues in researching traumatic stress in police officers. In Violanti, J.M. and Paton, D. (eds.) *Police Trauma: Psychological Aftermath of Civilian Combat.* Springfield, IL: Charles C. Thomas.
6. Beale, D. (1999) Monitoring violent incidents. In Leather, P. *et al.* (eds.) *Work-Related Violence: Assessment and Intervention.* London: Routledge.
7. Reid, J.L. (2000) *Crisis Management Planning and Media Relations for the Design and Construction Industry.* New York: Wiley.
8. Scott, M.J. and Stradling, S.G. (1992) *Counselling for Post-Traumatic Stress Disorder.* London: Sage.
9. Mitchell, J.T. and Everly, G.S. (1993) *Critical Incident Stress Debriefing: An Operations Manual for the Prevention of Traumatic Stress among Emergency Service and Disaster Workers.* Ellicott City, MD: Chevron Publishing.
10. Homes, R. (1985) *Acts of War: The Behavior of Men in Battle.* New York: Free Press.
11. Pugliese, D. (1988) Psychological pressures. Media: Israeli Defence Forces confronts soldiers' frustrations. *Armed Forces Journal International* 28 May.
12. Lindermann, E. (1944) Symptomatology and management of acute grief. *American Journal of Psychiatry* 101, 141–48.
13. Dyregrov, A. (2000) Psychological debriefing: an effective method? *Traumatology* 4(2), Article 1 (http://www.fsu.edu/^trauma/).
14. Raphael, B. (1986) *When Disaster Strikes: A Handbook for the Caring Professions.* London: Unwin Hyman.

15. Rick, J., Perryman, S., Young, K., Guppy, A. and Hillage, J. (1998) *Workplace Trauma and its Management: A Review of the Literature*. Sudbury: HSE Books.
16. McCloy, E. (1992) Management of post incident trauma: a fire service perspective. *Occupational Medicine* 42, 163–66.
17. Richards, D. (1994) Traumatic stress at work: a public health model. *British Journal of Guidance and Counselling* 22(1), 51–64.
18. Tehrani, N. (1995) An integrated response to trauma in three post office businesses. *Work and Stress* 9, 380–93.
19. Letts, C. and Tait, A. (1995) Post-raid debriefing. *Occupational Health* 47(12), 418–21.
20. Gallagher, B. *Critical Incident Debriefing: An Evaluation of Officers' Understanding. Report to Strathclyde Police Occupational Health and Welfare Unit*. Glasgow: Glasgow Caledonian University.
21. Flynn, R. (1996) *Sitting in the Hot Seat: Leaders and Teams for Critical Incident Management*. Chichester: Wiley.
22. Tehrani, N. and Westlake, R. (1994) Debriefing individuals affected by violence. *Counselling Psychology Quarterly* 7(3), 251–59.
23. Tehrani, N. (1997) Preventing stress in the UK Post Office: a cost benefit analysis. Paper presented at the European conference 'Costs and Benefits of Occupational Health and Safety', The Hague, 28–30 May.
24. Tehrani, N. (2000a) Measuring the impact of traumatic stress. *Journal of Aggression, Maltreatment and Trauma* in press.
25. Lane, D. (1990) Counselling psychology in organisations. *The Psychologist Bulletin of the British Psychological Society* 12, 540–44.
26. Hofstede, G. (1991) *Cultures and Organizations: Software of the Mind*. Maidenhead: McGraw-Hill.
27. Rose, S. and Bisson, J. (1998) One-off psychological interventions following trauma a systematic review of the literature. *Journal of Traumatic Stress* 11(4), 697–710.
28. Hytten, L. and Hasle, A. (1989) Firefighters: a study of stress and coping. *Acta Psychiatrica Scandinavia* 80(suppl. 355), 50–55.
29. Rick *et al.* op. cit.
30. Deahl, M., Gillham, A.B., Thomas, J., Searle, M.M. and Srinivasan, M. (1994) Psychological sequelae following the Gulf war. Factors associated with subsequent morbidity and the effectiveness of psychological debriefing. *British Journal of Psychiatry* 165, 60–65.
31. Kenardy, J.A. (1996) Stress debriefing and patterns of recovery following a natural disaster. *Journal of Traumatic Stress* 9(1), 37–49.
32. Tehrani, N. (1999) Introducing trauma care into an organisation: from theory into practice. In Leather, P. *et al.* (eds.) *Work-Related Violence: Assessment and Intervention*. London: Routledge.
33. Lee, C., Slade, P. and Lygo, V. (1996) The influence of psychological debriefing on emotional adaptation in woman following an early miscarriage: a preliminary study. *British Journal of Medical Psychology* 69, 47–58.
34. Brady and Dickson op. cit.

35. Hobbs, M., Mayou, R., Harrison, B. and Warlock, P. (1996) A randomised trial of psychological debriefing for victims of road traffic accidents. *British Medical Journal* 313, 1438–39.
36. Dyregrov op. cit.
37. Bisson, J.I., Jenkins, P.L., Alexander, J. and Bannister, C. (1997) Randomised controlled trial of psychological debriefing for victims of acute burn trauma. *British Journal of Psychiatry* 171, 78–81.
38. Kraus, R.P. (1997) Psychological debriefing for victims of acute burn trauma. *British Journal of Psychiatry* 171, 583.
39. Rick, J. and Briner, R. (2000) Trauma management vs. stress debriefing: what should a responsible organization do? Paper presented at the British Psychological Society's conference 'Occupational Psychology', January.
40. Avery, A. and Orner, R. (1998) First reports of debriefing abandoned – the end of an era? *Traumatic Stress Points* 12, 3–4.
41. Avery, A., King, S., Bretherton, R. and Orner, R. (1999) Deconstructing psychological debriefing and emergence of calls for evidence base practice. *Bulletin of the European Society for Traumatic Stress Studies* 6(2), 7–10.
42. Tehrani, N. (2000b) Assessing the impact of traumatic incidents: the development of an Extended Impact of Events Scale. *European Journal of Traumatic Stress* submitted.
43. Tehrani, N., Walpole, O. and Berriman, J. (2000) A special courage: dealing with the Paddington rail crash. Paper presented at the British Psychological Society's conference 'Counselling Psychology', Liverpool, May.

Concluding comments

Bonnie Fisher, Vaughan Bowie and Martin Gill

As we enter the 21st century, violence at work has captured a prominent position on the policy agenda for employees, employers, unions and governments across the industrialized world. Global communications remind us daily that no one is immune from experiencing violence at work. All types of violence can and do occur in the variety of settings where people work. We are also reminded that the perpetrators are not limited to persons who are internal and external to the work environment but that violence can also be committed by groups, organizations or businesses, both large and small.

The 'traditional' forms of violence we know most about – from murder, rape and robbery to verbal abuse and threats – still exist, but added to them are 'new' and 'emerging' forms of violence at work. In the preceding chapters, the occurrence of new forms of violence, such as physical stalking and 'cyber violence' where offenders can use anonymous email messages to harass, degrade, and humiliate employees, has been documented. So, too, emerging forms of violence, such as air rage and the overflow of domestic incidents into workplaces, which have been increasingly highlighted in the media. We are at a point in time where we need more researchers to turn their attention to these and other types of 'yet to be discovered' workplace violence. This generation of work is much needed to inform and guide the development of innovative polices and programmes to address effectively these traditional, new and emerging forms of violence at work and to help discover types of workplace violence that are unknown today.

We also need more fully to examine and understand better the different levels and patterns of victimization against a greater variety of occupations. Such comparative work might usefully include peacekeepers, international aid workers, prostitutes, journalists, and seafarers, to name but a few 'under examined' areas of work. Only by better understanding different offence patterns can we realistically determine the factors that 'cause' or 'trigger' violence. And without this understanding attempts at prevention or reduction are little more than a hit-and-miss affair.

There is also a growing need to understand more comprehensively how group and organizational dynamics can exacerbate or minimize the various types of violence occurring within workplaces. At the same time we need to re-examine and critique current 'best practices' in aggression and violence management within organizations and devise more consensual, appropriate responses to this growing concern. Although we understand much already, there is much more we need to learn about the different aspects of, and responses to, violence in our ever-changing work environments.

In this book we have sought to encourage rethinking on violence at work by including chapters from researchers around the world who are at the cutting edge of developing creative ideas and producing original research findings. This international dimension is important given our interdependent global economy. Clearly, many industrialized countries face similar problems and so there are clear advantages to shared learning. This shared learning also involves learning from the experiences of developing countries and applying expertise from the 'developed countries' to the violence at work issues that emerging economies face. The sharing of knowledge is becoming technologically easier and faster, although it is still fairly uncommon. Our hope is that others will continue the discussion of sharing of knowledge and take the first steps to execute research.

We have not sought to summarize the findings and thoughts of those who have contributed to this book: we feel the authors have already undertaken this task in the chapters. However, we would like to draw attention to the need for more research informed by theory and in consultation with practitioners. We need to develop workable frameworks to guide policy and to advance both the research and policy agendas to the next level of understanding, theorizing, hypotheses testing, and implementing and evaluating newly developed prevention interventions. It is a process that must involve all interested parties – employees, employers, unions, practitioners and academics – working together and sharing their expertise. History tells us this process will not be easy, but there are real dangers for employees everywhere if these parties do not rise to the challenge. The warning bells are being sounded loudly. We have to make sure all these parties are effectively listening, communicating and responding. We hope the ideas and findings presented in this edited volume will help all those parties who are committed to understanding and preventing violence at work.

Index